CLARENDON LIBRARY OF LOGIC AND PHILOSOPHY
General Editor: L. Jonathan Cohen

THE COHERENCE
OF THEISM

THE COHERENCE
OF THEISM

RICHARD SWINBURNE

CLARENDON PRESS · OXFORD
1977

Oxford University Press, Walton Street, Oxford OX2 6DP

OXFORD LONDON GLASGOW NEW YORK
TORONTO MELBOURNE WELLINGTON CAPE TOWN
IBADAN NAIROBI DAR ES SALAAM LUSAKA ADDIS ABABA
KUALA LUMPUR SINGAPORE JAKARTA HONG KONG TOKYO
DELHI BOMBAY CALCUTTA MADRAS KARACHI

© *Oxford University Press 1977*

British Library Cataloguing in Publication Data
Swinburne, Richard
   The coherence of theism.—(Clarendon library
of logic and philosophy).

   1. God—Attributes
   I. Title
   211   BT153.S/

ISBN 0-19-824410-X

Printed in Great Britain by
Billing & Sons Limited, Guildford, London and Worcester

Acknowledgements

THIS book includes much material which has previously appeared in articles. These are: 'Omnipotence', *American Philosophical Quarterly*, 1973, **10**, 231–7; 'Confirmability and Factual Meaningfulness', *Analysis*, 1972–3, **33**, 71–6; 'Duty and The Will of God', *Canadian Journal of Philosophy*, 1974, **4**, 213–27; 'Analyticity, Necessity, and Apriority', *Mind*, 1975, **84**, 225–43; 'The Objectivity of Morality', *Philosophy*, 1976, **51**, 5–20; 'Personal Identity', *Proceedings of The Aristotelian Society*, 1973–4, **74**, 231–47; *Sense and Nonsense in Physics and Theology*, University of Keele Inaugural Lecture, 1973. I am grateful to the editors and publishers concerned for permission to use this material. (In the references to these articles and to articles throughout the book, the first number indicates the year of publication of the journal, the second number the volume, and the third number the pages of the journal in which the article is to be found.)

Very many different philosophers have helped me with criticisms of previous versions of papers which have become chapters of this book, and to them I express my thanks. But I am especially grateful to Dr. Christopher Williams, who provided detailed criticisms of the penultimate version of Part I, and to Professor D. M. Mackinnon who read the penultimate version of Part II and provided me with guidance on the topics discussed there.

I am also most grateful to Mrs. Rita Lee, Mrs. Yvonne Quirke, and Miss Jean Meredith for their patient typing and retyping of various sections of this book; and to my wife for correcting the proofs.

Contents

I

Introduction

By a theist I understand a man who believes that there is a God. By a 'God' he understand something like a 'person[1] without a body (i.e. a spirit) who is eternal, free, able to do anything, knows everything, is perfectly good, is the proper object of human worship and obedience, the creator and sustainer of the universe'. Christians, Jews, and Muslims are all in the above sense theists. Many theists also hold further beliefs about God, and in these Christians, Jews, and Muslims differ among themselves; and yet further beliefs, in which some members of each group differ from others. Christians assert, and Jews and Muslims deny, that God became incarnate in Jesus Christ. Roman Catholics assert, and Protestants deny, that Christ is 'really' present in the bread consecrated in the Mass. With beliefs of the latter two kinds this book is not concerned. It is concerned solely with the central core of theistic belief, that God exists, that there is a God. It is not concerned primarily with whether this belief is true or with whether we can know it to be true, but with the prior questions of what it means and whether it is coherent; what claim a man who asserts that there is a God is making and whether it is a claim which is coherent, a claim which makes sense to suppose could be true. It will, however, reach the conclusion that the question of the coherence of the belief that there is a God cannot altogether be separated from the question of its truth.

Clearly, not all combinations of words which a man may utter make coherent claims about the world. To start with, the

[1] I am using this word in the modern sense. Some theists of course also wish to maintain that God is 'three persons in one substance'. But in claiming this they are using 'person' in a special and rather different sense, as a translation (and, I suspect, a rather unsatisfactory one) of the Latin *persona* and the Greek ὑπόστασις.

words may not form a meaningful utterance at all. This may be because some of the individual words have no meaning: 'Shouki blah nouki' has no meaning because the words have no meaning. Or it may be because, although the words have meaning, they are not put together so as to form a grammatical sentence; adverbs may be put as subjects of verbs, or a noun appear in place of a verb. It is for such a reason that 'upon opens nervously Greece stone hope' does not make a coherent claim. But even when we have a grammatical sentence composed of meaningful words, the sentence may not make a claim about how things are. Instead it may constitute a command or a request, a wish or a question. 'I recommend you to go home' does not make a claim about how things are; nor does 'Help the poor'. Alternatively, while making a claim, a sentence may not make a coherent claim; since it is not coherent, does not make sense, to suppose that what it claims to be the case is the case. 'John is over six foot tall and under five foot tall' and 'My box is a cube with all its edges six foot long which is simultaneously in Keele and a hundred miles away', while being grammatically well-formed sentences, do not make claims which it is coherent to suppose are true. For in whatever conceivable way the world was different from our world the claims made by these sentences could not be true claims. Merely because of what the words mean, whatever the world was like, there could not be a 'John' who was both 'over six foot tall' and 'under five foot tall'. By contrast, 'Mr. Thorpe is now Prime Minister' makes a coherent claim, though a false one. The claim is coherent because it makes sense to suppose that the world is such that it is true.

This book is concerned with sentences which purport to affirm the existence of a being with one or more of the following properties: being a person without a body (i.e. a spirit), present everywhere, the creator and sustainer of the universe, a free agent, able to do everything (i.e. omnipotent), knowing all things, perfectly good, a source of moral obligation, immutable, eternal, a necessary being, holy, and worthy of worship. Such sentences are 'There is a holy being, creator and sustainer of the universe', or 'an omnipotent and eternal spirit exists', or 'God exists', where God is defined in terms of the list of properties which I have given. Such sentences I will term credal sentences. They are grammatical sentences, and given that the words which occur in them are ordinary words used in their normal senses or are technical terms (such as 'omnipotent') defined by such words, they are meaningful sentences. Some philosophers of recent years claim that, despite appearances, these sentences do not make claims about how things are, but rather express intentions to live in a certain way or exhortations to others to pursue a certain course of life. I shall briefly consider and reject this account of credal language in Chapter 6, and will argue that credal sentences do, as they appear to, express claims about how things are. Many other philosophers of recent years, while agreeing that credal sentences make claims, have argued that they do not make coherent claims, because it is not coherent to suppose that things are as described by such sentences. This book is devoted to investigating this philosophical thesis. I shall be examining what is meant by the claim that there is a God, and whether this claim is a coherent one.

I consider in Part I general questions about how theological language works. In Chapters 2 and 3 I investigate the conditions which need to be satisfied for a sentence to make a coherent statement and in particular a factual statement (one which it is coherent to suppose to be true and coherent to suppose to be false). I reject the view that for a sentence to make a factual statement it has to be in some sense verifiable or falsifiable, and I go on to propose a rival view. One question which arises here is whether the words used in theology are being used in the same sense as when they are used to describe ordinary mundane things. (When a man says 'God is wise' is he using 'wise' in the same sense as when he says 'Socrates was wise'?) In Chapter 4 I pursue the consequences of two alternative suppositions—that theology uses words in the same sense as when they are used to describe mundane things, and that it uses them in different senses. This chapter considers the problem that if the reality which theological or similar utterances purport to describe is as strange and marvellous as is suggested, how can it be described by the words which we use in ordinary life for describing mundane things. As this issue has been the subject of much medieval and some later philosophical thought, in Chapter 5 I compare and contrast the views which I set out in Chapter 4, with those of earlier writers, especially St. Thomas Aquinas. In Chapter 6 I consider and dismiss the view that credal sentences do not make claims but only express attitudes or commend ways of life.

Having thus considered very general problems about the claim that credal sentences make coherent claims, I turn in Parts II and III to investigate the details of credal claims. In Chapter 7 I consider whether it is coherent to claim that there exists a non-embodied person, a spirit, who is present in every place. In Chapter 8 I consider whether it is coherent to suppose that there exists a free agent who created and sustains the universe. And so on. In the case of each new property examined I consider whether it is coherent to suppose that a being could have it as well as the other properties previously examined. In the theistic tradition different definitions of 'God' have of course been provided by different writers or been taken for granted at different periods of history. But most of these definitions consist of conjunctions of predicates designating most of the properties which I shall investigate. My conclusion will be that claims that God exists, as defined by some such definitions, are coherent. In particular I claim that it is coherent to suppose that there exists eternally an omnipresent spirit, who is perfectly free, the creator of the universe, omnipotent, omniscient, perfectly good, and a source of moral obligation— given certain qualifications on the ways in which certain of these terms are to be understood. Part II is devoted to arguing the coherence of this supposition. The God of Part II is, however, a contingent God. If he exists, he just happens to exist and he just happens to have the above properties; it is a fortunate accident that he does. He might not have existed or might not have possessed those properties. However, writers in the Judaeo-Christian–Islamic tradition who have thought about their theism in any depth have wanted to deny that God just happens to exist or just happens to have such properties as those listed above. They have wanted to claim that in some sense God is a 'necessary being'. In Part III I investigate the coherence of the supposition that there exists a necessary being. I find that it could be coherent to suppose that there exists a necessary being who has necessarily the properties denoted by the terms considered in Part II, only if such terms as 'person' and 'omnipotent' are understood in new and analogical senses, senses in which their meaning is much less easy to grasp. If the terms in the definition of God are to be understood in analogical senses I cannot prove for certain that claims that there exists such a God are or are not coherent. I can only indicate the considerations which are relevant to showing their coherence or incoherence. My main conclusion will be that we only have good grounds for supposing such claims coherent if we have good grounds for supposing them true. Whether we do have such grounds is a question which lies outside the scope of this book. Normally we can show a claim to be coherent without having to produce any grounds for supposing it true. Not so for the claim in question.

For my assertion that it is coherent to suppose that the God of Part II exists I shall of course give arguments. I regard these as good arguments in favour of my conclusion. However, for reasons which I shall give in Chapter 3, I do not consider that any good arguments to prove the coherence or incoherence of suppositions are necessarily going to convince all reasonable men. Yet I retain the hope that the particular arguments which I offer will convince most reasonable men.

Although the over-all topic of this book lies squarely within the field of the philosophy of religion, I have found it necessary, in order to answer the questions with which I am concerned, to write lengthy sections on many general philosophical topics and then apply the results to the claims of theism. There are detailed discussions of such topics as meaningfulness, personal identity, free will, and the objectivity of morality—topics generally considered to lie within areas of philosophy other than the philosophy of religion. This is an inevitable and to my mind welcome consequence of the integrated character of philosophy. What is unfortunate, however, is that since so many central philosophical issues come into this discussion, they are dealt with too briefly. I have tried to remedy this defect to some extent by referring to books and articles where the issues may be followed up more fully. I have also tried to discuss the issues in ways which do not presuppose familiarity with current philosophical discussions, although such familiarity will obviously be of great help in understanding the issues.

The programme of this book, if not its results, will seem a natural and useful one to many interested in philosophy and lacking religious commitment. They feel rightly that bold and puzzling claims about the universe which command some measure of support need putting under the philosophical microscope. Yet many religious men, especially if influenced by modern Protestant theology, will view this programme with grave suspicion. Religion, they will tell us, is not a matter of affirming creeds, but of a personal relationship to God in Christ. The religious man may tell us that he knows that he at any rate has such a relationship, and that he knows what he means when he says that he has this relationship; on these points he 'cannot be mistaken'. So what is in our enterprise for him? Three points must be made in answer to this. First, even if affirming creeds were no part of religion, you can only have a personal relationship to God in Christ, if it is true that God exists. And it is true that God exists only if it is coherent to suppose that he exists. So our programme can show whether it is possible for the religious man to have the relationship he claims. The second point is that, although the religious man claims to know that he has the personal relationship to God in Christ, many people have claimed to know things about which they have subsequently been found to be confused or mistaken. If others are very sceptical about some claim which you make to knowledge of a very important matter, it is no bad thing to check your claim by considering whether their objections provide you with grounds for sharing their scepticism. The third point is that even if the religious man has no need to question the truth, let alone the coherence, of his beliefs and of the claim that he has a personal relationship to God, he has, at any rate on the Christian view, a duty to convert others. If they are to believe, those others need to have explained to them what the theist's claims mean. They often doubt the coherence of these claims. If the religious man could show the claims to be coherent, he would remove a stumbling-block which stands in the way of the conversion of the unbeliever.

Yet, while perhaps admitting the theoretical utility of such a programme, some religious men may feel that a book such as this gets too subtle and difficult, and may wonder what it all has to do with the ordinary man in the pew. This book is designed to argue the issues with considerable rigour and thoroughness. There are of course contexts where these qualities are not needed. But there are other contexts where they are needed. They are needed in a context where men are familiar with any of the arguments of modern analytic philosophers relevant to these issues. They are needed too where we are trying to be as clear as possible about the meaning of the central doctrines of theism, as is surely the case in any large-scale work of theology concerned with these central doctrines. It is for these contexts that this book is written. It is one of the intellectual tragedies of our age that when philosophy in English-speaking countries has developed high standards of argument and clear thinking, the style of theological writing has been largely influenced by the continental philosophy of Existentialism, which, despite its considerable other merits, has been distinguished by a very loose and sloppy style of argument. If argument has a place in theology, large-scale theology needs clear and rigorous argument. That point was very well grasped by Thomas Aquinas and Duns Scotus, by Berkeley, Butler, and Paley. It is high time for theology to return to their standards.

PART I

RELIGIOUS LANGUAGE

2

Conditions for Coherence—1

IN the next two chapters I proceed to examine what are the conditions which must be satisfied for a sentence to express a coherent statement. Armed with some general principles, we can then proceed to examine whether the credal sentences of theology express coherent statements.

Philosophers distinguish between sentences and statements. Sentences are words strung together in conformity with the rules of grammar. (Adverbs qualify verbs, and do not stand in the subject place, etc.) Sentences may be in various languages—French, or English, or Latin, etc. A sentence will express something if and only if it is a meaningful sentence, that is if the words which occur in it have a meaning.[1] However, a meaningful sentence is to be distinguished from what it expresses. For different sentences often express the same thing; and on different occasions the same sentence may express different things. The two sentences 'go away' in English and 'abite' in Latin express the same command. Whereas the one sentence 'are you ill?' asks a different question, according to whether it is addressed to Jones or to Smith. A meaningful indicative sentence normally makes a claim about how things are. The sentence 'you are ill' addressed to me makes the claim that I am ill. In such cases philosophers have called what the sentence

[1] As I am using this word, to be a sentence, a string of words must be grammatical, and so any word which occurs in a sentence must have a grammatical status, e.g. be a noun, but it can do that without having a meaning. To have a grammatical status, it must *purport* to have a meaning—e.g. 'nuzzy' may be so used as to purport to describe a possible property of objects, but it may fail to do so because there are no rules for determining whether or not an object is nuzzy. If anyone does not like my suggestion that the concepts of sentence and meaningful sentence are distinct it will be easy enough for him to amend my terminology in such a way that the main points of the next two chapters remain.

expresses a 'statement' or a 'proposition'. I shall call it a statement. Different sentences may make the same statement, and
the same sentence on different occasions of its use may make
different statements.

I wrote that a meaningful indicative sentence *normally* makes
a claim about how things are. It would be a mistake to suppose
that all meaningful indicative sentences make claims. One kind
of case where a meaningful indicative sentence clearly does not
make a claim is where it is performative.[2] The sentence 'I
promise to pay you £10' does not claim that anything is
happening. Rather, it effects something—it makes the promise.
'I advise you to tell him what happened' does not report the
giving of advice or anything else; it constitutes the giving of
advice. Many philosophers have claimed that indicative sentences of various other kinds do not make claims, but do other
jobs instead. They have claimed, for example, that sentences
which say that things are 'good' or 'right' or 'ought to be done'
are not making claims, but merely expressing approval or giving
advice. On this view 'capital punishment is wrong' does not
make a claim, but merely expresses disapproval of capital
punishment or advises men to campaign for its abolition. Of
course it may well do these latter jobs as well as the former job,
but the philosophically interesting claim is the claim that it
does not do the former job at all, that it does not make a statement. This claim is much debated in philosophy, and later
in this book I shall have occasion to oppose it. A statement,
unlike anything else expressed by a sentence, is true or false.
Commands, questions, or performative utterances are not true
or false. Some philosophers of religion seem to hold that credal
sentences do not make statements. I shall consider this view
in Chapter 6.

Among statements we must distinguish coherent from incoherent statements. A coherent statement is, I suggest, one
which it makes sense to suppose is true; one such that we can
conceive of or suppose it and any other statement entailed by
it being true; one such that we can understand what it would
be like for it and any statement entailed by it to be true. A

---

[2] Performative utterances were named and classified by J. L. Austin. See his
'Performative utterances' in his *Philosophical Papers*, ed. J. O. Urmson and G. J.
Warnock (2nd edn., Oxford, 1970).

statement p entails another statement q if and only if p and the negation of q are inconsistent. The negation of a statement q is the statement which says that things are not as q says. Thus the negation of 'all Englishmen are mortal' is 'it not the case that all Englishmen are mortal', or 'some Englishmen are not mortal'. 'All men are mortal' entails 'all Englishmen are mortal', because it is not consistent to say both that 'all men are mortal' and 'some Englishmen are not mortal'. If a statement p entails another statement q, then a man who asserts that p is committed also to the claim that q; the claim that q lies buried within the claim that p. Now a coherent statement, I am suggesting, is a statement such that we can conceive of it and any other statement entailed by it being true, in the sense that we can understand what it would be like for them to be true. This seems to be the sense of coherence at which philosophers have been aiming when they have talked of statements being coherent. A coherent statement may be false but it is one which it makes sense to suppose true. An incoherent statement by contrast is one which it makes no sense to suppose true; in that either it or some statement entailed by it is such that we cannot conceive of it being true. The supposition of its truth is nonsensical and can be shown to be so by drawing out what is involved in the supposition. 'All men are mortal', 'the moon is made of green cheese', and 'I am now writing', are all coherent statements. It makes sense to suppose that they are true. We can conceive of them and anything entailed by them being true. In fact the first and third such statements are true. The second is false but we know what it would be like for it to be true; and we can conceive of it and statements entailed by it also being true. For instance, we can conceive of 'there is a moon' and 'the moon is made of cheese' and 'the colour of the cheese of which the moon is made is green' all being true. By contrast 'honesty weighs ten pounds' and 'some squares have five sides', and 'three is the square of one' are all incoherent statements. Honesty is not the sort of thing which it makes sense to suppose weighs ten pounds. It might seem that it made sense to suppose that the square of one is three, but it does not. Although we may be able to conceive it being true we cannot conceive of the truth of a certain claim which is entailed by it. For to say that $1^2 = 3$ is to say that $1 \times 1 = 3$, and that is to say that $1 = 3$ and that is a claim which we cannot conceive to be true. (We may of course easily conceive of '$1 = 3$' making a true statement in a language other than our own; but what we cannot conceive of is the statement in fact made in our language, that is the statement made by the words having the meaning that they do in our language, by '$1 = 3$' being true.)

What I have called a coherent statement I shall also sometimes call a logically possible statement. I shall use the term 'proposition' also in the sense of 'coherent statement'. What I have called an incoherent statement some philosophers have called a 'meaningless' statement. But 'meaningless' is not an apt word for a statement of this kind. It is meaningful to claim that three is the square of one. If a man makes this claim we understand what he means. But the claim is false and could not but be false. This is because buried within the claim is something which cannot be conceived to be true, which it makes no sense to suppose true—whatever the world is like. A self-contradictory statement, one which says that something is so and also that it is not so—for example, 'it is Thursday and it is not Thursday'—is of this kind. All self-contradictory statements are of course incoherent. But many incoherent statements are not straightforwardly self-contradictory. 'Thursday jumps loudly over the moon' is incoherent but it does not say that something is so and also that it is not so.[3]

Analytic and Synthetic

Among coherent statements it is important to distinguish those of which the negations are also coherent, from those of which the negations are incoherent. I shall call a coherent statement whose negation is also coherent, a synthetic or factual proposition; and I shall call a coherent statement whose negation is incoherent, an analytic or logically necessary proposition. Thus 'all men are mortal' is a synthetic proposition, because

[3] We must distinguish conceiving of something from imagining it. Even if a claim is coherent, if we can conceive of it and everything involved in it being true, we may not be able to imagine it being true, in the sense of being able to picture it 'in the mind's eye'. I cannot picture all space occupied by dense steel, or a million ant-like creatures perching on the end of a pin. But this just shows the deficiency of my powers of imagination in the stated sense. I can conceive of these things being so in that I can think of them as being thus.

both 'all men are mortal' and 'some men are not mortal' make coherent claims. We may also say that 'all men are mortal' is a factual statement. It tells you a fact about the world—that it is a world in which all men are mortal—where it is coherent to suppose that the world might not be like that at all. By contrast, 'all bachelors are unmarried' and 'red is a colour' are analytic, because 'some bachelors are married' and 'red is not a colour' are incoherent. What they say (quite independently of how the world is) alone guarantees the truth of the former statements.

The definitions which I have given of 'analytic' and 'synthetic' are by no means the most common definitions of these terms in philosophical literature. I now go on to suggest that other current definitions of 'analytic' are either too narrow or confused, or are equivalent to mine in the sense that they classify the same propositions as analytic as does my definition.

The distinction between analytic and synthetic propositions begins with Kant. He defined an 'analytic judgement' as one in which 'the predicate B belongs to the subject A, as something which is (covertly) contained in this concept A'.[4] The judgement adds 'nothing through the predicate to the concept of the subject, but merely [breaks] it up into these constituent concepts that have all along been thought in it, although confusedly'. Thus the concept of having four sides is contained within the concept of a square, in that part of what we mean when we say that something is a square is that it has four sides. For this reason Kant would classify 'all squares have four sides' as analytic. A synthetic judgement, in contrast, was one in which 'B lies outside the concept A'. The concept of brown is not contained within the concept of my desk, and so the proposition 'my desk is brown' is synthetic. Kant's classification of judgements, or, as we should say, propositions, was only meant to apply to 'judgements in which a relation of a subject to the predicate is thought'. These are propositions which ascribe a predicate (e.g. 'is brown') to a subject (e.g. 'my desk'). For this reason later philosophers have considered Kant's definitions of 'analytic' and 'synthetic' too narrow. They have felt intuitively that the kind of distinction which Kant made had application not merely within the class of subject–predicate propositions but within the wider class of all propositions. Apart from

[4] I. Kant, *Critique of Pure Reason*, B 10 (trans. N. Kemp Smith, London, 1919).

subject–predicate propositions there are, for example, existential propositions, that is propositions which affirm the existence of something, such as 'there are unicorns'. There are also conditional propositions, such as 'if Algy is a unicorn, Algy has one horn'. Of these two propositions just cited later philosophers would be naturally inclined to classify the former with those which Kant called synthetic, and the latter with those which Kant called analytic. They have therefore sought definitions of 'synthetic' and 'analytic' which would have this consequence.

Sometimes it is said that a proposition is analytic if and only if it is a truth of logic or can be reduced to one with the help of definitions (which correctly report the meanings of the words defined).[5] Thus a square may be defined as a figure with four equal sides and four equal angles. Then by substituting this definition, 'all squares have four equal sides' reduces to 'all figures with four equal sides and four equal angles have four equal sides', which is a truth of logic because it has the form 'all things which are A and B and C are B', which is a truth of logic. This definition can, however, only be of use if there is an agreed set of truths of logic. There is not. Further, it does not seem at all obvious that many propositions which many philosophers would wish to classify as analytic can be shown to be so on this definition. One celebrated example is the proposition 'nothing can be red and green all over'.

A more hopeful approach to a definition of 'analytic' is one which defines an analytic proposition in terms of it getting its truth from the meanings of words. Thus one might wish to say loosely that what makes 'all bachelors are unmarried' true is simply the fact that the words 'all', 'bachelors', etc. mean what they do. Whereas what makes 'my desk is brown' true is not merely the fact that 'my', 'desk', etc. mean what they do, but something else—'how the world is'. It is unfortunate that some definitions of this type have been expressed very unhappily in the past. Thus Ayer: 'a proposition is analytic when its validity depends solely on the definitions of the symbols it contains'.[6]

---

[5] An example of such a definition is provided by W. V. O. Quine in 'Two Dogmas of Empiricism' in his *From a Logical Point of View* (2nd edn., Harper Torchbook edn., New York, 1963), pp. 22 f. A definition of this type is suggested by Frege. See G. Frege, *The Foundations of Arithmetic*, trans. J. L. Austin (Oxford, 1953), p. 4.

[6] A. J. Ayer, *Language, Truth and Logic* (2nd edn., London, 1946), p. 78.

Since arguments rather than propositions are normally said to be valid, let us substitute 'truth' for 'validity' in the definition. The more substantial difficulty is that it is not clear which symbols, i.e. words, a proposition contains since, as we have seen, sentences containing different symbols may express the same proposition. So let us try the following amendment: 'a proposition is analytic if and only if any sentence which expresses it expresses a true proposition and does so solely because the words in the sentence mean what they do'. The fact that the words in the sentence mean what they do, that is, is by itself sufficient to guarantee that the statement which the sentence expresses is true—how rocks are arranged on Mars or the Romans behaved in Gaul, etc. does not affect the truth value. This seems to me a perfectly satisfactory definition, and one which yields the same results as the earlier definition of 'analytic' which I have adopted. This I will now show. On my earlier definition a proposition, that is a coherent statement, p, is analytic if and only if its negation is incoherent. Now whether a statement is coherent or incoherent is solely a matter of what it says—the fact that it says what it does is alone sufficient to make it coherent, or incoherent, as the case may be. So if p is an analytic proposition, the mere fact that its negation, not-p, says what it does, is alone sufficient to make it false. That being so, that fact that p says what it does is alone sufficient to make it true. (The fact that the proposition that all bachelors are unmarried says what it does is alone sufficient to guarantee its truth.) That a sentence expresses the statement it does is a consequence solely of what the words in the sentence mean. (That the sentence 'all bachelors are unmarried' expresses the statement it does is a consequence solely of what the words 'all', 'bachelors', etc. mean.) If p is true just because of what it says, then any sentence which expresses it will express a true proposition solely because the words in the sentence mean what they do. (Since the proposition that all bachelors are unmarried is true just because of what it says, then any sentence such as 'all bachelors are unmarried' or sentences with the same meaning in other languages which express that proposition will express a true proposition, and will do so solely because the words 'all', 'bachelors', etc. mean what they do.) Hence if a proposition is analytic on the earlier definition, it will be analytic on the later definition too. Conversely, if a proposition p is analytic on the later definition, any sentence which expresses p will express a true proposition and do so solely because the words in it mean what they do. In that case the fact that p is true is a consequence merely of what it says. Hence that the negation of p, that is not-p, is false, is also a consequence merely of what it says. So the assertion of the negation will be in words which have such a meaning that the falsity of the negation lies buried in them. Hence the assertion of the negation contains its own falsity buried within it and so is incoherent. Hence any proposition analytic on the later definition will be analytic on the earlier definition also.

So the definitions are equivalent. Another favoured definition is that an analytic proposition is one whose 'negation is self-contradictory'. If it is meant by this that the negation has explicitly to claim that a certain thing is so and that that thing is not so, then this definition is obviously far too narrow—even 'all bachelors are unmarried' fails to come out as analytic. But if the self-contradictoriness of the negation need only be implicit we need to be told how it is to be recognized. This point suggests the following amended definition: 'a proposition is analytic if and only if its negation entails a self-contradictory statement',[7] i.e. a statement which claims explicitly that a certain thing is so and that that thing is not so.[8] By this test 'all bachelors are unmarried' comes out as analytic. The entailment can be demonstrated as follows. 'It is not the case that all bachelors are unmarried' entails 'some unmarried men are not unmarried', which entails 'there are certain persons, x's, such that x's are unmarried and x's are not unmarried'.[9]

I believe that this definition of 'analytic' is also equivalent to my original definition in the sense that any proposition which satisfies the one will satisfy the other, and conversely. This will

[7] This account of analytic propositions has its origin in the account which Leibniz gives of truths of reason. These are those propositions which, by analysis, can be resolved into 'identical propositions, whose opposite contains an express contradiction'; *Monadology*, 33–5 (Leibniz's *Philosophical Writings*, trans. Mary Morris, London, 1934).

[8] It may do this either by having the form 'p and not-p' (where p is a statement) or the form 'there is an x such that x is ϕ and x is not ϕ' (where x is an object and ϕ is a property).

[9] This derivation assumes what is called the existential commitment of 'all', that is that 'all A's are B', is true only if there are A's. If this is not assumed, a different derivation can be given instead.

be so if any incoherent statement is also a statement which entails a self-contradictory statement, and conversely. I now proceed to show that this is so. Clearly if a statement p entails a self-contradictory statement, then p is incoherent—for it has buried in it a claim that something is so and that it is not so—and it is not conceivable that things should be thus. The converse needs a longer proof. There are a number of kinds of statements which logicians have codified. Among them, as we saw earlier, are subject–predicate statements, existential, and conditional statements. There are too relational statements which affirm that a certain relation holds between two or more named objects—e.g. the statement 'John is to the left of James'. Now let us take a statement of one of these forms. Let us take a simple subject–predicate statement, such as 'John is bald' or 'I am old'. Such a statement will have the form 'a is ψ'. If such a statement is incoherent, then being a must be being an object of a certain sort, being which is incompatible with having the property of being ψ. For if there were no incompatibility between being the sort of thing which is a, and the sort of thing which can be ψ, how could there be any incoherence in a thing being both a and ψ? So there is an incompatibility between being a and being ψ, and so there will be buried within 'a is ψ' a contradiction which can be brought to the surface by deriving from it what is entailed by the statement. Examples bear out this point. Take a typically incoherent statement of the above form, e.g. 'honesty weighs 10 pounds'. 'a is honesty' entails 'a is not a physical object'. (Physical objects and honesty, one may say loosely, are different kinds of thing.) 'a has weight' entails 'a is a physical object'. (Only a physical object, something with spatial location, is the kind of thing that can have weight.) Hence 'honesty weighs ten pounds' entails 'there is something which both is and is not a physical object', that is a self-contradictory statement. This type of argument can clearly be generalized for statements of other forms to show generally that if a statement is incoherent it entails a self-contradictory statement.[10] From the results of this paragraph it follows that any proposition whose negation is incoherent will be a proposition

[10] Philosophers have often tried to produce a theory of types which would group entities together in one type if and only if certain predicates can be predicated 'significantly' of all of them. Thus persons might form one type because 'is smiling',

whose negation entails a self-contradictory statement, and conversely. From this it follows that this latest definition and my original definition of 'analytic' are equivalent.

There is a well-known kind of objection to the applicability of definitions of the kind which I have been discussing which is due to Quine. He points out that such definitions will only be of use if the terms which occur in them such as 'entails' or 'negation' have clear meanings. He doubts if they do.[11] However, definitions *can* be provided of these terms by other expressions, such as 'consistent' or 'a statement which says that . . . is not so', which have a perfectly regular use in non-philosophical discourse, a use which can be made clear to those unfamiliar with them with the help of examples.

So then I claim to have shown that two well-known accounts of the nature of analyticity yield definitions of an analytic proposition equivalent to the one with which in the main I will operate; this will enable me to use the other definitions on occasion. Earlier I defined a synthetic proposition as a coherent statement whose negation is also coherent. Equivalently, on any of these definitions of 'analytic', we may say that a synthetic statement is a coherent statement which is not analytic. The class of propositions, or coherent statements, is thus divided without remainder into the analytic and the synthetic.[12] As stated, I shall use 'logically necessary' in the same sense as 'analytic', and 'factual' in the same sense as 'synthetic'. In philosophical writing 'necessary' by itself (rather than 'logically

---

'is thinking', 'is dreaming', etc. can all 'significantly' be predicated of persons such as Socrates, or Plato, or Alexander. Whereas numbers might form a different type because these predicates cannot 'significantly' be predicated of numbers, such as 2 or 7. 'Significantly' seems to mean 'coherently'. But I do not see how you can show which entities belong together in a type except by considerations of the sort which I have sketched in the text. I do not see how you could first establish a theory of types, and then use it to establish claims about coherence or incoherence. Philosophers who have attempted to establish a theory of types have in fact assumed that they knew what was predicated 'significantly' of what. For this point and an account of theories of types, see James W. Cornman 'Types, Categories, and Nonsense' in N. Rescher (ed.), *Studies in Logical Theory* (*American Philosophical Quarterly* Monograph, No. 2, Oxford, 1968).

[11] See his 'Two Dogmas of Empiricism'.

[12] Some writers have provided a very different kind of definition of 'synthetic' from that which they have provided of 'analytic', which means that it needs to be argued that there are no coherent statements other than analytic and synthetic ones. A classification of the kind which I have adopted seems much neater.

necessary') is often used to mean the same as 'analytic'. This use seems to blur important distinctions. There may well be other kinds of necessity than that which arises from the incoherence of alternatives, and in a later chapter I shall argue that there are indeed such kinds of necessity. The opposite of 'necessary' is 'contingent'. I shall not assume that the contingent is the same as the synthetic (although I shall use 'logically contingent' to mean the same as 'synthetic'), nor shall I equate 'empirical' with 'synthetic'. Many philosophers have also tended to assume that propositions which are analytic are *a priori*, and conversely. An *a priori* proposition is (very roughly) one which is true and can be known to be true merely by considering what it says, without 'looking at the world' to see if it is true. It is not very easy to give a clear definition of an *a priori* proposition, but however we do define an *a priori* proposition (along the lines just given) it *may* well be the case that there are *a priori* propositions which are not analytic, statements whose negations are not incoherent but which we can know to be true 'without looking at the world'. So I will not assume in this book that all propositions which are analytic are *a priori*, or conversely. The opposite of *a priori* is *a posteriori*. Very roughly, an *a posteriori* proposition is one which can only be known to be true by 'looking at the world' to see if it is true. I shall not assume that any proposition which is synthetic is *a posteriori*, or conversely.[13]

Many theological sentences, like many sentences in other disciplines, seem to express analytic propositions. 'If God exists, then he is worthy of men's worship' is a sentence which almost certainly expresses an analytic proposition, on our normal understanding of 'God'. A being would not count as God unless he was worthy of worship. It is the fact that the words mean what they do which alone makes the proposition expressed by them true. However, many other theological sentences, and in particular those which I have termed credal sentences, seem to express claims which it is not incoherent to deny. If 'God' is defined as on page 1, it does not seem incoherent to claim that 'God does not exist'. 'God exists' does

[13] In my paper 'Analyticity, Necessity, and Apriority' (*Mind*, 1975, **84**, 225–43) I discuss more fully the issues treated in this section, and reach conclusions about the relation between the *a priori* and the analytic.

not seem to express a true proposition just because 'God' and 'exists' mean what they do. What makes it true, if it is true, is something else, 'how things are'. Hence credal sentences, if they *do* make coherent statements, would *seem*[14] to make factual rather than logically necessary statements; and so if they do not make factual statements, they make incoherent statements. In that case a certain fashionable doctrine, the verificationist theory of meaning, could have application, for it provides a criterion for a statement being factual. I propose to argue, however, that there is no good reason for believing this doctrine to be true in any of its forms, and so no good reason for relying on it to help to solve questions about the coherence of anything expressed by credal sentences.

The Weak Verificationist Principle

The doctrine was first put forward by the logical positivists of the late 1920s. In its earliest form it claimed (in our terminology) that to be factual a statement had to be verifiable 'in principle' by an observation–statement or, more loosely, by observation. By 'verifiable' was meant 'conclusively verifiable'. An observation–statement is one which reports something observed, or, in a wide sense, experienced. By a statement being verifiable 'in principle' by observation was meant that the statement was such that it made sense to suppose an observation might verify it if that observation could be made, even if it was not in practice possible to make the observation. 'This table is brown' is a factual statement, on this form of verificationist doctrine, because it is possible 'in principle' for someone to make an observation which would conclusively establish that the table is brown. It makes sense to suppose that someone could make an observation which would consist in seeing that the table is brown—even if in fact the table is not brown, it *makes sense* to suppose that a man could make such an observation. That the star Sirius has five planets is not something which

---

[14] I here assume what seems to be the case, that credal sentences do not express logically necessary propositions. Some philosophical theologians of the past, such as Descartes and perhaps Anselm, seem to have held a different position. My assumption is made only for the purposes of argument in the context of this chapter and nothing further depends on it. An argument is given in favour of the assumption in Ch. 14.

anyone could conclusively verify at present. But one day tele-
scopes or space travel might be so developed that the observation that Sirius has five planets, it makes sense to suppose,
could be made.

The above form of verificationism may be called the strong
verificationist theory. It is generally agreed to be false. The
argument most influential in persuading logical positivists to
abandon it was the argument that it would show all universal
statements to have no factual meaning; and since clearly some
such statements have factual meaning, the theory must be false.
A universal statement is a statement of the form 'all A's are B'
where the class of A's is an open class, that is A's are such that
however many A's you have observed, it always makes sense
to suppose that there is another one. The class of ravens is open.
The class of the twelve Apostles is not. Examples of universal
statements are 'all ravens are (at all times) black', 'all material
bodies near the surface of the earth are (at all times) subject to
an acceleration towards the earth of $c.$ 32 ft/sec.^{2}'. Such statements cannot be conclusively verified. However many ravens
you have observed to be black, there may always be another
one and that one may be white.

So the logical positivists abandoned strong verificationism and
tried the strong falsificationist principle that to be factual a
statement had to be falsifiable in principle by an observation-
statement. A statement is falsifiable 'in principle' if it makes
sense to suppose that it be (conclusively) falsified. A universal
statement 'all A's are B' is falsified by finding an A that is not B,
and if an A which is not B is the sort of thing which can be observed, then 'all A's are B' can be falsified by an observation-
statement. 'All ravens are black' would be falsified by observing
a white raven. However, although at any rate many universal
statements prove to be factually meaningful on this criterion,
existential statements asserting the existence of a member of an
open class do not. An existential statement is a statement
asserting the existence at some time or other of an object of a
certain kind, such are 'there is, was, or will be a man with two
heads' or 'there is, was, or will be a centaur (somewhere)'. No
observation can falsify such statements. However many observations you make and fail to find a two-headed man, there
may be one somewhere where you have not looked, or one may

be born tomorrow. Yet clearly such existential statements are factual.

One might suggest that to be factual a statement has to be *either* conclusively falsifiable *or* conclusively verifiable 'in principle' by an observation-statement. But counter-examples, of what are clearly factual statements, to this principle are also not hard to find. Consider what are known as mixed-universal-and-existential statements, such as 'all badgers are mortal', that is 'all badgers die at some time or other'. You cannot conclusively falsify such a statement. For however old a badger you find, he may die one day. Nor can you conclusively verify such a statement, for however many badgers you find which eventually die, there may be yet another one which you have not yet found which will live for ever. Faced with these difficulties logical positivists retreated to what I shall call the weak verification-or-falsification criterion, or, for short, the weak verificationist principle. This is that a statement *q* is factual if and only if either it is itself an observation-statement or there are observation-statements which, if true, would confirm or disconfirm *q*. By 'confirm' I mean 'raise the probability of', that is 'count as evidence in favour of'; by 'disconfirm' I mean 'lower the probability of' or 'count as evidence against'. Thus although you cannot conclusively verify 'all ravens are black', you can make observations which would count as evidence in favour of this statement. Observing many ravens in different parts of the world and finding them all to be black would count as good evidence favouring 'all ravens are black'. And even though you cannot conclusively verify or conclusively falsify 'all badgers are mortal', you can have good evidence in favour of it—e.g. that all of many reliable reports available to you about the lives of many badgers show that all have died within at any rate fifty years.

The weak verificationist principle expresses the very weak form which verificationism reached in A. J. Ayer's influential *Language, Truth and Logic*, first published in 1936. Much subsequent philosophical controversy has been devoted to attempting to state criteria for when one statement confirms another. But whether or not any simple general account can be given of this matter, that has no tendency to cast doubt on the applicability of the weak verificationist principle itself. So long as we can recognize intuitively when one statement confirms another (as of course we often can) we can apply the principle. In *Language, Truth and Logic* Ayer seems at times to be introducing the principle as a definition of a 'factual' or 'synthetic' statement. If so, the only objection which can be made to his procedure is that it is misleading. There may well in that case be non-analytic propositions which are not 'synthetic', and as propositions are generally supposed to be either synthetic or analytic, a definition which allowed an intermediate category is out of accord with normal philosophical usage, and might mislead someone who was not paying close attention to Ayer's peculiar usage. However, at other times Ayer seems to assume that if a statement is 'meaningful' (i.e. coherent) and non-analytic it must be synthetic. On that understanding of 'synthetic' the weak verificationist principle is an interesting further claim about 'synthetic' or 'factual' propositions. Most philosophers have understood the principle in this way, and many have taken for granted that it is true. I shall also understand it in this way and shall investigate whether or not it is true.

Let us begin, however, by noting a preliminary point. Even if the principle were true, it would not be of great value in sorting out factual statements from others. Like other forms of verificationism, it relies on the notion of an observation-statement. An observation-statement is a statement which reports an observation which could 'in principle' be made. But what does 'in principle' mean? An observation could be made 'in principle' if it makes sense to suppose that it could be made, if it is coherent or logically possible to suppose that it be made. So what has happened is that being uncertain about whether a statement is a factual statement, that is a statement which is logically possible while its negation is also logically possible, the advocate of the weak verificationist principle suggests that a statement is factual if and only if either it describes a logically possible state of affairs which is observable or it would be confirmed or disconfirmed by some statement which described a logically possible state of affairs which is observable. Hence the principle will be useful only if men are agreed better about which statements report observable logically possible states of affairs than about which statements report logically possible states of affairs in general. Are they? I doubt it. Consider all the things that some men have claimed to be observable: 'the end of the world', 'my own death', 'the devil', 'heaven', 'the fourth dimension', 'Poseidon', 'men turned into stones', etc. etc. Some men have held these things to be observable 'in principle' and others have denied it. Is there any simple way to settle the issue? One way which has been suggested is to suppose that the observable must be describable by some simple sensory vocabulary; to suppose that we can *really* observe objects which are square or round, red or blue, move, utter noises, etc.; but that we cannot observe quarrelsome men, a lump of gold, or the planet Venus; and that when we claim to have observed the latter, we ought rather to claim to have inferred these things from things of the former kind which we can truly be said to have observed. But this kind of move constitutes a highly arbitrary restriction on the normal use of 'observe'. Philosophers now recognize that there is no simple and obvious limit on the observable—we can observe bacteria (under a microscope), the moons of Jupiter (in a telescope), Harold Wilson (on the television). So if men claim to have observed the objects and events cited earlier how can we show them wrong? One or two of the purported observations *might* be eliminable in virtue of some logical property of the word 'observe', such as that it is not logically possible to observe the future. From this it would follow, for example, that an inhabitant of the world cannot observe its end. For many p, however, the proof, if it can be given, that p is not something which it is logically possible to observe, will, I suspect, consist of a proof (by means other than the weak verificationist principle) that p is not logically possible *simpliciter*. So although men may be agreed *by and large* about which statements are observation-statements, I see no reason to suppose that the degree of consensus is vastly greater here than over which statements are factual. And if that is so, the weak verificationist principle is not going to be of great help in clearing up the latter.

Even if men were to agree for any given statement about whether or not it is an observation-statement, there is a second difficulty which arises with any attempt to show that the statement expressed by some sentence is *not* a factual statement. To show this you have to show that it is not confirmable or disconfirmable by *any* observation-statement. Yet we hardly have before us a catalogue of types of observation-statement which we can run over quickly to see whether they have any confirmation relations to some given statement. So we may easily make a mistake in concluding that a statement p is not confirmable or disconfirmable by any observation-statement through not having thought of a certain observation-statement q, which does in fact confirm (or disconfirm) p.

For these reasons, but primarily the first, I conclude that the weak verificationist principle may not be of much use in separating 'factual statements' from others. Nevertheless the principle may be true. Is it? I know of only two arguments in its favour. The first is the argument from examples; that if we consider any statement which we judge to be factual, we will find that it is confirmable or disconfirmable through observation (or experience in a wide sense). The trouble is, however, that there are plenty of examples of statements which *some* people judge to be factual which are not apparently confirmable or disconfirmable through observation. For example:

p_1. There is a being like men in his behaviour, physiology, and history who nevertheless has no thoughts, feelings, or sensations.

or p_2. Some of the toys which to all appearances stay in the toy cupboard while people are asleep and no one is watching, actually get up and dance in the middle of the night and then go back to the cupboard, leaving no traces of their activity.

Now such statements are apparently unconfirmable—to all appearances there is no possible evidence of observation which would count for or against them. If it is known that something looks like a man, has the body of a man, reacts like a man, talks like a man, and has been born and has grown up like a man, there is no further observational test which could be done to show whether or not he really feels anything when you stick a pin into him and he screams. So the claim that (somewhere in the universe) there exists a being of the kind described in p_1 cannot be confirmed or disconfirmed. Some philosophers think that such statements are nevertheless factual, and others deny this. If the former are right, the weak verificationist principle is false; and if the latter are right, that perhaps counts in its favour. But you cannot show that the weak verificationist principle is true by appealing to examples, because people disagree about whether the statements cited as examples are factual. Only if you can prove by some *other* acceptable principle that the disputed statements are not factual can you use them as evidence for the verificationist principle.

The other argument in favour of the weak verificationist principle is the following. It is claimed that a man could not understand a factual claim unless he knew what it would be like to observe it to hold or knew which observations would count for or against it; from which it follows that a statement could not *be* factually meaningful unless there could be observational evidence which would count for or against it. But then the premiss of this argument seems clearly false. A man can understand the statement 'once upon a time, before there were men or any other rational creatures, the earth was covered by sea', without his having any idea of what geological evidence would count for or against this proposition, or any idea of how to establish what geological evidence would count for or against the proposition. Surely we understand a factual claim if we understand the words which occur in the sentence which expresses it, and if they are combined in a grammatical pattern of which we understand the significance. It may be that, as I shall argue in the next chapter, in order to understand the words we have to have observed cases where they would be correctly applied or where terms definitionally related to them would be correctly applied—or at least to have observed events which are evidence for or against the occurrence of such cases. And it may be that in order to understand the significance of the pattern in which the terms are combined (e.g. a subject–predicate sentence) we have to have observed cases where such a sentence-pattern would be correctly used. But none of this shows that in order to understand a particular statement we have to know what it would be like to observe *it* to hold or know which observations would be evidence for or against *it*.

I conclude that arguments in favour of the weak verificationist principle do not work.[15] We have no reason for supposing this

---

[15] Gareth B. Matthews also argues that there is no reason for accepting the principle in his 'Theology and Natural Theology', *Journal of Philosophy*, 1964, **61**, 99–108.

principle to be true. If we did have such reason, and if we were able to apply the principle without begging crucial questions, we would have a test which we could apply to credal sentences to see if they expressed factual statements. We could ask whether credal sentences made observation-statements or made statements which were confirmable or disconfirmable by observation-statements. Yet our conclusion is that, despite the verificationist's arguments, there may well be factual statements which no evidence of observation can count for or against. Hence, even if it could be shown that credal sentences did not make observation-statements or statements which evidence of observation could count for or against (and I do wish to suggest that this could be shown), that would not show—without further argument—that they did not make factual statements. Verificationism does not provide principles which are of use for settling the character of theological sentences.

3

Conditions for Coherence—2

HAVING shown the failure of the verificationist account of
factual meaning, I now return to the general question of when
a sentence expresses a coherent statement. I shall in this
chapter develop the account given in the last chapter more
fully, and consider not merely what it is for a sentence to
express a coherent statement, but how we can show that it does.
Once we can pick out coherent statements, we can then if we
wish distinguish factual statements from analytic ones by the
criterion that the negation of a factual statement is a coherent
statement, whereas the negation of an analytic statement is not.

Since our interest in the question of when a sentence expresses
a coherent statement derives from interest in whether credal
sentences make coherent statements, we need not look for a
general definition of coherence. (I doubt whether any very useful
one can be given.) Instead we can start from the fact that there
are millions of sentences which we would all recognize without
question to make coherent statements—such as 'today is
Monday', 'Mr. Heath often goes sailing', 'there are over 2,000
students in the University of Keele', etc. etc. And there are also
plenty of sentences which we can recognize without question
not to make coherent statements—in particular any sentence
which makes a self-contradictory statement, such as 'he is over
6 feet tall and he is not over 6 feet tall', does not make a claim
which, it makes sense to suppose, could be true of the world—
for it states and denies something at the same time. Given these
points, we can now go on to investigate how to show whether
puzzling sentences such as 'positrons are electrons travelling
backwards in time' or 'there are places which have no spatial
relations to (i.e. are not in any direction or at any distance from)

the place where we are now' or credal sentences can be shown to be in one or other category. Often one cannot give a general definition of the meaning of some term, but one can show how to show that it is or is not correctly applied to some doubtful case. I cannot give a definition of 'green'. There are many paradigm cases of green objects—leaves in springtime, grass, unripe apples, runner beans, and so on. To say that an object is green is to say that it is like these objects in the way in which they are like each other, that is in respect of colour. And the test for whether a disputed object is green is whether it looks to most people in normal light that it has the same colour as the standard objects. So although one cannot give a definition of 'green', one can show how to test whether some object of unknown colour is or is not green, how to test, that is, whether it is like the standard objects. So even if one cannot give a general criterion for a sentence to express a coherent statement, one may be able to give a criterion which enables one to determine whether some sentence of dubious status expresses a coherent statement, i.e. to determine whether it is like the standard cases in this respect.

Meaningfulness

If a sentence is to express a coherent statement, it must be an indicative sentence, and the words which occur in it must have meaning. In that case the sentence will have a meaning; it will be meaningful or significant. For a string of words to form a sentence, the string has to be grammatically well formed. To say that it is well formed is to say that the words are put together in such a way that if the words have meaning, then the resulting sentence has meaning. I shall not put forward any general doctrine of when strings of words are grammatically well formed, supposing this to be fairly obvious in particular cases.

To have a meaning, words must be *either* words which have a use in standard cases of sentences expressing coherent statements and are purportedly used in their normal sense *or* words whose meaning is introduced by new syntactic and/or semantic rules. By a syntactic rule for use of a word 'φ' I mean one which states in words how to use 'φ', by laying down general conditions governing its use. A syntactic rule may give a verbal definition, that is a phrase of equivalent meaning, e.g. 'a philatelist is some-one who collects postage stamps or who knows about different kinds of postage stamps'. Or it may tell you in words how a word is used, without giving a verbal equivalent, e.g. 'when you say "if so-and-so" you are making the supposition that so-and-so is the case. You are not stating that so-and-so is the case, but you are temporarily supposing it.' Or it may merely tell you some restriction on the use of a word without giving any general in-dication of its meaning: 'you cannot say that someone knows so-and-so, when so-and-so is not the case'. By a semantic rule for the use of a word 'φ' I mean a rule which points out or describes coherently examples of particular objects or kinds of object to which the term 'φ' is correctly applied, and/or examples of objects to which 'φ' is not correctly applied (or circumstances in which the word is, and/or circumstances in which it is not, correctly used in a sentence of some kind). A very simple seman-tic rule for the use of a name is one which points out the object to which the name is correctly applied, e.g. 'John is the second boy from the left in the front row'. A semantic rule for the use of a descriptive term such as 'turquoise' will point to various objects which are turquoise and contrast them with various objects which are not: 'these objects over here are turquoise; the objects over there are not—they are blue or green but not turquoise'. To give a semantic rule for the use of a term is to convey its use by showing examples of the circumstances in which it is correctly used. The semantic rule must make clear the role of the objects pointed to. In saying that a certain object is 'φ', the rule must make it clear whether 'φ' is a name for a particular object (John), or a descriptive term describing a kind of object ('university teacher' or 'turquoise'). If 'φ' is a descriptive term, we shall normally (if we rely almost entirely on semantic rules to convey the meaning) need to be shown several objects which are 'φ' and have them contrasted with objects in many ways similar to the former objects but which are nevertheless 'not-φ', if we are to convey the meaning. If a music teacher wants to teach a pupil what a fifth is, it is no good him playing just one pair of notes. Various pairs of notes need to be played, in order for the pupil to get the idea that being fifths is what they have in common. Normally a new object will be φ if it resembles the standard examples in the respect in which and to the degree to which they resemble each other. An object is red if it is like English pillar-boxes, ripe strawberries, tomatoes, and fire-engines in the respect in which and as much as they resemble each other. But the examples presented may sometimes not be intended as a spectrum of objects which are φ but only a narrow subclass of such objects. You might be able to show a man what a ship was by pointing only to rowing boats, canoes, and dinghies. In that case you would need to provide some indication of how other kinds of ship differ from those shown. This could be done by a syntactic rule ('ships are things which can be used to convey men and goods across water'). Or it could be done by contrasting the set of φ-objects with objects which are not φ and saying that a new object is φ if it resembles the former more than it resembles the latter in the respect in which they resemble each other. Even if all the blue objects you had were light blue, you could still use them to convey the meaning of 'blue' if you also had red and green and yellow objects. You could say that an object is blue if it resembles the blue objects in the respect in which they resemble each other more than it resembles the red and green and yellow objects.

A word is often introduced by both syntactic and semantic rules. A syntactic rule succeeds in giving the meaning of a word if it states under which circumstances it is correct to use the word and under which it is not, and it is coherent to suppose that a man could follow the rule.[1] A semantic rule succeeds in giving the meaning of a word, if, as a result of understanding the rule,[2] hearers often agree among themselves for some set of circumstances whether or not it is correct to use the word in those circumstances; and if often when there is dispute among them whether or not it is correct to use the word, they agree what further procedures would settle the issue. If I tell you that this note and that note are both 'middle C', I have only con-

---

[1] Recall that we are only giving an account of when statements of dubious status are coherent. There is therefore not necessarily any circularity in using the notion of the coherence of some other statement (viz. the statement that a man follows a certain rule), in analysing the coherence of a statement of dubious status.

[2] Men understand the rule for 'φ' if they understand which are the standard cases of φ-objects, and if they understand in general terms by how much or in what respect objects have to resemble the standard objects in order rightly to be classified as 'φ'. They may do this without agreeing over particular objects whether they do resemble the standard objects.

veyed the meaning of 'middle C', if, as a result of this instruction, you are often in agreement with others whether or not some note is middle C; or if you find yourself disagreeing with others about a certain note (e.g. when it is not loud enough, or there are competing sounds), you know how to settle the dispute—by making the conditions more suitable for listening. When syntactic and semantic rules are used together to give the meaning of a word, they will succeed in doing so if it is coherent to suppose that a man follow both rules, and if those who understand the rules agree in the way just described about whether or not the word applies in various circumstances. If syntactic and semantic rules for the use of a word do not lead to men agreeing when the word is correctly used, they have failed to give meaning to the word. This may be for various reasons. It may be, for example, because there is conflict between rules (i.e. because it is not coherent to suppose that a man follow both rules) or it may be, in the case of a semantic rule, that men cannot see any property which the standard objects have in common, of which they can then recognize new instances.

Three qualifications must, however, be added to what has just been said. The first is that the process of giving a word a meaning may give it only a very vague and unclear meaning. This will happen if those who understand the rules by which the word has been introduced disagree or are uncertain over whether or not it is correct to use the word in a large number of cases. You may be told that an object is 'φ' if it is like a number of standard objects a, b, c, and d in the ways in which these resemble each other; but you may see so little in common between a, b, c, and d that you are uncertain with respect to most new objects (but not all new objects) whether or not they are to be classified as 'φ'. You may, for example, be shown a number of buildings between which you do not see a great deal in common and be told that they are all examples of 'Rococo' architecture. Although that might put you in a position to apply the term to one or two further clear cases, you might feel generally uncertain about whether or not to apply it to new cases. If you were typical of those to whom the word was introduced, the process of introducing the word would have given it some meaning, but only a very vague and unclear one.

The second point is that in some circumstances a semantic rule may give a word a meaning (and a very clear one) although a large number of those who understand the rule find themselves uncertain or in disagreement about subsequent use of the word. This will occur if, after the semantic rule for the use of a word 'φ' has been given, there is a more or less clear division between two classes of hearers—one class of hearers who do agree among themselves (by and large) as to when it is and when it is not correct to use the word 'φ', and one class of hearers who are quite unable to apply the word or agree when to apply it. The natural description of this situation is to say that 'φ' has been given a meaning but that some people have not succeeded in learning what that is, and so remain φ-blind. Only if there is no group which can agree in identifying circumstances when it is and when it is not correct to use the word 'φ', has 'φ' not been given a meaning. We can see that this is the right understanding of when 'φ' has been given a meaning by the following example. Suppose that many of us know nothing about wines. An expert then invites us to taste some which, he tells us, are 'full-bodied', an expression which, let us suppose, has not been used before; and he invites us to taste other wines which, he tells us, are not 'full-bodied'. If as a result of this process, we agree with him in our subsequent judgements, made independently of the expert and of each other, about which wines are 'full-bodied', then 'full-bodied' has been given a meaning. If only half of us come to agree in our subsequent judgements, then 'full-bodied' has still been given a meaning but some of us have palates too poor to recognize full-bodiedness. But if in general none of us agrees in our subsequent judgements, then 'full-bodied' seems not to have been given a meaning in the language.

The third point is that the same word may on occasion be used ambiguously in language, through being introduced into language by more than one process, so that for some people it means one thing and for some another. Thus some may be taught that any animal that lives in the sea is a 'fish' and others may be given a more precise zoological definition of 'fish' ('vertebrate, breathing through gills, with a heart having one auricle', etc.). What has happened is that each group designates a different concept by the word 'fish'. Not realizing this they may dispute about whether whales are fishes, and fail to see that the same interrogative sentence ('are whales fishes?') is being used to ask two different questions (one in which 'fish' has the first meaning, and one in which it has the second). Ambiguity leads to much philosophical trouble, but it is in principle possible to detect when words are being used ambiguously. One just has to keep a look-out for this kind of thing. One has to ensure that in so far as syntactic rules fix the meaning of a word, all men agree on what those rules are, and in so far as the meaning of a word is given by semantic rules all men accept each other's examples as paradigm cases of its applicability. If two men accept the same rules as governing the use of a word, they are using it in the same sense; otherwise they are not. Ambiguity is thus to be distinguished from vagueness. A word is vague if the rules do not give clear guidance on use; a word is ambiguous if there are two distinct sets of rules for its use.

It is evident that if a sentence is to express a coherent statement, the words which occur in it must be meaningful. The claim here is if words are to have meaning either they must be ordinary words used with their ordinary meaning or they must be words whose meaning is explained by means of ordinary words or observable phenomena; the words must be empirically grounded. Obviously I have said nothing meaningful when I say 'Gobbledegook is wise' unless I say who or what 'Gobbledegook' is. I must tell you whether 'Gobbledegook' is the name of a person or thing, or a description, e.g. a word designating a property or kind of event or object. If 'Gobbledegook' is a name, I must point to, and/or give you a description (in familiar words) of, the object referred to in order for you to understand what I have said. I may say 'Gobbledegook is the student over there with the short hair'. If 'gobbledegook' is a descriptive term, I must give you in familiar words an expression which means the same or show you what it means by giving you examples of things which are 'gobbledegook' and contrasting them with examples of things which are not. Further, if I claim to be using 'wise' in an abnormal sense, I must explain by similar procedures what that sense is if my sentence is to say anything meaningful. Words are meaningful if they have an established use in the language. Otherwise they are not—until a use is given to them, the procedures for doing which I have briefly outlined.

That the meaningfulness of a statement depends on the empirical cashability of the words which occur in the sentence which expresses it is a view held by writers as diverse as St. Thomas Aquinas and David Hume. Aquinas held that the meanings of predicates applied to God 'are known to us solely to the extent that they are said of creatures'.[3] Hume held that words which purport to denote 'ideas' or, in more modern terms, properties in fact do so only if we have had 'impressions' of them, or, again in more modern terms, have observed instances of them: 'When we entertain, therefore, any suspicion that a philosophical term is employed without any meaning or idea (as is but too frequent), we need but enquire *from what impression is that supposed idea derived*? And if it be impossible to assign any, this will serve to confirm our suspicion'.[4]

If the words of a sentence have meaning, then the sentence is meaningful. Normally (but as we saw earlier not always) a meaningful indicative sentence makes a statement, that is a claim about how things are. It makes a statement if it is coherent to suppose that what it says is either true or false, if it makes a claim about how things are. In view of the normal use of indicative sentences, the onus is, I think, on a man who claims that indicative sentences of a certain kind do not make statements, to produce arguments in favour of his case. In Chapter 6 I shall consider arguments in favour of the view that credal sentences do not make statements, and I shall find them inadequate.

One sufficient condition of a sentence making a statement is that there be established ways of arguing for or against what it expresses, where the arguments are recognized as tending to establish conclusions. (The verificationist of course wishes to argue that this is both a sufficient and a necessary condition of factual meaningfulness; but that is not my claim here.) If p is evidence for q, then q is a claim about how things are. I am not saying that the established ways of arguing will necessarily

[3] St. Thomas Aquinas, *Summa contra Gentiles*, I.33.6 (Bk. I, trans. Anton C. Pegis under the title *On the Truth of the Catholic Faith*, Bk. I, New York, 1955).
[4] David Hume, *An Enquiry Concerning Human Understanding*, ed. L. A. Selby-Bigge (2nd edn., Oxford, 1902), p. 22.

always (or even often) yield true results—whether they can be guaranteed to do so depends rather on the field of discourse in question and the structure of the argument—but merely that the existence of such ways of arguing for them shows that we are dealing with claims about how things are which are either true or false.

Proofs of Coherence and Incoherence

Given that a certain sentence expresses a statement, makes a claim, what further must be the case if it is to express a coherent claim? We saw in Chapter 2 that if a statement expresses an incoherent supposition, it will entail a self-contradictory statement—which henceforward I will often call, simply, a contradiction. The statement expresses an incoherent supposition, for buried in it is a claim that a thing is so and that it is not so— and it is not coherent to suppose that that could be. It follows that if a statement does not entail any contradiction, then it expresses a coherent supposition.

Such are formal conditions for coherence and incoherence, but how can they be applied? Can we use them to prove of any given statement of doubtful status that it is or that it is not coherent? It certainly looks as if one could prove a given statement incoherent by proving that it entails a contradiction. But how, in order to show a statement coherent, can we prove that it does not entail any contradiction? One cannot list all the entailments of a statement, for any statement entails an infinite number of statements. Generally, we cannot prove a statement p to be coherent by proving what it *entails*. The fact that it entails many coherent statements would not show it to be coherent; for all statements, coherent or not, entail many coherent statements. 'Some squares have five sides' is incoherent, but it entails 'some squares have sides' which is coherent. Our only hope of proving a statement p to be coherent is by showing that it *is entailed by* some other statement r; and that would prove it to be coherent if and only if r was coherent. So to prove one statement coherent you need to assume that some other statement (or conjunction of statements) is coherent. You can prove p to be coherent if you can show that it follows deductively from another statement r which is coherent. For if r makes a coherent claim about the world and p follows deductively from r and so is involved in the claim that r, p must also be coherent. Put another way, if r is coherent, no contradiction follows from r, and therefore, since p follows from r, no contradiction follows from p, and so p is coherent. But proof only gets off the ground if you assume that a certain other statement r is coherent. So you have to assume the coherence of one statement in order to prove the coherence of another. Further, proofs of both coherence and incoherence depend on assumptions about what entails what, which means in effect assumptions about other statements being incoherent. For a statement p entails a statement q if and only if p and not-q are inconsistent, that is 'p and not-q' is an incoherent statement.

A proof is a good deductive proof if it starts from true premisses and is valid (that is, the premisses entail the conclusion) No. doubt many good proofs of coherence and incoherence can be given along the above lines, although I see no reason to suppose that for any statement of dubious status such a proof of coherence or incoherence can be given. But proofs will only be useful, will only convince rational men, if men accept the premisses and the rules of inference by which the conclusion is reached and that applies to proofs of coherence and incoherence as much as to other proofs. A proof of coherence or incoherence may be valid, but it will only convince (and will rightly only convince) if the hearers accept that a certain statement entails a certain other statement, and that a certain statement is coherent, or that a certain other statement is contradictory. So only if we can reasonably assume certain statements to be coherent, to be contradictory, or to entail other statements straight off can any proof of the coherence or incoherence of some dubious statement get off the ground. (Maybe any statement can be up for question at some time, but only if other statements are not up for question at the same time.) We can indeed reasonably assume some statements to be coherent straight off, as was argued earlier, and the same surely applies to entailments. Some entailments obviously hold. 'John has red hair' obviously entails 'someone has red hair'. 'All men are mortal and Socrates is a man' obviously entails 'Socrates is mortal'. We can see straight off that these entailments hold, because we can see straight off that 'John has red hair, but no one has red hair' and 'all men are mortal, and Socrates is a man, but he is not mortal' are incoherent statements. We have enough initial consensus on coherence and incoherence, consensus that certain statements are coherent and certain other statements are incoherent, for some proofs that further statements are coherent (or incoherent, as the case may be) to be given which are not merely good proofs, but ones which will convince all reasonable men.

For example, here is an easy proof of incoherence. Suppose that a physicist much influenced by Eastern thought tells us that 'all physical objects which exist, including ones many miles apart, are composed of the one and only particle a which exists, a particle of maximum diameter 10^{-8} cm'. He assures us that he is using words in their ordinary senses. In that case it follows that 'there exist two physical objects which are many miles apart, of which the first is composed of particle a, and the second is composed of particle a.' It follows from that that 'particle a has a diameter of many miles'. For a particle can only be in two different places at once if it is partly in one place and partly in the other place, and so extends over the space between them. Hence it follows from the original statement that 'a has a diameter of more than 10^{-8} cm and no diameter of more than 10^{-8} cm'—which is a contradiction. The incoherence of the original statement has been demonstrated by bringing to the surface a contradiction buried in it.

Here next is an easy proof of coherence. A physicist claims 'light behaves sometimes like a stream of particles and sometimes like waves'. A philosopher suspects that the physicist is talking nonsense. The patient physicist persuades the philosopher. He says: 'you surely agree that the following statement is coherent: "rays of light bend round obstacles in their way, in the way in which waves do; and very weak light, when passed through a slit to reach a photographic plate on the other side, makes spots on the plate, in the way that a stream of small particles would".' The philosopher agrees that this statement is coherent. The physicist then points out to him that that statement entails the statement 'light behaves sometimes like a stream of particles and sometimes like waves'. The philosopher is brought to see that the latter statement is coherent by having a detailed story told to him of a set of circumstances which would make it true. The proof will be made especially strong if the physicist can actually show the philosopher the phenomena described by his statement, and so long as the philosopher agrees that the statement does describe the phenomena exhibited by the physicist, he will have to agree that the physicist's claim is coherent.

Proofs of coherence or incoherence such as those given depend, as we have seen, on assumptions about other statements being coherent or contradictory, and claims that one statement entails another. If an opponent agrees with the proponent of a proof in his claims over these matters, the proof will persuade. But with the more controversial cases, an opponent is liable to jib at the proponent's assumptions, and then the proof, though it may be in fact valid, will not be seen to be valid and so will not persuade. Thus in my view 'positrons are electrons travelling backwards in time', a suggestion seriously put forward by the physicist R. P. Feynman,[5] is an incoherent supposition, and 'there are places not spatially related to other places' is a coherent supposition. But these are highly controversial claims. I should attempt my proof of the incoherence of the first statement on the following lines: Let s_1 be a state of a positron at t_1, and s_3 be a state of that positron at a slightly later time t_3. Now if the positron is 'travelling backwards in time', this entails that (part of) the cause of s_1 is s_3. But necessarily, if a state s_3 is (part of) the cause of another state s_1 ,then (in the absence of other interfering factors), by preventing the occurrence of s_3 I prevent the occurrence of s_1. Even if it be not physically possible, it is nevertheless logically possible for me so to act at any time prior to t_3, including a time t_2 lying between t_1 and t_3, to prevent the occurrence of s_3. But it is not logically possible for me to act at t_2 so as to prevent the occurrence of s_1, which has already happened. So, I suggest, 'positrons are electrons travelling backwards in time' entails the contradiction 'there are states of affairs such that is both logically possible and not logically possible for an agent acting at a certain specified time to prevent their occurrence'.

Now some opponents *may* be convinced by this argument, but others will not be, because they will not accept my claims about what entails what. An opponent might deny that my entailment

[5] R. P. Feynman, 'The Theory of Positrons', *Physical Review*, 1949, **76**, 749–59.

holds by denying any of the stages of my argument. These involve subsidiary claims about what entails what and claims about what is or is not logically possible, i.e. is a coherent supposition. The opponent may deny that if something travels backwards in time, then (part of) the cause of one of its states s_1 is a state of it s_3 at a later time. Or he may claim that it is logically possible for me to act at t_2 so as to prevent what has already happened at t_1.

Similar difficulties arise with coherence proofs. I say that 'there are places not spatially related to other places' is coherent.[6] An opponent denies this. To persuade him I argue thus: 'Imagine the following: every night when you go to sleep you wake up in a world where things behave in as regular and predictable a way as in this world, and you meet there people who look and behave like people in this world. When you go to sleep in that world you wake up again in this one. Yet however far anyone were to travel in this world they could not find the place where you spend your nights; nor however far anyone were to travel in the other world could they find any places of this world.' I thus attempt to describe a coherent state of affairs. Suppose you accept that I have done so, that I have uttered coherent statements. I then say that those statements entail that there are places not spatially related to other places. If you also accept that the entailment follows you must withdraw your claim that 'there are places not spatially related to other places' is incoherent, for you have accepted that it would be true in a perfectly coherent state of affairs. But of course you may deny that the entailment follows or that the purported description of the imaginary state of affairs which I have given ('every night when you go to sleep . . . ', etc.) is coherent.

So both these, and generally all other, attempted proofs of coherence or incoherence may fail to convince through an opponent in all honesty failing to accept a proponent's claims about what follows from what, and what else is coherent. Fortunately that is not the end of the matter. For one thing, the proponent of incoherence or coherence can attempt a different proof. Or he can try to show his opponent that the original

---

[6] This example, and the kind of argument by which its coherence is supported, is taken from Anthony Quinton, 'Spaces and Times', *Philosophy*, 1962, **37**, 130–47. For discussion see my *Space and Time* (London, 1968), Ch. 2.

proof really does work. Suppose that the disagreement turns on whether a statement p does entail another statement r. A man attempting to prove an incoherence wishes to show that it does. Argument that one statement p entails another one r relies, as we have seen, on other claims about entailments and so on claims about what are incoherent suppositions. The opponent of the argument does not accept that p entails r because he does not accept one of these subsidiary claims. Then argument can be produced for these subsidiary claims on just the same lines as before. This argument may convince the opponent, or it may not—because he cannot 'see' the truth of some sub-subsidiary claim about entailment or coherence being put forward in the course of backing up the subsidiary claim.

Thus suppose that my attempted proof of the coherence of 'there are places not spatially related to other places' is not accepted by an opponent because in all honesty he cannot 'see' the coherence of the more detailed supposition which I made; ' . . . every night when you go to sleep you wake up in a world where things behave in as regular and predictable a way as in this world'. My opponent objects: 'I think that what you ask me to imagine is incoherent. If a man wakes up, he wakes up at the place at which his body is. A body is a material object. It is not coherent to suppose that a material object moves from one place to another without moving in a continuous path. For even if a material object a is very like another one b which was at a distance from it, unless a has travelled along a path from where b was, a must be merely very similar to b, not the same object as b.' So I must attempt to show my second and fuller supposition coherent if I am to show the original supposition coherent. I can do that if I can describe a state of affairs yet more fully so that my description entails the second supposition, and my opponent admits the new description to be coherent and the entailment to hold. Alternatively, I can show the coherence of the original supposition if I can actually show you circumstances which make the supposition true, and you are prepared to agree that the circumstances do make the supposition true. Of course in this particular case to show you such circumstances might be a bit difficult! and even so you might try to insist that one of the 'worlds' was only a 'dream world'. Alternatively, as in this case, an opponent's failure to accept that my second purported description is coherent may arise from its clashing with some principle which he holds about coherence. The principle in this case is that it is not coherent to suppose that a material object moves without moving along a continuous path. In that case the best strategy for me is to attempt to show either that this principle is false or that my purported description does not clash with it. I can do the former if I can produce a coherent description of a case where a material object moves non-continuously; and you will see that the principle is wrong if you 'see' that I have produced a coherent description. I may show that my purported description does not clash with my opponent's principle if I claim in my story that when a man goes to sleep he leaves his body behind and wakes up with a new body. An opponent may now agree that with this qualification I have given a coherent description; or he may say in all honesty that he still fails (or fails 'even more') to see its coherence. And so we go on, each trying again to convince the other.

Your opponent may not accept the particular claims which you make about entailment and coherence but you can go on attempting to prove them to him by similar methods, trying to find a common starting-point and a route of proof that he will accept as valid. If a man can give an acceptable proof on these lines then he has indeed proved coherence or incoherence, as the case may be. But if he cannot (and cannot adduce other reasons in favour of his claim) there is no reason for anyone else to accept his claims about what does or does not make sense. Yet many men do convince others by producing proofs along the lines which I have sketched. Even when a man fails to convince his opponent it may well be that if he attempted to justify the claims made in the course of his purported proofs with yet further proofs he would succeed. Maybe if men argued hard and long enough they would by such proofs finally reach agreement about all such matters, as they do about some. Yet I must admit to feeling some scepticism about this matter, some doubt about whether men have enough initial consensus about what is coherent and what entails what, are clever enough and have enough imagination to reach agreed proofs which would settle all disputes about whether a statement is coherent or incoherent.

The question therefore arises as to whether reasons less strong than compelling proofs can be given for thinking some statements coherent and others incoherent. An interesting parallel from mathematics suggests the answer. There are many mathematical statements which, if true, are logically necessary or, if false, logically impossible, and yet which have not been proved to be one or the other by the normal way of showing them or their negations to be deductive consequences of axioms. Yet indirect but by no means compelling evidence has been produced giving reasonable men considerable grounds for assenting to their truth or falsity. For example, no one has ever proved Goldbach's conjecture to be true, that every even number is the sum of two prime numbers. Yet it has been shown to hold for all of the very many even numbers for which it has been tested. This is generally supposed and surely rightly supposed to count in favour of the truth of Goldbach's conjecture, although not conclusively so. Even though the question whether a statement is coherent, like the question whether a mathematical statement is true, is a question to which the answer is logically necessary, nevertheless when deductive proofs fail to answer the question, non-deductive arguments may provide reliable guidance as to what is the right answer.

Let us understand by an inductive argument an argument from premisses to a conclusion in which the premisses count in favour of,[7] provide evidence for, the conclusion, without entailing it. Empirical science of course depends crucially on inductive arguments. When the scientist argues from his observational data to his scientific theory or to his predictions about the future, he can give only an inductive argument. The past behaviour of sun, moon, and planets counts in favour of such and such predictions about their future behaviour without making them certain. For any prediction you like would be compatible with observations which have been made so far; some predictions, however, are very much more likely to be true than are other predictions. Philosophers of science have

---

[7] Although we do say, and, I have urged, rightly say with respect to the mathematical examples that the evidence 'counts in favour of' the conclusion, it should be pointed out that talk about 'counts in favour of' does not in that case conform to the usual axioms of the probability calculus. I have argued this in my *An Introduction to Confirmation Theory* (London, 1973), see Ch. 4.

done much work in codifying inductive criteria, that is setting out those features of premises p and conclusions q which make an argument from p to q a strong inductive argument, that is one in which p provides considerable evidence for q. The criteria of inductive evidence are such criteria as that if a theory gives successful predictions over a wide area that is evidence of its truth; or that if a certain kind of thing (described in a natural way) has happened in the past under certain circumstances, that is evidence that it will happen again in future under similar circumstances. Thus the fact that Newton's theory of motion or the atomic theory of chemistry gave successful predictions over a wide area was evidence of its truth, and the fact that all copper so far has been found to expand on heating, is evidence that on another occasion if a new piece of copper is heated it will expand.

Now what kind of inductive arguments could there be to show the coherence or the incoherence of a statement? Clearly there could be either arguments which had as their premises non-factual statements, or ones which had among their premises factual statements. It is hard to see how one could have a useful argument of the former kind of any inductive strength. The obvious candidates for non-factual premises would be claims that certain statements were coherent or that they were incoherent. So one would have an argument for example, from 'q is coherent', 'r is coherent', 's is coherent', to 'p is coherent'. If it is an inductive argument, the conclusion will not be entailed by the premises. So how can the coherence of q, r, and s make it likely that p is coherent? Perhaps in this way. q says 'an object is both φ_1 and ψ_1'; r says 'an object is both φ_2 and ψ_2'; s says 'an object is both φ_3 and ψ_3' (where φ's are similar properties to each other, and ψ's are similar propeties to each other); p says 'an object is both φ_4 and ψ_4'. So the evidence of the compatibility of a number of pairs of properties, one of each pair from each group of properties, counts as evidence in favour of the compatibility of another such pair. This argument seems to exemplify a standard pattern of inductive inference. Thus from the premises that it is coherent to suppose that an object be both red and square, that an object be both orange and octagonal, that an object be both brown and triangular, one might conclude that it was probable that it is coherent to suppose that an object be both green and round. But although such an argument could be given, I find it hard to think of an example where the premisses could be known to be true, and yet the conclusion could not be known to be true by a normal deductive argument. For only in such a case would an inductive argument to a conclusion that a proposition p was probably coherent be of any use—that is in getting someone rationally to believe what he would not otherwise rationally believe. Inductive arguments are of use only if deductive ones cannot be had, and arguments are only of use if their premisses are known to be true. In the kind of example cited if we reflect on the coherence of the statements considered in the premisses, we will in practice come to see (not merely infer as probable) that all statements of the form 'there is an object which has a property of type φ, and also a property of type ψ' are coherent, and so the conclusion—'it is coherent to suppose that an object is both φ_4 and ψ_4'—is deducible with certainty from premisses known to be true; it does not need to be supported by a mere inductive argument. Thus in the particular example considered, reflection on the premisses will show us that all statements ascribing to an object both a colour and a two-dimensional shape are coherent, and so the conclusion can be known with as much certainty as its premisses. There is here a crucial disanalogy with normal inductive arguments of similar form from factual premisses to factual conclusions. 'a is φ_1 and ψ_1', 'b is φ_2 and ψ_2', 'c is φ_3 and ψ_3' may have the same form as 'd is φ_4 and ψ_4' and yet the former have been observed to be true and the latter not yet so observed. But where we are dealing, not with factual claims, but with coherence claims, the notion of observing (in the literal sense) does not come in. We 'see' metaphorically that the premisses are true. But in a case such as we have cited, we could also, if we thought about it, 'see' that the conclusion was true, and so we would not need the inductive argument to give it support.

However, an inductive argument from factual premisses is of more interest. We could have an argument from some datum of observation q which by normal inductive criteria counts as evidence in favour of some non-analytic claim p. If p is true, it must be coherent. So q counts as evidence in favour of the coherence of p. Such an argument could certainly be useful. For in this case (unlike in the previous case) a man's grounds for believing p to be coherent are his grounds for believing p to be true; and, p being non-analytic, it could easily be that the only evidence he could get of the truth of p was inductive evidence, codified in an argument from premises known to be true. As the example below and later examples will illustrate, mere reflection on p or attempts to construct normal deductive arguments might give no grounds for supposing p to be coherent; and the inductive argument alone might provide these grounds. Normal inductive evidence that an object is both φ and ψ is evidence that these are compatible properties, that a claim that an object is both is coherent. Of course if we already know that φ and ψ are incompatible properties (i.e. this knowledge is already part of our evidence) no new evidence can have any tendency to show that a particular object is both φ and ψ. But lacking that knowledge, if we find other good reason to believe that an object is both, we have found good reason to believe that the properties are compatible.

Here now is an example of how factual evidence can count in favour of the coherence of a statement. Let p be the statement 'there is a strip of paper with only one surface' (i.e. the surface on one side cf the paper is continuous with that on the other side). A group of men cannot agree whether this is a coherent supposition, nor produce acceptable proofs that it is or that it is not. The matter would of course be settled if such a strip could be produced for observation, but we suppose that no one has been able to produce one. Then a number of travellers arrive from a distant land, claiming to have seen such a strip, although they do not know how to make one. They produce their stories independently and prove to be reliable witnesses over other matters. Surely by normal inductive criteria their general reliability (what they say on other occasions being true) is some evidence of their reliability on a particular occasion, in which case it is some factual evidence of the truth and so of the coherence of p. Certainly, if we *knew* that p was incoherent it would be no evidence at all of their reliability in this matter. But if we do not know that p is incoherent, I suggest that our common intuition in these matters reveals that the testimony of generally reliable witnesses to the truth of p is evidence of its coherence. I, we say about the mathematical examples that inductive evidence can count in favour of their truth (even though, if true, they are true of logical necessity, and, if false, they are false of logical necessity), in consistency we must say the same about coherence claims (which also, if true, are true of logical necessity, and if false, are false of logical necessity).

There could not be an inductive argument of the same kind from factual premisses in favour of incoherence, because while evidence that a statement is true is evidence that it is coherent, evidence that it is false is hardly evidence that it is incoherent. For a statement is true only if it is coherent; but it can easily be false without being incoherent.

So although I do not rule out the possibility of useful inductive arguments of other kinds to the coherence of statements, the only kind of inductive argument for which I see much future is one of the above kind from known factual premisses p, to a non-analytic claim q; evidence for q's truth being evidence that q is coherent. Such an argument I shall call an indirect argument for the coherence of q, and I contrast such arguments with the normal deductive arguments for coherence or incoherence, which I discussed earlier. My main concern in this book will be with these latter arguments which I call direct arguments. Obviously we need only concern ourselves with indirect arguments, if we cannot marshal direct arguments to prove the coherence or incoherence of the claims with which we are concerned. In general I have assumed in this book so far that it is one thing to show the coherence of a supposition and another to show its truth. If, unfortunately, we have to rely on an indirect argument for coherence, the only evidence we have of coherence is also evidence of truth.

4

The Words of Theology—1 Words with Old and New Senses

IF the credal sentences of theology are to make coherent claims the words which occur in them must have meaning. In the next two chapters we shall consider how the words of theology get their meaning. This is crucial. In order to know whether credal sentences make coherent claims, we must know what claims they make, and that depends on how their words get their meaning. I propose in this chapter to develop in detail the consequence of two alternative suppositions—that theology uses the words of ordinary language in their normal senses, and that theology gives new senses to the words of ordinary language. Almost all the words used by theology are words which have a perfectly ordinary and non-ambiguous use in talking about non-theological matters. 'Person', 'wise', 'good', 'body', etc. are such words. The meaning which they have when used to talk about ordinary or non-theological matters I will call their mundane meaning. There are certainly some words used by theology which are peculiar to it—for example, 'omnipotent', 'omniscient', and 'incarnate', but it is plausible to suppose that these can be given a verbal definition by the ordinary words; that is, a number of ordinary words can be found which together are equivalent in meaning to the technical terms. 'Omnipotent', for example, might plausibly be said to mean 'able to do anything'; 'omniscient' might plausibly be said to mean 'knowing all things', and 'incarnate' 'having taken to himself the body of a man'. (More careful definitions of two of these technical terms will be provided in subsequent chapters, but they too will use ordinary words.) The crucial issue is in what senses are the ordinary words used.

Theology using Ordinary Words in Ordinary Senses

I will begin by investigating in detail the consequence of the supposition that theology uses only ordinary words in their mundane senses, together with words which can be given verbal definitions in terms of the former. How on this supposition can theology tell us of a strange and marvellous world so different from the ordinary world of human experience? The answer must be that although the theologian uses ordinary words to denote ordinary properties, he claims that the properties cited are manifested in unusual combinations and circumstances and to unusual degrees. God is a powerful person—but a very very much more powerful person than any with whom we are ordinarily acquainted. His power, unlike the power of human rulers, is combined with great goodness. Human persons have bodies; he does not. And so on. That we can conceive of a very unfamiliar world by postulating the properties of the familiar world existing in very unfamiliar combinations was the point made by Hume when he claimed, in his terminology, that although simple ideas must conform to impressions, complex ideas need not do so. (Very roughly— impressions are things immediately experienced; ideas are concepts. Simple ideas are the ideas of such basic properties as blueness, hardness, roundness, etc. Complex ideas are ideas formed out of these.) Hence, Hume writes, 'I can imagine to myself such a city as the *New Jerusalem*, whose pavement is gold and walls are rubies tho' I never saw any such'.[1] In a similar way, we can describe the existence of people with two heads, or animals with one horn in the centre of their heads, or men made of wood. We can also describe a world different from ours in that the temporal successions of things are different from those in ours. Curses uttered by anyone who carries a certain wand are immediately followed by the fulfilment of the

---

[1] David Hume, *A Treatise of Human Nature* (first pub. 1739), ed. L. A. Selby-Bigge (Oxford, 1888), 1.1.1.

curse. Teeth planted in the ground are followed by the appearance of men, etc. Further we can describe worlds different from ours in that properties are exemplified to very different degrees.[2] We can talk about a world where men are two inches tall or alternatively a world where men are twenty foot tall; and a world where objects shine with a brightness brighter than any object in ours, and there are animals far stronger than the strongest elephant we know. We can do this because we have derived from experience the concepts of various properties exemplified in differing degrees, and can thus conceive of an object which has even more of the property than one which we have observed. Schematically, we observe several objects, a, b, c, d, each of which is more-φ than its predecessor. Thus we derive from experience the concept of being more-φ than some other object. Then we can conceive of an object which is more-φ than d, although we have never observed one. So for both these reasons we can use our old words to describe worlds very different from ours.

Some science clearly uses familiar words in familiar senses to describe things beyond our experience. The proponent of the atomic theory of chemistry tells us that solids, liquids, and gases consist of millions of molecules; that molecules are groups of atoms; that atoms are very small particles. Here it seems that 'particle', 'group', and 'consist of' are being used in their ordinary senses; but the chemist is claiming that there are particles different in size from those previously known. (An account of this kind would not be a plausible account of what the physicist is doing when he attempts to describe the world below the atomic level, but we shall come to this point later.)

Of course as we saw in the last chapter not all properties can coherently be postulated to coexist; nor, analogously, can all properties coherently be postulated to exist to any degree. The issue arises whether the theologian or scientist is contra-

[2] This second point was inadequately appreciated by Hume. If he had properly appreciated it, he would have been less worried by his example of the missing shade of blue. (See his *Enquiry Concerning Human Understanding*, Sect. 2.) Why we can conceive of a certain shade of blue, and indeed imagine it, although we have never observed an instance of it, is because we have observed instances of other shades of blue and instances of the concept of being darker-in-blueness-than. We can thus conceive of a shade darker in blueness than a certain shade which we have seen.

dicting himself in prising words out of their normal context and postulating their application to an object of a very different kind from that to which they are normally applied. If all φ's so far observed have been ψ, does it make sense to talk of φ's which are not-ψ? Thus Flew points out that the crucial terms in the theologian's definition of God 'are all essentially personal: not only is God required to be in general personal; he is also, in particular, to have a will and, as maker and preserver, to be an agent. Goodness, which in some contexts belongs to things, is also here presumably personal: indeed the New Testament writers often prefer to speak of love.' Flew goes on to claim that 'precisely because' these characteristics are 'so distinctively personal, they cannot without losing all their original meaning, be thus uprooted from their peculiarly human habitat and transferred to a context so totally different'.[3] A similar objection could readily be made to the scientist's activity. A scientist talks of atoms having mass, diameter, and charge. Yet the original context of these terms was that of describing medium-sized material objects. The procedures for measuring the mass, etc. of the latter are procedures which cannot be used to determine the mass, etc. of an atom—you cannot weigh individual atoms in a balance. Hence a Flewian might say that 'precisely because' mass, length, etc. are properties so distinctively characteristic of medium-sized material objects, 'they cannot without losing all their original meaning be thus uprooted' from that habitat and be 'transferred to a context so totally different'. He might say that if atoms and molecules are to be said to have 'mass' and 'length', these latter terms must have a completely different sense from their mundane sense.[4]

[3] Antony Flew, *God and Philosophy* (London, 1966), p. 37.

[4] We do not have to look far in the philosophy of science to find just such an objection actually made. It was the hallmark of operationalism that a concept is defined by the set of operations which establish whether or not it is instantiated. P. W. Bridgman illustrated this doctrine with reference to the concept of length. The normal operations which establish the length of an object are to lay rulers alongside it. But there are of course other operations often used—e.g. light-signals. However, he writes, 'if we have more than one set of operations, we have more than one concept, and strictly there should be a separate name to correspond to each different set of operations'. (P. W. Bridgman, *The Logic of Modern Physics*, New York, 1927, p. 10.) 'What is the meaning of the statement that the diameter of an electron is 10^{-13} cm? The answer is found by examining the oper-

We saw earlier in the chapter that it certainly does not follow from the fact that the only φ's we have ever seen are ψ that it is not coherent to suppose that there are φ's which are not-ψ. Even if the only persons we have seen have bodies, perhaps it is coherent to suppose that there is a person without a body. What is needed is detailed argument to show that this supposition is or is not coherent (and Flew attempts to provide this). The kind of argument needed to show this kind of thing was analysed in the last chapter. I shall be producing detailed arguments of this kind myself in subsequent chapters.

Note that if we do say that such a word as 'good' is being used in the same sense in 'God is good' and in 'Florence Nightingale was good', that does not mean that God's goodness is not very different from Florence Nightingale's. This is clear from trivial examples. I and my filing cabinet are both said (without these words being used ambiguously) truly to 'weigh ten stone'. Yet my ten-stone weight is very different from (i.e. itself *has* very different properties from) that of my filing cabinet in many ways. It is ten stone of flesh and blood as opposed to ten stone of steel and paper for a start. My ten stone can be reduced by my eating less and taking more exercise; the ten stone of the filing cabinet cannot be reduced in these ways. But all of this does not mean that 'weighs ten stone' is being used in different senses, to denote different properties. It is simply that the property of weighing ten stone amounts to something different in different kinds of thing.

Theology using Words in New Senses

The alternative to supposing that theology uses familiar words in their normal senses is to suppose that it gives to old

---

ations by which the number 10^{-13} was obtained.' (Ibid., p. 22.) So, strictly speaking, Bridgman claims, we cannot talk of length or mass outside the range measurable by ruler or balance. If we do, we are using 'length', etc. equivocally. However, it is not at all obvious that this view is correct. The methods by which we ascertain the 'mass' of objects of various kinds very much overlap. There is not one set of methods for objects of one kind and an entirely different set of methods for objects of another kind. As one reads through a scientific textbook, it looks as if when the scientist talks of the 'mass' of an atom, he is talking about the same property as when he talks about the 'mass' of a lead ball, but one to find the value of which in practice we need different techniques.

words a new sense; that 'wise', 'powerful', 'person', etc. are given new senses in their introduction into theology. Now quite obviously such words are not given *entirely* new senses in such a case. There is more in common between 'wisdom' attributed to God and 'wisdom' attributed to man than between 'wisdom' attributed to God and 'folly' or 'weighing ten stone' attributed to man. That being so, the process of giving a new sense to old words must take the form of amending the meaning of old words. This could be done either by amending the semantic rules or by amending the syntactic rules for the use of old words, or by both. Semantic rules for the use of a word 'φ' could be amended either by introducing new examples of the circumstances in which it is correct or incorrect to use it, or by altering our understanding of the role of existing standard examples.

Before spelling out my positive account, I need, however, to rebut one suggestion as to how new meanings are given to old words in theology. It may be suggested that the old words such as 'person', 'good', 'wise', 'powerful', and 'merciful' are given new meaning by new standard examples of their correct application being provided by the peculiar and private experiences of the religious believer. If you want to know what the 'mercy' of God means, an evangelical Christian may say, get down on your knees and ask God to forgive your sins and you will feel it. If you want to know what the 'power' of God means, ask for his help and you will feel it. I am expressing this view by rather crude examples, but they do illustrate the basic idea, that the meaning of theological terms is to be explained in part through the experiences of the religious believer. If this view is adopted, it does of course explain why some people justifiably believe in God and others do not. The difference lies in the former alone having had experiences which they rightly characterize as experiences of God. Clearly the experiences would have to be, not special and semi-public experiences like visions, which most religious believers do not claim to have, but the private experiences given to a believer in his prayer and worship.

Suggestions of this sort have at times received unduly short shrift from philosophers. It has been said that the most which men could experience on the above account would be their own feelings (e.g. of being overwhelmed), not something objective and apart from their feelings (e.g. a source of mercy, or even God himself); the latter would be an unjustifiable inference from the former. But this will not do. Quite clearly ordinary men have visual sensations and, thereby, as a result, see public objects such as desks and tables and chairs. Why should not the religious believer through having a peculiar experience be aware of a reality beyond that experience to which he gives the name 'God'? But then a second objection arises. The object purportedly experienced is not a public object, since only some people (viz. religious believers) claim to experience it. Hence they do not really experience it. For if there was a public object there, all men would be aware of it. Hardly. Those without a sense of smell cannot smell roses, but the smell of roses is real enough. Some men are blind and cannot see the rainbow, but it is there all the same. We saw in Chapter 3 that agreement between a number of persons about what they claimed to experience sufficed to show that there was something public experienced. That others claim to experience nothing does not damage the claim of some to have experienced something.

But this is the point at which the analogy with smell and sight breaks down. When the rainbow is there, a number of observers, who claim to have sight, will, if they take the trouble to look, agree that it is there; they can provide detailed descriptions of it which coincide, and say how long it lasts. But those who have religious experiences do not claim to have them simultaneously. One man on his knees may claim to have an experience, while the man next to him (equally given to making claims about religious experiences) may not on that occasion have any such feeling. Even if two men kneeling together both claim to have a religious experience at the same time, they may give very different descriptions of it. All of this is not to deny (or to affirm) that veridical religious experiences occur. But it is to point out that they are not a sufficiently public and objective phenomenon for them to be a means of giving a meaning to words. If a word 'φ' is to be given a meaning through such a process, then the learner must be shown examples of things which are φ and have them contrasted with examples of things which are not-φ. But if no one knows when the learner is having a religious experience of some object or property φ (because no one else is necessarily having one at the same time), then no one else can tell him that the experience which he is having is an experience of φ.

Further, many devout religious believers claim to have no peculiarly religious experiences. They would say that their experiences during prayer and worship can be fully described in mundane terms, such as 'sense of peace', 'conscious of life being worth while' in which the words have the same meaning as when they are used to talk about other matters. (And all those one-time religious believers who have subsequently ceased to be believers have usually wanted to say just that about their former 'religious experiences'.) The religious believer who feels that his experiences can be adequately *described* in non-religious terms will of course normally add that they cannot be fully *explained*, without reference to God, their source. But that is not what is at stake here. The issue is whether some form of religious experience is necessary to give meaning to the terms of theological language. And our conclusion must be that, if it is, many who call themselves religious believers do not fully understand that language. But they appear to enter into theological discussion with those who claim to have peculiarly religious experiences without there occurring any very obvious failure of understanding. And those who do claim to have peculiarly religious experiences would not, I think, in general wish to say of other religious believers that they do not understand theological language. For these reasons I conclude that the suggestion that ordinary words are given a new sense in theology through new standard examples of their correct application being provided by the experiences of the religious believer is not a fruitful one. Nor do I think that it is plausible to suppose that ordinary words are given a new sense by new public examples of their correct application being provided. The theist never gives you any other public examples of 'persons' than those which we would normally call persons, of 'good' deeds other than those which we would normally call 'good'.

If the theist does give a new sense to such words as 'person', or 'wise', or 'powerful' when he says that God is 'a person', 'wise', and 'powerful', he is clearly using the words in wider senses than the normal ones. For he does not normally wish to deny that things ordinarily called 'persons', or 'wise', or 'powerful' are really so. So if the meaning of these words is changed, it must be extended or loosened up. Given that no new standard examples are introduced, there are two ways in which this can be done. One is to modify the role of the standard examples in the semantic rules. The other is to abandon some of the syntactic rules. I shall illustrate these processes for a word 'W' normally used for designating a property W (e.g. the word 'blue' normally used to designate the property of being blue). In describing these processes I shall assume that the semantic and syntactic sets of rules are sets of rules for 'W' both of which have to be satisfied in order that the word may apply correctly to an object. (My point would need to be expressed differently if I supposed that satisfaction of one *or* other set of rules sufficed for an object correctly to be called 'W'.)

The first process is to change the semantic rules so that the role therein of the standard examples becomes a different one. We saw in Chapter 3 that the normal way in which the semantic rules operate is that certain standard examples are provided, and then an object is said to be correctly described as 'W' if it resembles the standard objects in the respect in which they resemble each other to the extent to which they resemble each other. The modification to the rules consists in saying that in the new use an object is correctly called 'W' if it resembles the standard examples of W objects in the respect in which they resemble each other either as much as they resemble each other or more than it resembles standard examples of objects which are not-W. This modification will tend to have the effect that the word will now apply to a wider class of actual and conceivable objects than it did before. However, if this modification is to produce any significant effect it must be accompanied by a modification of the syntactic rules. The syntactic rules tie the meaning of 'W' to the meanings of other terms which are partly defined by examples. Thus it may be a rule that if an object is 'W' then it is 'X', and if it is 'X' then it is either 'Y' or 'not-Z'. 'Y' and 'Z' may, like 'W', be terms defined in part by examples, that is by semantic rules. Suppose that the meaning of 'Y' and 'Z' is not changed and so that their semantic rules remain the same; and that the syntactic rules for 'W' remain the same. Then although the new semantic rules for 'W' might by themselves allow various objects rightly to be called 'W' which were not so called before, nevertheless by the semantic rules for 'Y' and 'Z' those objects might count as 'Z and not-Y'. In that case, since both sets of rules have to be satisfied, if the syntactic rules remain the same the objects will be 'not-X' and hence 'not-W'. What the modification to the semantic rules would by itself let in to the class of 'W' objects, is kept out if the syntactic rules remain the same. This is not to say that amending the semantic rules by themselves would not let some new objects into the class of 'W' objects, only that there needs to be amendment to the syntactic rules if the modification is to have much effect. Clearly the more syntactic rules we drop, the wider becomes the class of 'W' objects. The amendments to the syntactic rules will be ones which have the consequence that we can infer less from an object being 'W'. Maybe before we could infer from an object being correctly described as 'W' that it was 'not-P' (e.g. from its being correctly described as 'blue' that it was 'not-red'). The modification may consist in so amending the syntactic rules that these by themselves no longer allow this as a legitimate inference.

It may be a simple matter so to amend the syntactic rules. There may be a single isolated rule which says that you can deduce from 'X is W' that 'X is not-P', which can be dropped. Or it may be that the concepts of W and P are interwoven with many other concepts, so that a number of syntactic rules have to be altered in order that the cited inference no longer hold. Thus 'X is W' may entail 'X is Q' which may entail 'X is R' which may entail 'X is not P'. We would need to amend some other rule, e.g. the rule allowing us to deduce 'X is Q' from 'X is W', in order to ensure that the inference no longer held. Or it might be that an amendment to the semantic rules was also necessary. For it could be that it is not coherent to suppose that an object resemble the standard 'W' objects and also the standard 'P' objects to the extent necessary.

Let me illustrate this point about the different kinds of amendment to rules needed to secure some result, from a recent philosophical controversy. Consider the word 'cause'. The vast majority of philosophers agree, as I shall need to urge in Part II, that it is not logically possible that a cause be later in time than its effect. But why is this not logically possible?

It may be that there is an isolated and detachable syntactic rule to this effect, viz. a rule that says that 'E happened at t_1' entails 'if E has a cause, that cause did not occur later than t_1'. A number of writers have in effect urged this when they have claimed that the temporal priority of causes was a 'mere convention for the use of words'[5] which does not reflect anything deep about reality. Their claims seems to amount to the claim that if you dropped the explicit syntactic rule (and perhaps one or two other closely connected syntactic rules), but kept most of the syntactic rules and all the semantic rules, then you would have a concept of 'cause' very similar to our present one, but such that it is logically possible for a 'cause' to follow its 'effect'. Other writers have urged that the syntactic rule in question is not isolatable but follows from other syntactic and semantic rules, many of which would have to be scrapped if we were to allow a 'cause' to follow its 'effect'. Thus R. M. Gale has claimed that a whole range of syntactic and semantic rules would have to be altered—the rules connecting 'cause' with 'action', 'intention', 'memory', 'past', 'future', etc. and the (syntactic and semantic) rules for the use of these terms.[6] I do not pronounce on which of these views is correct, but merely use the controversy to illustrate my point about the different kinds of amendments to rules necessary to secure some result.

When the meaning of a word 'W' is modified by changing the role of examples in the semantic rule for its use (*viz.* saying that to be 'W' an object has only to resemble the standard objects more than objects which are standard cases of 'not-W' objects, but need no longer to resemble the former to the extent to which they resemble each other) and by loosening some syntactic rules (so that some inferences are no longer valid), I shall say that the word 'W' has come to be used (by comparison with its old use) 'analogically'.[7] The loosening of rules means that 'W' comes to designate a different property $W*$. The new concept of $W*$-ness will be internally coherent if the old one was. By a concept

[5] See Roderick M. Chisholm and Richard Taylor 'Making Things to have happened', *Analysis*, 1960, **20**, 73–8. 'This seems to be merely a point of vocabulary'. 'If we do not thus secure the principle by stipulation . . . then there seems to be no reason for supposing that causes must precede their effects' (74).

[6] See R. M. Gale, 'Why a Cause cannot be later than its Effect', *Review of Metaphysics*, 1965, **19**, 209–34.

[7] I shall, however, discuss a different use of 'analogically' in Ch. 5.

being internally coherent, I mean that it is logically possible that it apply to some object, that the word which designates the concept has a meaning. Hence a concept is internally incoherent only if it is not logically possible that it apply to anything. But the effect of loosening-up can only be that the new concept applies to more things than the old one did. So if it was logically possible that the old concept apply, it will be logically possible that the new one apply. An effect of the loosening-up may, however, be that sentences which previously expressed incoherent suppositions now express coherent ones (and conversely).

It may well be now that although it was not coherent to suppose that an object be W and also P, it is coherent to suppose that it be both W^* and P. Or, if that be not coherent, the word 'P' denoting P could be given an analogical sense so that it now denoted P^*, and it could be coherent to suppose that an object be both W^* and P^*. The normal coherence and incoherence proofs could in theory apply and show that these suppositions were or were not coherent. The best proof of coherence would be to exhibit such an object. In default of that you might be able to give an evidently coherent description of one using ordinary words in ordinary senses. This might be difficult to do, however, if the postulated object differed radically from objects with which we are familiar—any attempted description might be far from being *evidently* coherent.

However, once we give analogical senses to words, proofs of coherence or incoherence become very difficult. The less syntactic rules we have for the use of a word, the harder it is to deduce a conclusion from a statement expressed by a sentence which contains the word, or to deduce from some other statement a statement expressed by a sentence containing the word. Yet, as we saw, to prove coherence or incoherence, we need to do just such deducing. Again, if the semantic rule for the use of 'W' is that an object is correctly called 'W' if and only if it resembles certain standard objects in the respect in which and to the extent to which they resemble each other, we have a fairly clear idea of the limits to the use of 'W'. But if we loosen the rule and say that an object is correctly called 'W' even if it does not resemble the standard objects as much as they resemble each other, so long as it resembles them more than it resembles certain standard 'non-W' objects, then we are a great deal less clear about what kind of objects there could be which we have not experienced which would be correctly called 'W'. One man may think that it is evidently coherent to suppose that an object be 'both W and P', and another man be altogether unsure about this. But to prove the coherence of some supposition, we need to point to some other supposition which is evidently coherent. But in so far as now strange unexperienced things quite dissimilar from standard examples of W-objects could be correctly termed 'W', it becomes unclear what suppositions about things which are $W*$ (viz. things correctly called 'W' in the new use of this term) are evidently coherent.

If theology extends the meanings of words in the ways which I have described, it is in no way unique in this.[8] Science does so, and I shall shortly illustrate this from Quantum Theory. One can also readily conceive of men other than professional scientists giving words analogical senses in order to describe phenomena which evade normal description, and I shall give an example of this first.

Non-theological Examples of Words being used in Analogical Senses

Imagine a community of men born blind isolated from men with sight. They are intelligent and have their other senses well developed. They learn to distinguish between the objects of touch, the objects of hearing, the objects of smell, and the objects of taste. They learn to describe the objects of touch as hard or soft, sharp or blunt, rough or smooth, etc.; the objects of hearing as loud or soft, high or low; of smell as sweet or acrid; of taste as sweet or sour, etc. They learn that the objects of touch are the real constituents of the world, the public objects whose public properties all men feel. The objects of hearing, smell, and taste are mere effects produced by the public objects. So to say that an object is rough entails that it is a public object which can be learnt about by feeling. A blind man of genius then suggests that although 'we' have only four senses, it is

---

[8] There is a powerful plea to philosophers to recognize the value of using words in extended senses in order to express ideas which would otherwise be inexpressible, in F. Waismann's 'Analytic-Synthetic' (published in his *How I See Philosophy*, London, 1968; see pp. 172 ff.).

conceivable to suppose that men might have a fifth. Through that fifth sense men would learn about other properties of objects undetectable by the four senses. He attempts to describe these properties. All surfaces, he says, are characterized by them; but they differ from the properties detectable by touch. You do not have to be close to an object to detect these new properties. Words fail him to describe the properties adequately, but he suggests that 'loud' and 'soft' in analogical senses would be quite good descriptions of them. In suggesting analogical uses of these terms, he suggests amending the syntactic and semantic rules governing their use in two ways. He suggests that the semantic rules be amended as follows. In order for an object to be 'loud', it has now to resemble standard examples of loud objects in the respect in which they resemble each other, no longer as much as they resemble each other, but merely more than it resembles standard examples of non-loud objects; e.g. it has to be more like the noise of men shouting than like the noise of men whispering. The man of genius also suggests an amendment to the normal syntactic rule that if something is 'loud' it is a 'noise' (and for that reason the effect of a material object and not a property of a material object). He proposes that it should no longer follow deductively from something being 'loud' that it is a 'noise'. However, most other syntactic rules for the use of the term remain, e.g. that if an object is 'loud' it is not at the same time 'soft'.

The man of genius suggests that it is possible that there be material objects or surfaces thereof which are loud' in the new sense. If the man could actually show you such an object that would prove his point. If he could describe such an object in an evidently coherent way using ordinary words in ordinary senses then he would also have shown that there could be such objects. But if the object is, from the point of view of the blind community, as strange as it is said to be, it is doubtful whether a sufficiently full and evidently coherent description of it using ordinary words in ordinary senses could be given for it to be deducible that in the suggested analogical sense the object is 'loud', but is a material object or surface thereof and not a 'noise'. It may well be that he cannot prove the coherence of his supposition. In that case the supposition is unlikely to be very well received in the community, and many a sophist may attempt a quick proof of its incoherence. And if the man of genius is not very explicit about the analogical senses in which he is using his words, many may be convinced by the sophists. But if the man of genius makes it clear what he is doing, the proofs of incoherence will be less easy to obtain. For there are the same difficulties in proving incoherence as in proving coherence. The less rules there are to delimit the application of the term 'loud', the less easy it will be to show that it could not apply to an individual of a certain kind, viz. a material object or surface thereof.

What will settle the matter? Apart from seeing the object perhaps very little. It is hard to think of any compelling proof of coherence or incoherence which did not involve giving the blind men sight. But there is the less compelling indirect kind of argument which might in fact convince. The blind men would have such an argument if they had inductive evidence of the existence of a material object or surface which is more like loud objects (in the respect in which they are like each other) than like objects which are not loud, yet all the same not very like loud noises in the respect in which they are like each other. The inductive evidence might be of various kinds. It might be that other men reported that they had seen such an object, or that some public phenomena were best explained by postulating such an object. Suppose that there meet with the blind community other men who describe properties of material objects and surfaces with which they are not in contact, which they call 'colours' and which they claim to observe straight off. They use words such as 'red', 'yellow', 'pale', 'light', and 'dark', 'multicolour', 'of uniform colour', 'bright', and 'dim' in describing these properties. Asked for an account of the meaning of these terms, the newcomers are for a start much puzzled as to how to give an account. But they then say such things as follows: 'The difference between bright and dim is rather like the difference between loud and soft or between sharp and blunt. The difference between multicoloured and of-uniform-colour is like the difference between rough and smooth' or, following Locke[9] 'scarlet is like the sound of a trumpet'. The

---

[9] John Locke, *Essay Concerning Human Understanding*, III.4.11. Locke *seems* to teach that his 'simple ideas', that is particular tastes, sounds, colours, etc., have virtually nothing in common, do not resemble each other significantly more or

newcomers prove in general trustworthy people, and they corroborate each other's testimony about 'colours'. This gives to members of the blind community grounds for believing what they say, and so far holding that the man of genius made a coherent claim. For they can now see that he is proposing to use the words 'loud' and 'soft' to mark a difference which the strangers mark by using the words 'bright' and 'dim'. The strangers whom there is reason to believe, say that the difference between bright objects and dim objects is like the difference between the objects which they ordinarily call 'loud' and those which they ordinarily call 'soft'. From that it follows that you can use the latter words in an analogical sense to pick out that difference. With his suggested use of words, what the man of genius has suggested is (on the evidence available to the community) probably true and hence probably coherent.

A different and yet importantly similar example of words being given analogical senses comes from modern physics. What is light? Since the sixteenth century there have been two views—that light radiating from a source consists of a stream of particles, and that it consists of a wave. Up until the beginning of the twentieth century it was thought that one or other view was the correct one, and they held alternate dominance. The wave theory originally held that light was a disturbance in a material medium, ether, which filled all space; the propagation of light consisted in the propagation of a disturbance in that medium. Later it was held that the wave was an electromagnetic wave; that is, the propagation of light consisted in a continuous change of the electromagnetic field (which is a field of force and not a material thing) at all the points of space involved. But on both versions of the wave theory what was propagated was a disturbance, a change in the state of things at the points along the path of the wave without any material object moving along that path. Whereas on the particle theory the propagation of light along a path consisted in the motion of particles, material objects, along that path. Since

---

less. The quoted sentence is used to make the point that the blind could not come to know much about colours by knowing just that. However, Locke's doctrine seems simply false. Of course one colour can be more like a second colour than like a third; and there are significant resemblances between objects of different senses——scarlet is somewhat like the sound of a trumpet, smooth surfaces are like soft noises, bitter tastes are like acrid smells, etc.

1905, however, neither theory can be regarded as in exclusive possession of the field. Many phenomena are known which are fully explained by the theory that light is a wave and seem quite inconsistent with the particle theory. Among these are diffraction and interference. Yet many other phenomena are known which are fully explained by the theory that light consists of particles and seem quite inconsistent with wave theory. Among these are the photoelectric effect and the Compton effect, and, above all, the fact that when very weak light irradiates a photographic plate, a lot of tiny blobs appear on the plate (not a very weak smear over the whole plate, as wave theory would suggest). So neither theory seems fully adequate to the phenomena. There have been many attempts to construct more adequate theories, but no theory which gives an easily comprehensible account of the nature of light has had any success in prediction. What we do have is Quantum Theory, a highly sophisticated piece of mathematics, which allows us to predict within a range how light will behave (once, that is, we have learnt the conventions for applying it to a concrete situation); and also allows us to predict a vast number of other physical and chemical phenomena. But science is not merely a predicting device. Another function which science has successfully fulfilled in so many other fields is to tell us what the world really consists of, what the entities are of which the world is made, and what are the basic laws of their interaction. The atomic theory of chemistry was not merely a predicting device —it told us what a pint of water consisted of, a large finite number of molecules, and what each of these consisted of: two atoms of hydrogen and one of oxygen. What now of Quantum Theory in this respect? What does it tell us about the world on the small scale?

One alternative, basically that adopted by what is known as the Copenhagen Interpretation, is to abandon this ideal of describing the world. According to the Copenhagen Interpretation Quantum Theory is just a predicting device, and does not tell us about what the world is like. It cannot do so— because if it did it would have to say either (a) light is sometimes particles and sometimes a wave or (b) light is always particles and always a wave. But neither (a) nor (b) will do. (b) is self-contradictory—light either is or is not a material object. Yet it will not do to say (a), that the beam of light forced to show interference phenomena was a wave, and that forced to show the photo-electric effect was really a stream of particles. For all our evidence is that any one beam can be made to show either effect.

Yet to adopt the Copenhagen Interpretation is not merely to abandon the scientific ideal of describing the world; it is to do so when the two accounts of what light is are in their respective fields remarkably successful. In exhibiting inter-ference phenomena light behaves exactly like a wave; in making blobs on a photographic plate light behaves exactly like a stream of particles. The alternative to the Copenhagen Interpretation is to say that light is both 'particles' and 'wave', only in extended senses of the terms which do not exclude each other. Light is a stream of 'particles', in a sense of 'particle' in which grains of sand and everything else we would call 'particles' are particles, but in a sense in which some things which we would not call 'particles' are particles. Light is a 'wave', in the sense in which a water wave and everything else which we would call 'waves' are such, but in a sense in which some things which we would not call 'waves' are waves. I believe that this second, realist alternative is that adopted by the majority of scientists. It seems at any rate to be a possible alternative. If it is, what is happening is that in the face of pressure to say two incompatible things about light, words are being given an analogical sense to remove the incompatibility.

In giving analogical senses to 'wave' and 'particle' we loosen the semantic rule by stating that an object is a wave if it is like water waves, air waves, waves in oil and lemonade, or electro-magnetic waves, in the respect in which they are like each other more than it is like standard examples of objects which are not waves (e.g. books or grains of sand). And similarly for 'particle'. We also drop the explicit syntactic rule that if anything is a 'wave' (a disturbance in a medium) it is not also a 'material object' or a group of such.

With the new analogical senses of 'wave' and 'particle', is it coherent to suppose that light is both a stream of 'particles' and a 'wave'? I know of no straightforward proof that it is or that it is not. But there is clearly indirect evidence that there exist such objects and so that it is coherent to suppose that there are. The indirect evidence is that light exhibits so many of the properties of waves and particles; that Quantum Theory of light is a very successful scientific theory, and that the only remotely possible way to interpret it, to say what the 'light' is about the behaviour of which it is telling us is to say that it is something which is (in analogical senses) both 'wave' and 'particle' (for other answers to the question what the light is are *evidently* not coherent).

With the Quantum Theory interpreted thus realistically we have what I shall call a two-model situation. Philosophers of science have often used the notion of a 'model' to analyse the activity of scientists. When a scientist postulates some entity *a* to explain certain phenomena, and says that *a* is like and behaves like some familiar observable entity *b*, we may say that *b* is a 'model' for *a*. Thus the atomic theory of chemistry seeks an explanation of various observable chemical phenomena, such as the fixed ratios of combination by weight of chemical substances to make new substances, and the fixed ratios of combination by volume of gases to make new gases (when kept at the same temperature and pressure). The chemist postulates that all observable substances consist of very large numbers of molecules specific to each substance (a pint of water consists of a very large number of water molecules, etc.). Each molecule consists of a number of atoms. There are atoms of some hundred types only. Some molecules consist of atoms of one type only. Thus hydrogen molecules each consist of two identical atoms which are therefore called hydrogen atoms. Other molecules consist of some atoms of one type and some of another. Thus a molecule of water consists of two hydrogen atoms and one oxygen atom. Every molecule of a given substance consists of exactly the same number of atoms of the same types. Chemical combination consists in the breakdown of molecules of the original substances and the rearrangement of their atoms to make molecules of new substances. All of this and various other postulated facts explain the observed chemical phenomena. The chemist is not content merely to provide a formula which allows prediction of new chemical combinations. He wishes to tell us what chemical substances really consist of and what is really going on, as a result of which we observe the phenomena that we do. He must therefore tell us something about these 'atoms'. He says that they are very small particles. They are like billiard-balls—not of course in many ways (in being red, shiny, and used for playing billiards) but in many other ways (in being hard, round, and inelastic). In postulating an entity a in many respects like a known entity b he has a 'model' for a. The billiard-ball or particle is the model for the atom.[10] The respects in which the model is known to resemble the postulated entity Mary Hesse calls the positive analogy; the respects in which it is known not to resemble it she calls the negative analogy; and the respects in which it is not known whether or not it resembles it she calls the neutral analogy. The model suggests that the postulated entity resembles it in these further ways (the neutral analogy) also. It suggests directions for extending the theory. I. T. Ramsey introduced the terminology of models profitably into theology.[11] He speaks of 'models and qualifiers', the qualifiers being expressions stating the respects in which the model does not apply (Hesse's 'negative analogy').

Now the situation in Quantum Theory is a two-model situation. The postulated entities, such as photons, the units of light, have some of their properties in common with waves and some with particles and there is no one model which we can provide of them. There is around us no familiar phenomenon which resembles the postulated photons more than either of these, and they resemble it very much equally. Maybe one day Quantum Theory will be overthrown and we will have a theory in its place susceptible of interpretation by one model—e.g. then maybe we will be able to say that really light consists of 'particles' in the ordinary sense of the term. But until then we have to make do with the two models. If we have two models for a postulated entity, we have necessarily to use words in analogical senses if we are to describe that entity. For since it cannot resemble both of its models very closely (since they are different models), we can only describe it in terms of the two models by giving extended senses to the words used for describing the

[10] The most useful discussion of the role of models in science remains Mary B. Hesse, *Models and Analogies in Science* (London, 1963). I use 'model' in her 'model₂' sense (see her pp. 10 f.) For other discussion see Peter Achinstein, *Concepts of Science* (Baltimore, 1968), Chs. 7 and 8.

[11] See, e.g., his *Religious Language* (London, 1957). I discuss Ramsey's account of religious language in Ch. 5.

models. The fact that we can give such an analogical interpretation of theories which do not admit of an interpretation with
words used in ordinary senses is of great interest. For our
ability to do this is clearly independent of the truth of Quantum
Theory. If it can be done for Quantum Theory when we have
grounds for believing it to be true, it can be done for some other
theory when we have grounds for believing it to be true.

I shall argue in due course that some claims which the theist
wishes to make about God will only be coherent if some of the
words which occur in the sentences by which they are expressed
have a different sense from the normal sense. In that case, the
words must be being used in an analogical sense (in my sense
of 'analogical'); since for reasons given above it is not plausible
to suppose that the meanings of words have been changed in
other ways. Some extension of meaning of some words is
necessary for the theist's task. But clearly the more words are
used in analogical senses, and the more stretched those senses
(i.e. the more the rules for the use of the words are altered), the
less information does a man who uses the words convey. For
words used in analogical senses have wide applications and
woolly boundaries. It is a great deal less clear what we are
saying of an object when we say that it is W^* than when we say
that it is W. If theology uses too many words in analogical
senses it will convey virtually nothing by what it says. The
claim that he is using a word in an analogical sense must be
for the theist a last resort to save his system from a charge of
incoherence which would otherwise stick. He must claim that
he is using many words in ordinary senses. For similar reasons
the more the theist loosens up the semantic and syntactic rules
for the use of a given word in order to give it its analogical
sense, the less will be said by the use of the word and the less
clear it will be what is being said. In giving to words analogical
senses the theist must avoid loosening up their meaning too far.
The 'analogical sense' card is a legitimate one, as the examples
which I have adduced should show, but it must not be played
too often—for the more it is played, the less information will
be conveyed by what is said.

Unless there is reason to suppose otherwise, clearly we ought
to assume that theists are using words in their ordinary mundane senses. In any discourse it is reasonable to make the initial

assumption that words are being used in ordinary senses, unless the speaker indicates otherwise. I shall argue that on some versions of theism there is never any reason to suppose that words are ever being used in other than ordinary senses—for these versions of theism make coherent claims on the supposition that words are being used in ordinary senses. I shall, however, argue, as I have said, that most theists have wanted to make claims which will only be coherent if we suppose that some words are being used in analogical senses. But even so, we need not suppose that all words are being used in analogical senses. When the theist says that God is 'good', 'good' is, I suggest, being used in a perfectly ordinary sense. The only extraordinary thing being suggested is that it exists to a degree in which it does not exist in mundane objects. But when theists say that God is a 'person' who is 'necessarily' able to 'bring about' any state of affairs and 'knows' all things, I shall suggest that if what they say is to be coherent some of these words must be being used in somewhat analogical senses. For if they are not (and if no other account can be given of how these words are being given unusual senses), the claims are straightforwardly incoherent. Even if words are being used in analogical senses, the claims expressed by credal sentences are not necessarily coherent. Having brought out the senses in which I believe the words are being used, I shall prove unable to give a direct proof either that the claims are coherent or that they are incoherent. There remains the possibility of an indirect argument for coherence based on any inductive evidence that the claims are true, that there exists a being with the cited properties; but whether there is such evidence is beyond the scope of this book.

However, I shall seek to establish that some credal claims are coherent, that others can be coherent only if words are being used in analogical senses, but that purported direct proofs that they are or that they are not coherent in the latter case, fail.

5

The Words of Theology—2
Medieval and Modern
Accounts

THE view that theology uses ordinary words in somewhat special ways in order to describe a strange reality beyond ordinary experience is one which has occurred naturally to most of those who have thought seriously about theological language. Those who have written on the subject have not, however, always made very clear what are the 'special ways' in which the ordinary words are used. In this chapter I intend to compare and contrast the views stated in the last chapter with the views of philosophers and theologians who have written on this subject. It is only at two periods in the history of thought that men have thought at length and systematically about these matters—the later Middle Ages and the twentieth century. I therefore propose to confine my remarks to thinkers of these periods.

Later Medieval Accounts of Religious Language

The concern of writers in the later Middle Ages was whether words used to describe properties both of God and of creatures were used univocally (i.e. in the same sense) or equivocally (i.e. in different senses). John Duns Scotus taught that predicates such as 'good' and 'wise', and above all 'exists' are applied univocally to God and man. When we say that 'God is wise' and that 'Socrates is wise' we are using 'wise' univocally and so attributing the same property to God and to Socrates. Certainly wisdom amounts to something different in God and Socrates. But to say that a thing is wise does not in itself mean that that thing has the finite wisdom of creatures; it may have the infinite wisdom of God. Only when we know what sort of thing it is do we know what wisdom amounts to in it:

Take, for example, the formal notion of 'wisdom' or 'intellect' or 'will'. Such a notion is considered first of all simply in itself and absolutely. Because this notion includes formally no imperfection nor limitation, the imperfections associated with it in creatures are removed. Retaining this same notion of 'wisdom' and 'will', we attribute these to God—but in a most perfect degree. Consequently every inquiry regarding God is based upon the supposition that the intellect has the same univocal concept which it obtained from creatures.[1]

The meaning of words such as 'good' and 'wise' is learnt by seeing them applied in mundane situations. The only difference when we use them in theology is that we combine them in unusual ways or suppose the properties denoted to exist in higher degrees than in the mundane objects to which we originally applied the words:

Creatures which impress their own proper species on the intellect can also impress the species of the transcendentals which are common to themselves and to God. Then the intellect in virtue of its own power can make use of many such species simultaneously, in order to conceive at one time those things of which these are the species. For instance it can use the species of 'good', the species of 'highest', the species of 'act', to conceive the 'highest good which is pure act' ... The imagination is able to use the species of different things perceptible to the senses and thus imagine a composite of these different elements, as is apparent, for instance, when we imagine a gold mountain.[2]

So we have clearly in Scotus the first view of theological language which I stated in the preceding chapter. The later

[1] J. Duns Scotus, *Opus Oxeniense*, I, dist.III.q.i, trans. Allan Wolter in *Duns Scotus: Philosophical Writings* (London, 1962), p. 25.
[2] Ibid. The word translated 'species' would be translated more satisfactorily as 'concept'.

scholastic philosopher, William of Ockham, held similar views.[3] In claiming that predicates applied to God and man were used univocally, they might appear to oppose the earlier position of St. Thomas Aquinas. He claimed that (at any rate almost all) predicates used of God and man are used neither univocally, nor purely equivocally, but in a way which he called analogical. However, Scotus makes a remark which I believe to be true of Aquinas, that 'those masters who deny univocity with their lips really presuppose it'.[4]

Aquinas classifies types of analogy in different places in his works in different ways, and subsequent commentators such as Cajetan have attempted to detect a uniform system of classification underlying the different remarks which he makes. I shall not attempt to present a uniform Thomist doctrine of analogy, but simply concern myself with the account which he gives of the analogical use of predicates attributed both to God and to creatures in the *Summa Theologiae* (Ia.13) and the *Summa contra Gentiles* (1.30-5).

Aquinas holds that we learn all words from their application to mundane objects. In theology we then apply them to an extra-mundane object, God. In such a case the property signified by the predicate, the *res significata*, is the same, but the *modus significandi*, the way in which the predicate signifies the property, or, better, the way in which the property is present in the object of the type in question, differs. Aquinas wants to say that in such a case when we apply a term to an entity of a radically different kind from those by reference to which we originally learnt to use the term, we are using it 'analogically'. He is emphatic that the term is not being used 'equivocally', that is with a completely different meaning. He has a very

---

[3] Ockham distinguishes three senses of 'univocal' (see his *Reportatio*, III. Q. 8, trans. in P. Boehner, (ed.), *Ockham: Philosophical Writings*, London, 1957, pp. 106–13). In the first sense a word is univocal if it denotes a concept which applies to things which are perfectly alike in all essentials, i.e. it only applies to members of the same species. In the second sense a word is univocal if it denotes a concept which applies to things similar in some essential respects and dissimilar in others, e.g. members of the same genus. In the third sense a word is univocal if it designates a concept common to many things. 'In this manner, every concept which applies to God and to creatures is univocal to them.' In one sense of 'analogical', Ockham writes, 'it is taken for a univocal concept of the third kind, which is neither purely equivocal nor purely univocal'.

[4] *Reportata Parisiensia*, 1.3.1., no. 7.

powerful argument repeated by his successors against those who claim that when God is said to be 'wise' or 'good', we do not mean by these words at all what we mean when we say that men are wise or good:

A name is predicated of some being uselessly unless through that name we understand something of the being. But if names are said of God and creatures in a purely equivocal way, we understand nothing of God through those names; for the meanings of those names are known to us solely to the extent that they are said of creatures. In vain therefore would it be said or proved of God that He is a being, good, or the like.[5]

Aquinas is equally emphatic that we do not and cannot use terms univocally of God and creatures. His reasons for his view are of a motley kind, which it would not be useful to discuss in detail, but underlying them seems the basic reason that the 'wisdom', 'goodness', etc. attributed to God are very different from 'wisdom', 'goodness', etc. attributed to men. So he would seem to argue that when we say that God is 'wise' and Socrates is 'wise' we must be using 'wise' in somewhat different senses. For example, he gives as a reason for 'wise' not being univocal when applied to God and man that in a man his wisdom is 'distinct from his essence, power, or existence' whereas in God this distinction does not exist. But, as we noted in the last chapter, the fact that 'wisdom' amounts to something very different in God from what it amounts to in men does not show that the term is being used non-univocally—at any rate if 'univocally' means 'in the same sense' in our sense.

As we have seen, Aquinas claims that a non-equivocal term is being used analogically in two cases if its *modus significandi* differs in each. He teaches that non-equivocal terms 'φ' predicated of different objects a, b, c, etc. denote the same property in each (i.e. the *res significata*, the thing attributed to a and b, when we say 'a is φ' and 'b is φ' is the same) but the *modus significandi*, the way in which it signifies, may differ. Now, for every object, what being φ amounts to will vary with the kind of object. Weighing ten stone amounts to having ten stone of flesh and blood if what weighs ten stones is myself; weighing ten stone amounts to having ten stone of steel if what weighs ten stone is my filing cabinet. However, Aquinas does not want to say that the *modus significandi* of a term 'φ' differs with each different object of which it is predicated. The *modus significandi* differs only if the objects are of radically different kinds, for example of different genera. Thus he writes: 'God is more distant from any creature than any two creatures are from each other. Now there are some creatures so different that nothing can be said univocally of them—for example when they differ in genus. Much less, therefore, could anything be said univocally of creatures and God.'[6] An obvious example which brings out what Aquinas is getting at is one which he himself uses—knowledge in men and animals. Men and animals are both said to know things. A common property is apparently attributed to each. And it might appear that we can to some extent analyse this common property in the way in which philosophers have done. If '*A* knows that *p*', then '*A* believes that *p*', and '*p*', and maybe other propositions too, are entailed (e.g. '*A* has good evidence for *p*', '*A* believes that *p* on the basis of that good evidence'). These entailments hold whether *A* is a man or an animal. So to some extent it might seem that we can state what is the common element in knowledge, to whatever kind of being the knowledge is attributed. However, the tests for the presence of these characteristics of knowledge are rather different in the case of men and animals (with babies perhaps forming an intermediate case). Evidence that *A* believes that *p* in the case of animals is of only two kinds—there is evidence that *A* has been provided with evidence that *p* (i.e. evidence that certain stimuli impinge on *A*) and evidence that *A* acts on *p* (i.e. that *A* with such purposes and intentions as we can reasonably attribute to him assumes that *p* in attempting to realize them). Evidence that *A* believes that *p* in the case of humans is supplemented by evidence of what *A* says, and this I think means that we pay less attention to whether *A* has been provided with evidence that *p* in assessing whether *A* believes that *p*—but not perhaps in assessing whether *A* knows that *p*. Again what counts as having been provided with evidence that *p* is going to vary very much with animals and men. Because of the kind of creature each is, the sort of evidence it can have will be very

[6] *Summa Theologiae*, vol iii (London, 1964; trans. H. McCabe, O.P.), Ia.13.5.

different. For people evidence that p may be constituted by a complicated mathematical proof that p; for animals this cannot be. So in 'A knows that p' there is a common element of knowledge (the *res significata* of 'knows') attributed to A; but the way in which this is exemplified in A (the *modus significandi* of 'knows') differs with the kind of being A is.

Aquinas then goes on to claim that when God is said to know things, the *res significata* of 'know' remains again the same whereas the *modus significandi* differs from the *modus significandi* of 'know' when knowledge is attributed to men or animals. The *modus significandi* is now one peculiar to divine knowledge. God's knowledge that p, like human knowledge, entails belief that p, and p, and various other thigs; but it differs from human knowledge in various ways arising from the difference between God and man. All things are before God's eyes. He therefore does not need to make (possibly) fallible inference from the observed to the unobserved in order to gain knowledge. Further he so completely sees things that he cannot err in his claims to knowledge about what he sees. Hence divine claims to knowledge are not subject to error as human ones are, and so on. Further to say of a man that he knows that p, does not imply that he is currently thinking about p. Divine knowledge, however, is ever before the divine mind. These points of Aquinas are illustrated by his discussion of divine knowledge in *Summa Theologiae*, 1a.14. An objection is raised to the claim 'there is knowledge in God' as follows: 'Knowledge is a disposition, which God cannot have since it is intermediate between potentiality and actuality.'[7] Knowledge would be a disposition if it were an ability to recall items. Yet in God there is no potentiality —no ability to develop, to realize as yet unrealized qualities. The answer which Aquinas gives to the objection is as follows:

The perfections which go out from God into creatures are in God in a higher way, as we have said above; therefore whenever a description taken from any perfection of a creature is attributed to God, we must eliminate from its meaning all that pertains to the imperfect way in which it is found in the creature. Hence knowledge in God is not a quality nor a habitual capacity, but substance and pure actuality.[8]

[7] *Summa Theologiae*, vol. iv, (London, 1964; trans. T. Gornall, S.J.), Ia.14.1. obj.1.
[8] Ibid., 1a.14.1. ad obj. 1.

Aquinas's distinction between the *res significata* and the *modus significandi* of a term seems appropriate in the kind of case considered, knowledge in men and animals. But there is no sharp border between cases where a term is being used with different *modi significandi* and cases where it is being used with the same *modus significandi*. Where there is a sharp division between entities of two kinds, and φ-ness amounts to something very different in each, there we can clearly talk of 'φ' having different *modi significandi*. But what where the division is not so sharp, where there is a whole continuum of intermediate cases; or where φ-ness, while amounting to something different in different cases, does not amount to something *very* different in each case? Knowledge amounts to something very different in men and animals, but what of sight and smell? If I say 'men see things' and 'cats see things' does 'see' have a different *modus significandi*? 'Weighs ten stone' presumably has the same *modus significandi* when attributed to monkeys and men; so what of 'sees', 'smells', and 'feels'? What too of knowledge in babies? Is the *modus significandi* of 'know' in 'the baby knows' and 'the man knows' the same or different? Border-line cases, it is true, do not show the non-existence of genuine distinctions, but they do bring out their significance. And of course, on the theist's assumptions, God is so different from anything else that any predicate applied to him is bound to be applied with a different *modus significandi* from when it is applied to anything else.

Given then what the distinction between *res significata* and *modus significandi* amounts to, why say that when a term 'φ' is used to denote the same *res significata* with a different *modus significandi* it is being used, not 'univocally', but 'analogically'? One can of course introduce technical terms with any meaning which one chooses. But if 'univocally' means what it appears to mean, i.e. 'in the same sense',[9] then surely a word is being used

[9] On the definition of univocity provided by Scotus, 'good', 'wise', etc. turn out to be univocal. Scotus writes that he designates 'that concept univocal which possesses sufficient unity in itself so that to affirm and deny it of one and the same thing would be a contradiction' (*Ordinatio*, l.dist.3.q.1; trans. in Wolter, op. cit., p. 20). In other words the word 'φ' is univocal (denotes one concept, we would say) if '*a* is φ' contradicts '*a* is not-φ'. Since 'God is not wise' contradicts 'God is wise', only one concept is denoted by 'wise'. Whereas 'God is not indifferent' does not necessarily contradict 'God is indifferent', for in one sentence 'indifferent' may be used in its old sense of 'impartial' and in the other sentence in its modern sense of 'not caring'. Note 3 of this chapter shows Ockham denying the apparent

univocally if it denotes the same property, even if having that property amounts to something very different in different things. At any rate Aquinas does not seem to be denying that in our sense of 'univocally' predicates attributed to God and man are being used univocally. His position ultimately boils down to that of Scotus, but in the course of expounding it he has drawn our attention to the vast differences between the wisdom of God and the wisdom of Socrates, the power of God and the power of Stalin, etc.

So then the later medievals held that predicates ascribed to God and to creatures, and in general words used inside and outside theology, were used in the same senses. And they held that the words used inside theology were not words given new senses but were ordinary words used in ordinary senses. Their arguments for this were that otherwise we could not understand, let alone have evidence for, the claims of theology. But this argument only shows that if theology introduces new senses for words, it must show what those senses are by giving semantic and syntactic rules (with the help of ordinary words) for their use, not that theology cannot introduce words in new senses.

Aquinas, however, clearly felt that there is something special about theological language. I have nevertheless argued that despite this feeling, Aquinas's official theology is that words are used in theology in the same sense (in our sense of 'in the same sense') as outside it. Not everyone will agree with my interpretation of Aquinas. Nothing of philosophical substance turns on whether my account of Aquinas's doctrine is correct. Nevertheless, I thought it right to treat of him at length and set his doctrine within the context of my treatment of theological language, because of the wide influence exerted by his discussion of the topic. Historically Aquinas lies between, on the one hand Scotus and Ockham, who undoubtedly held the view just cited, and, on the other hand many earlier writers who, impressed by the vast difference between God and man, urged that words ascribing predicates to God had an entirely different meaning in theology from that which they had outside it. There is, for example, a long tradition in Jewish, Christian, and Muslim

---

contradiction between the views of Aquinas and Scotus, and claiming that in one sense of 'univocal' and one sense of 'analogical', the univocal could be analogical.

theology before Aquinas of the *via negativa*, according to which all that we can say of God is what he is not, not what he is. To say that God is 'good' is, on this view, just to say that he is 'not evil' (in the ordinary sense). But this view failed lamentably to give an adequate account of what theists have wished to say about God. Sticks and stones are 'not evil'; but to say of God that he is good is clearly to say more of him than that he is, like sticks and stones, not evil. Aquinas tried to give a more plausible account of theological language which allowed it to convey substantial information about God, while continuing to emphasize the differences between God and man. If I am right, he had really crossed over to Scotus's account, which is not altogether adequate as a full account of theological language. Aquinas did not succeed in providing the *via media* between the earlier account and the Scotist account which, he rightly saw, must be provided.

Twentieth-century Accounts of Religious Language

So much for the scholastics. The twentieth century has shared their great interest in religious language. The continental theologians, many of them in the Existentialist tradition of philosophy, Bultmann, Tillich, Barth, etc., have had much to say about it. But codifiable doctrines as to exactly how words used in theology are similar to or different from words used outside theology are hard to find in their works. It is to writers in the British empiricist tradition that we must look for more careful statements. The Logical Positivists and other writers in the tradition in the 1930s and 1940s tended to assume without argument that words in theology meant precisely what they did outside. The 1950s saw some moves away from this position. One such move was in the direction of attitude theories, that certain kinds of word, which outside theology described things, were used inside theology to commend values or express attitudes. I shall discuss attitude theories in Chapter 6. However, a few writers in the British Empiricist tradition accepted that at any rate the credal sentences of theology did have to some extent a descriptive role and they sought to elucidate carefully the role which on that supposition words played in theology. The two best-known of such writers are Ian Ramsey and I. M.

Crombie, and it is with their views that I shall now briefly
compare and contrast my own.

Ramsey[10] stresses that in theology we use one or more different
'models'[11] to get across the meaning of theological claims. Thus
to bring out the meaning of 'atonement' in the Christian
doctrine that Christ on the cross 'atoned' for the sins of the
world, we compare 'atonement' to the process in a law court
where the judge declares the prisoner innocent (or, alternatively,
treats him as innocent by imposing no penalty), to the process of
ransoming captives, to the process of propitiating an angry
deity, etc. All of these processes form models for atonement.
However, the atonement made by Christ is not quite like any
of these, and we are misled if we take these models too literally.
As well as models we need 'qualifiers' to bring out the limits to
the application of the models. Thus although Christ ransomed
us, there was no person to whom the ranson was paid (e.g. the
Devil).[12] So we must qualify the model. Again, to take other
examples of Ramsey's, God is the cause of the Universe, wise and
good. But we must qualify these claims (these models or pictures
of God) by saying that he is the first cause (the end of the backward series of causes), infinitely wise, and infinitely good. To
make the latter qualifications makes the point that to say, for
example, that God is infinitely wise is not just to place him
further along the scale of worm, dog, three-year-old child,
O-level candidate, undergraduate, university lecturer, Einstein;
he is somehow 'outside the series'.[13] When a theologian presents
us with such examples, we may for a little while not see what
he is getting at, and then 'the penny drops', a 'disclosure', or
'discernment' occurs, 'with which is associated, by way of response, a total commitment'.[14]

This account of religious language is a somewhat vague one
and does not answer in detail such crucial questions as when
models and qualifiers are used legitimately, and when they are
not. But it seems to me that in Ramsey's account there is

[10] See, among other works, his *Religious Language; Models and Mystery* (London,
1964); and *Christian Discourse—Some Logical Explorations*, (London, 1965). The last,
a short work, is in some ways clearer and more satisfactory than the others.
[11] See Ch. 4 of this book for brief consideration of the role of models in science.
[12] See *Christian Discourse*, pp. 51 f.
[13] See *Religious Language*, Ch. 2.
[14] Ibid., p. 49.

implicit an advance from the doctrine of Scotus and Ockham that the words of theology are ordinary words used in ordinary senses. Certainly Ockham would have been quite happy to use Ramsey's terminology and talk of the 'model' of a wise person being 'qualified' by the qualifier 'infinitely'; of 'cause' being qualified by 'first'. But for Ockham the words 'cause' and 'first' are used in their ordinary senses. I think that Ramsey is implying that they are not always so used. For if they were being used in their ordinary senses we should not need a 'disclosure' in order to see what was being got at by saying that God is 'infinitely wise'. Although I feel some hesitation in my interpretation, what Ramsey *might* be suggesting is the following. We are shown how 'infinitely' works in mathematics, and then are told that it is being used in a much wider sense which allows us to talk of something being 'infinitely wise' (a sense which does not carry the normal mathematical implications of 'infinite'). Likewise in order to explain what 'atonement' is, we are shown various situations (a ransom, a verdict of acquittal, etc.) which, we are told, are very imperfect instances of it. Words are given new senses in theology by our being shown instances of their application and being given directions for their wider use. But to grasp the meaning of a word introduced by examples, we do of course need the requisite ability to see what is common to the instances. (You may need to show a child many 'verbs' and distinguish them from 'nouns' before he suddenly 'sees' what a verb is.) If this is what Ramsey is getting at, then of course it adumbrates my suggestion that theology sometimes alters the semantic and syntactic rules for the uses of words.

A more careful and systematic account of theological language is given by I. M. Crombie in his influential paper 'The Possibility of Theological Statements'.[15] Crombie considers statements apparently affirming predicates of God, such as 'God loves us' or 'God became incarnate in Christ'. He claims explicitly that such statements make factual claims. In order to show what these claims are we have to make clear what we are talking about (i.e. fix the reference of 'God') and what we are saying about him (e.g. say what 'loves us' means). We cannot fix the

[15] In B. Mitchell (ed.), *Faith and Logic* (London, 1957), pp. 31–83 (the first four of the six sections of the paper are reprinted in B. Mitchell (ed.), *The Philosophy of Religion*, London, 1971.)

reference of God by pointing to him literally or giving a description since the 'descriptions which are sometimes offered as uniquely characterizing Him ("the first cause", "the necessary being") are such that nobody can say what it would be like to conform to one of them'.[16] However, we get some idea of what we are referring to by considering the attributes of people which cannot be analysed in purely materialistic terms—'loving, feeling, hoping, even seeing are obvious examples'. Considering these characteristics which 'have a relative independence of space' we get 'the notion of a being independent of space', 'a spirit', or rather 'not a conception, but the hint of a possibility of something we cannot conceive, but which lies outside the range of possible conception *in a determinate direction*'.[17] Using the word 'spirit' as anything other than an abstract noun involves 'the deliberate commission of a category mistake under the pressure of convictions which require us to depart from normal language-practice in this way'.[18] Crombie then goes on to show how some sense is given to 'infinite', in order by the phrase 'infinite spirit' to fix the reference of 'God'. In order to show the meaning of the predicate 'loves us' we show examples of love (the love of Christ revealed in the gospels), and explain that 'love' means 'care for' rather than 'wish to fondle'. In all cases the predicates such as 'loves' are used of God not because they fit exactly but because they are the nearest words we have for what we want to say. We use the word 'love' because we 'believe in some kind of resemblance or analogy between, say, human love and divine love'.[19] In using such words of God, we 'affirm a parable'. Further, to affirm the words is to claim that thought on this line (e.g. of God as loving, or dwelling in the believer) will prove progressively illuminating in the experience of the believer.

[16] Ibid., p. 43.

[17] Ibid., pp. 57 f. This idea of religious language telling us about something which lies 'in a determinate direction' is similar to Aquinas's idea that religious language tells us that certain predicates such as 'wise' apply to God *eminentiori modo*, that is 'in a superior degree' to that in which they apply to men. We cannot, according to Aquinas, form much conception of what that degree is but having some idea of the degrees of wisdom of men and animals we know that God's wisdom is more than theirs, and so we know the direction in which his degree of wisdom is to be sought (e.g. we know that God's wisdom is not at all like that of a monkey, but a little closer to that of a man.)

[18] Ibid., p. 60.

[19] Ibid., p. 71.

With the basic themes of Crombie's account I believe my
own account to coincide. My claim that the use of words in
theology involves the introduction of new syntactic rules is what
is involved in Crombie's claim that theology makes 'category
mistakes'. I claimed that theology understood its semantic rules
in a loose way, such that to say that an object is φ is just to say
that an object is more like standard cases of φ-objects than like
standard cases of objects which are not-φ. This is Crombie's
point that in affirming 'love' of God, for example, we are merely
affirming the existence in God of a property similar to human
love.[20]

I conclude then that the analyses provided by Scotus and
Ockham affirm in essence that theological language uses words
in the same sense as they are used outside theology. I shall argue
in later chapters that theological language certainly does this
to some extent. The analyses of Ramsey and Crombie in the
modern Empiricist philosophical tradition claim that theology
gives a somewhat different sense to words from their ordinary
one. Their analyses largely support the account which I gave in
Chapter 4 of how this is done. I shall argue in later chapters that
theology also sometimes does this.

Henceforward when I claim that a word is being used
'analogically' I shall mean thereby that it is being used in a
sense which results from loosening up the syntactic and semantic
rules for its use in the way described in Chapter 4. Having discussed in this chapter other ways of understanding 'analogical'
meaning, I shall henceforward understand it in the way described in Chapter 4.

---

[0] Crombie's concern has been with statements of the form 'God is so-and-so'
and so he asks his question in two parts—how do we know the reference of 'God'
and how we know the meaning of 'is so-and-so'? But since we fix the reference
through a description 'infinite spirit' rather than by pointing literally, the same
kind of answer is needed and provided for both questions (viz. in terms of how to
understand the descriptions given).

6

Attitude Theories

In the last two chapters I have given an account of how the words of theology come to have meaning—either by having meaning in their mundane sense or by being given meaning in an analogical sense in a way which I have described. Whether this account is correct must be judged by its ability to give a plausible account of what the theist wishes to say by means of credal sentences. In Parts II and III of this book I hope to give such an account on the assumption that the words of theology get their meaning in the stated ways. However, I also hope that the last two chapters have made it initially plausible to suppose that the words of theology are meaningful. In consequence, as we saw earlier, the sentences in which they occur will be meaningful. Normally, meaningful indicative sentences make statements, claims about how things are. Credal sentences look as if they are doing just that, making claims about a reality beyond the world of sense which accounts for the ordinary things around us.

However, a number of recent writers have denied that 'religious' or 'theological' 'assertions' make statements, and since credal sentences obviously have a central place among such assertions, the claim would seem to involve the claim that credal sentences do not make statements. For them religious assertions, including credal sentences, express intentions to live in certain ways, or express attitudes of approval for certain patterns of life or do something else other than stating how things are. In this chapter I will examine this view.

The clearest of such writers is R. B. Braithwaite who presented in his well-known Eddington lecture[1] the view that 'a

[1] R. B. Braithwaite, *An Empiricist's View of the Nature of Religious Belief* (Cambridge

religious assertion is the assertion of an intention to carry out a certain behaviour policy, subsumable under a sufficiently general principle to be a moral one, together with the implicit or explicit statement, but not the assertion, of certain stories'.[2] The stories about the life, death, and resurrection of Jesus Christ, or the creation of the world, or the life of the Buddha, may or may not in a literal sense be believed. The important thing is that the stories show examples of a certain kind of behaviour, and in 'affirming' the network of stories which are associated with a religious system taken together in a religious context, what the believer is doing is committing himself to that kind of behaviour. We find out what kind of behaviour is associated with the stories of religion by 'asking [the religious man] questions and by seeing how he behaves . . . I myself take the typical meaning of the body of Christian assertions as being given by their proclaiming intentions to follow an agapeistic way of life, and for a description of this way of life—a description in general and metaphorical terms, but an empirical description nevertheless—I should quote most of the thirteenth chapter of 1 Corinthians.'[3] So, to simplify crudely but not, I think, unfairly, the meaning of 'there is an omnipotent, omniscient spirit who cares for man' is in the end 'show great consideration for all men'. A religious 'believer' is, according to Braithwaite, misleadingly so called; 'neither the assertion of the intention [to carry out a certain behaviour policy] nor the reference to the stories includes belief in its ordinary senses'.[4]

Now it may well be that someone who utters a credal sentence thereby commits himself to pursuing a certain course of behaviour. But even if this were so (and I do myself think that it is), that would not show that that is *all* that is done by uttering a credal sentence. And on the surface Braithwaite's account seems glaringly false. Men other than Christians may express intentions to pursue much the same course of behaviour as Christians, and they might illustrate the kind of behaviour they intend to pursue by reference to the Christian stories (e.g.

1955). Reprinted, among other places, in B. Mitchell (ed.), *The Philosophy of Religion*, pp. 72–91. My page references are to the latter volume.

[2] Ibid., p. 89.
[3] Ibid., pp. 81 f.
[4] Ibid., p. 89.

'Behave towards foreigners as Jesus did towards Samaritans').
But they would not express those intentions by means of the
credal sentences typically offered by Christians (e.g. 'There is a
God who became incarnate in Christ'). Nor would they be
called Christian 'believers' just because they affirmed those
intentions. When men 'lose their faith', they do not necessarily
lose their intention of following a certain behaviour policy. But
they cease to assert credal sentences (unless they utter them in
order to deceive) because they lose their conviction of the truth
of certain metaphysical claims which to some degree provide
a rationale for the behaviour policy.[5] Further, men often
express their 'belief' in at any rate some of the 'claims' of
traditional theism, while at the same time affirming that they
are not going to let their 'belief' affect their behaviour at all.
A man may say 'I believe that there is a God, although I doubt
whether he's very interested in me; but anyway I don't intend
to do anything about it now.' He thus distinguishes having a
belief expressed by credal sentences from following a certain
behaviour policy. Ultimately, if anybody really thinks that
credal sentences merely affirm intentions to pursue behaviour
policies, the only way to settle whether they do or not is by a
sociological and literary survey of what people who use credal
sentences think that they are doing and have thought that they
were doing over the past two thousand years.[6] But I do not
think that the vast majority of readers who reflect on the simple
points that I made a few sentences back will feel the need to
wait for the result of such a survey.

Why did Braithwaite suppose that credal sentences merely
assert intentions for behaviour? His lecture shows the reason
clearly. Religious assertions are not, he claims, statements about

[5] It may be claimed that although the non-Christian could affirm his commitment to much the same behaviour as a Christian (e.g. in respect of his family, his
neighbours, and society as a whole), he could not affirm his commitment to
exactly the same behaviour as a Christian. For a Christian is committed to
certain peculiarly religious behaviour—e.g. saying prayers. But it is certainly
logically possible for a non-Christian to express his intention of saying his prayers,
that is of uttering from time to time the words which Christians utter when they
pray. Why it would be odd for him to do this is that the activity has no point unless
the doer believes that there is a God who hears prayers. The Apostles' Creed justifies
the activity, by claiming that there is such a being.

[6] A plea for such surveying to settle the issue between contrasting philosophical
analyses of religious discourse is made by Anders Jeffner in his *The Study of Religious
Language* (London, 1972).

particular empirical facts, or scientific hypotheses, or propositions of logic and mathematics. We see that because we see that they are not open to verification in the same way. So we have to look around for some sort of assertion to which religious assertions are akin and we find that moral assertions are akin to religious assertions. Moral assertions are not 'verifiable' (in the sense that their truth value can be ascertained), but they have a use—in guiding conduct. Braithwaite seems to assume, though he does not state, that assertions of the three former kinds are the only kinds of statements which there are. Even if that were so, why should not religious statements be like scientific hypotheses? Braithwaite's answer is that scientific hypotheses must be 'refutable' by experience and religious assertions are not. If Braithwaite means, as he appears to mean, by 'refutable' 'conclusively falsifiable', then there are good reasons[7] to suppose that he is mistaken about science, that scientific hypotheses are not refutable by experience. Even if he were claiming only that scientific hypotheses must be confirmable or disconfirmable by experience, he would need to prove this arguable point, and then go on to show that religious assertions, to be factually meaningful, must be like scientific hypotheses in this respect. In our discussion in Chapter 3 of the weak verificationist principle we have argued that there are no good reasons to suppose that it applies universally.

A number of writers over the past thirty years have given in vaguer and more obscure language the kind of account of religious language which Braithwaite gave so clearly in his Eddington lecture. Similar objections tell against them all. Credal sentences do not *merely* affirm intentions. Nor do they merely express emotions or hopes. At any rate one thing which they do is to express claims about how things are. Most of these writers do not require separate discussion. However, one group of writers who in a way oppose the view that credal sentences make factual claims does require more lengthy treatment. This is the group of those who expound a view sometimes called Wittgensteinian fideism, of whom the best known is perhaps D. Z. Phillips.

[7] See, e.g., Imre Lakatos, 'Falsification and the Methodology of Scientific Research Programmes' in I. Lakatos and A. Musgrave (eds.), *Criticism and The Growth of Knowledge* (Cambridge, 1970), pp. 91–195.

Wittgenstein wrote very little explicitly about religion, but his writing about language-games in the *Philosophical Investigations* has given rise to the account given by Phillips and others of religious language. A language-game is the use of a certain kind of talk. A language-game may be a very simple kind of language, such as a language in which there are a few simple commands which are given and obeyed. Or it may be a segment of a complicated language, as, for example, 'giving orders and obeying them; describing the appearance of an object, or giving its measurements; constructing an object from a description (a drawing); reporting an event; speculating about an event; forming and testing a hypothesis; presenting the results of an experiment in talks and diagrams; making up a story, and reading it; play-acting. . . .'[8] To study a language-game is to study how and when the different sentences of a kind of talk are uttered (in what circumstances, in response to what other sentences). Thus to study the scientific language-game of 'forming and testing a hypothesis' is to study when scientists announce hypotheses, when they reject them, when they judge them confirmed, which experiments they do to test them, etc. Wittgenstein lays down no rules for when one language-game ends and another begins, nor does he claim that there are no logical connections between language-games. Quite obviously there are, if we take the examples of language-games given in Wittgenstein's list. Obviously the 'report' of an event can count crucially against a scientific 'hypothesis'.

However, writers such as D. Z. Phillips have written of the 'religious language-game' as an activity in which religious people indulge which has no logical connections with any other language-game—assertions of the religious language-game do not entail assertions of any other language-game, and conversely. The religious language-game certainly *presupposes* the occurrence of certain mundane events, such as birth and death describable in non-religious terms, in which religion finds a meaning.[9] But

---

[8] L. Wittgenstein, *Philosophical Investigations*, trans. G. E. M. Anscombe (Oxford, 1953), I.23. In his earlier *Blue Book* (Oxford, 1969), p. 17, Wittgenstein wrote that 'the study of language-games is the study of primitive forms of language or primitive language'. In the *Investigations* there is the wider understanding of 'language-games' described above. See Ch. 9 of Anthony Kenny, *Wittgenstein* (London, 1973), for discussion of Wittgenstein's treatment of language-games.

[9] Phillips brings this out in his reply to critics in 'Religious Beliefs and Language

it does not predict such events; nor does their occurrence entail its truth (nor does any weaker relation such as 'making probable' hold between statements of the two disciplines). To understand what religious utterances such as credal sentences mean, one must study when and where they are uttered and the point of uttering them. Other writers, Phillips writes, 'have assumed too readily that words such as "existence", "love", "will", are used in the same way of God as they are used of human beings, animate and inanimate objects'.[10] 'The criteria of the meaningfulness of religious concepts are to be found within religion itself.'[11] The language-game of religion, like that of science or history, is played. What can be said—that God loves this and hates that, hears these prayers and forgives those sins—cannot be determined by arguments which use the criteria of other discliplines. Religious discourse has its own criteria which determine what can be said. History and science have their own criteria of truth; so too with religion. Disciplines cannot be judged from without; they have their own standards within.

From here Phillips proceeds to give his own account of the meaning of religious sentences, and, stressing the alleged autonomy of religion, he asserts that they make no claims of a historical or scientific or any other non-religious kind. Phillips has written mainly about prayer and eternal life, and a few quotations from his writings on these subjects will give the flavour of his account of theological language. 'To know how to use [religious] language is to know God.' Prayer is, however, 'not a conversation'.[12] Like the will of the dead, the will of God cannot be 'bargained with'. One thanks God—but not for doing this rather than that. One thanks him, as one would not thank human benefactors, for good and evil. God's being good does not mean that things are going to happen one way rather than another. 'When deep religious believers pray *for* something, they are not so much asking God to bring this about, but in a way telling him of the strength of their desires. In prayers of confession and in prayers of petition, the believer is trying to

---

Games', *Ratio*, 1970, **12**, 26–46, reprinted in B. Mitchell (ed.), *The Philosophy of Religion*, pp. 121–42.

[10] *The Concept of Prayer* (London, 1965), p. 8.

[11] Ibid., p. 10.

[12] Ibid., p. 50.

find a meaning and a hope that will deliver him from the elements in his life which threaten to destroy it.'[13] To think of prayer as an attempt at influencing the divine will is 'superstition'. 'Eternal life for the believer is participation in the life of God'[14], not survival after death. 'In learning by contemplation, attention, renunciation, what forgiving, thanking, loving etc. mean in these contexts, the believer is participating in the reality of God; *this is what we mean by God's reality*.'[15] Although Phillips has written comparatively little explicitly about credal sentences, one quotation will give the flavour of his approach to them. In 'From World to God?' he advocates a view in which 'the love of God is manifested in the believer's relationship to people and things. In this sense he can be said to have a love of the world. To see the world as God's world, would, primarily, be to possess this love. To say that God created the world would not be to put forward a theory, hypothesis, or explanation of the world.'[16] (A footnote explains that Phillips wrote 'primarily' 'because of the possibility of other responses to seeing the world as God's, e.g. rebellion, fear, or aspiration'.)

These various quotations illustrate Phillips's general approach. It is, I think, fair to extrapolate from them the following account of credal sentences. The credal sentences of theology do not state claims which could in any way conflict with claims of any other discipline. To suppose otherwise is 'superstition'. Theology makes no claims about the past history of men or the future experiences of any individual; and no claims about any suprasensible reality which explains the observable world. Credal sentences concern rather the religious meaning of the world, which is something different from what any other discipline is concerned with. The point and appropriateness of uttering them is revealed by studying the pattern of prayer and worship. Phillips does not say explicitly whether or not we would be right to say that credal sentences make statements, but I think that he would feel that it would be misleading to do so. For on his view theology does not tell us of facts which are the concern of other disciplines, nor of facts additional to those of

[13] Ibid., p. 121.
[14] D. Z. Philips, *Death and Immortality* (London, 1970), pp. 54 f.
[15] Ibid., p. 55 (Phillips's italics).
[16] D. Z. Phillips, 'From World to God?', *Proceedings of the Aristotelian Society*, Suppl. Vol., 1967, **41**, 133–52.

which other disciplines tell, but tells us rather about the right way to regard the ordinary facts (reported by other disciplines). To say that theology makes statements would, I think, on Phillips's view, make it appear too much like history or science.

Phillips's account of religious language is subtle and coherently developed, reflecting Wittgenstein's immense sensitivity to the different uses of language. It seems, however, to me to be in essence plainly false as an account of what the vast majority of normal users of religious language during the past two millenniums have meant by the words and sentences which they have uttered. The vast majority of those who have prayed petitionary prayers have hoped that their prayer would make a difference to the way things happen. They would admit of course that God in his wisdom might choose not to grant the prayer, but they have hoped that he would grant it, in the way in which a ruler might grant a petition. (Jesus himself in his parable of the unjust judge—Luke 18: 1–8—likened petitionary prayer to God to petitionary prayer to an earthly ruler.) The vast majority of those who have expressed in the Nicene Creed their belief in 'the Resurrection of the Dead, and the Life of the World to come' have believed in survival of death. For they have been moulded in this thought by the words of the Creed, and by St. Paul's explicit affirmation of this in 1 Corinthians 15. They have supposed that they would meet their loved ones in a future world. And to turn to an expression of more immediate concern to us, the vast majority of those who have used religious language have certainly treated the affirmation that God created the world as the confident propounding of a hypothesis explaining its existence. This can be seen by the fact that they have abandoned their faith if they have come to believe that 'matter alone exists' or 'there is nothing beyond the Universe and the people in it' or some such claim. They have thought of God as a person who can always intervene in history to make a difference to things, though he may choose not to. This is the clear and unambiguous picture of God in the Old and New Testaments, and Jews and Christians have formed their idea of God by continual study of the Scriptures. If Phillips was right in his account of religious language, it remains an immense puzzle why religious people should use the words which they do. Why affirm their belief in God as 'loving', 'creator', 'saviour', etc. etc. if these words do not have a meaning similar to their normal meaning? Certainly God's love may not be quite like human love, and theists may only use the word 'love' because it is the word nearest in meaning to the word which they would like to use but have not got. But if God's 'love' is not similar to the love of a person, shown by care for well-being, readiness to forgive faults, etc. etc., why talk of 'love'? And so on. Phillips's account of religious language might serve as a useful reinterpretation of the sentences traditionally uttered by theists, for someone who for some reason wished to continue to utter them but did not wish to utter them with their normal meaning. But as an account of the meaning of the sentences uttered by the vast majority of theists down the past two millenniums Phillips's account is false. Once again, if anyone still doubts this, perhaps only an extensive sociological and literary survey of what the utterers of theological sentences suppose to be implied by what they say will convince them. But my hope is that a brief reflection on the points which I have made will render this unnecessary.[17]

I conclude that attitude theories of credal sentences are mistaken. Credal sentences, do, as they appear to, make statements, although they may use words in stretched senses in order to do so. The rest of the book will be concerned with whether the statements made by typical credal sentences are coherent statements.

[17] For more extensive criticism see Kai Nielsen, 'Wittgensteinian Fideism'', *Philosophy*, 1967, **42**, 191–209.

A CONTINGENT GOD

7

An Omnipresent Spirit

The Task of Part II

I CONCLUDED in the last chapter that credal sentences do, as
they appear to, make claims—given that the words which occur
in them have their mundane senses or are given analogical
senses, or are defined by means of ordinary words used in
mundane or analogical senses. The topic of this book is what do
those claims mean and are they coherent? In this part I shall
consider what it means to claim that there exists eternally an
omnipresent spirit, free, creator of the universe, omnipotent,
omniscient, perfectly good, and a source of moral obligation,
and whether this is a coherent claim. I shall argue that this
claim (expressed in the words just used, either used in their
mundane senses, or given natural definitions by other words
used in mundane senses) is a coherent one—given certain qualifications on the way in which the words 'omnipotent' and 'omniscient' are understood. I shall do this by taking one or two of the
above properties in each chapter and considering whether the
claim that there exists a being with these properties is a coherent
one, and whether it is coherent to suppose that there exists a
being with the properties in question as well as properties discussed earlier. Thus in Chapter 7 I consider whether it is
coherent to suppose that there exists a spirit, that is a person
without a body, who exists everywhere, that is, is omnipresent.
In Chapter 8 I consider whether it is coherent to suppose that
there exists an omnipresent spirit who has free will and is the
creator of the world. And so on.

I argue for the coherence of these claims in two ways; first by
attempting to refute arguments purporting to show that the

claims in question are incoherent, and secondly by attempting to construct positive proofs of their coherence. I attempt the latter in the only way in which, as we saw in Chapter 3, this is possible. I attempt to describe in some detail what it would be like for them to be true, to describe circumstances under which they would be true, that is to give descriptions of circumstances which entail that the claims hold. By filling out the picture of what is claimed I hope to make sense of it. Yet for the reasons given in Chapter 3, my arguments may not convince everyone. It may seem to them that my descriptions are themselves incoherent, or alternatively that the theological claims do not follow deductively from them, that is that the former are not descriptions of circumstances under which the claims hold. I try to argue for my claims about coherence but my arguments may not suffice to convince all. However, I hope that they will convince most, and in that hope I see no need to consider the less direct methods of attempting to show coherence referred to in Chapter 3.

To repeat, the full claim which I consider in this part is that there exists eternally an omnipresent spirit, free, creator of the universe, omnipotent, omniscient, perfectly good, and a source of moral obligation. In understanding this claim, I argue, we may understand the words in which it is expressed in their mundane senses, or as given a syntactic definition by words used in mundane senses—so long as 'omnipotent' and 'omniscient' are understood in ways more restricted than their etymology would suggest. If this is done, the claim is a coherent one. I argue that to understand the latter words in the senses which I specify, rather than the wider senses, does not make the being whose existence is being asserted any less worthy of worship, and so that there is no reason why a theist should refuse to understand the words in the former senses. If, however, he insists on understanding the words in the senses other than those which I specify, I argue that the claim is not coherent—unless one or more words in it are understood in analogical senses. If the words are to be understood in analogical senses, I can give no straightforward proof of the coherence or incoherence of the claim. There is, however, I argue, no need for the theist to plead 'analogical senses' for his words at this point. A place at which this plea is necessary will be located in Part III.

What is a Person?

This chapter, then, considers what it means and whether it is coherent to suppose that there exists an omnipresent spirit. By a 'spirit' is understood a person without a body, a non-embodied person. By 'omnipresent' is meant 'everywhere present'. That God is a person, yet one without a body, seems the most elementary claim of theism. It is by being told this or something that entails this (e.g. that God always listens to and sometimes grants us our prayers, but does not have a body) that young children are introduced to the concept of God.

In setting out to make sense of the concept of a non-embodied person I shall not discuss the compatibility of the doctrine held by all theists that God is such a person, with two specifically Christian doctrines—the doctrines of the Trinity (that God is three 'persons' in one substance) and the doctrine of the Incarnation (that God did at one time take to himself a human body, the body of Jesus of Nazareth). This book is concerned only with the most general doctrines about God common to theists, not with specifically Christian doctrines. Some theists have attempted to effect reconciliation of the view that God is a person with the view that he is 'three persons in one substance' by abandoning the former and saying that really God is 'personal but not a person'. However, I am making the assumption that a man who says this is giving a specialized sense to the expression 'a person', and that he in no way wishes to deny that in the ordinary sense of the word it is more or less true that God is a person. At any rate this latter is the view with which I am concerned and I think that it is held by very many theists. Some recent Protestant theologians seem to have had a different reason for saying that God is 'personal but not a person'. I think that the main point of their saying this was to bring out that God is not an object in the world alongside others, but something very different from objects in the world. The writers concerned felt that to describe God as a person would be to picture him as too much like ordinary created persons. There seems to me no need for this reason either, to refrain from saying that God is a person—so long as you bring out the difference between the person which is God and other persons by other devices (e.g. by ascribing to him all the other predicates which I shall be going on to discuss).[1]

So then we move to consider whether it is coherent to suppose that there exists a person without a body who is present everywhere. Let us begin by considering what it is for something to be a person. We first learn what a person is by having examples pointed out to us—we ourselves are said to be persons, and so are our parents, our brothers and sisters, other children and their fathers and mothers. These, like many things around us other than persons, can properly have ascribed to them what P. F. Strawson[2] has called M-predicates, e.g. 'weighs ten pounds', 'is six foot tall'', 'consists largely of water', 'grows in size for the first eighteen years of existence', and so on. The fact that such predicates can be truly ascribed to persons may be described by saying that persons, or at any rate those with which we are initially acquainted, are material bodies (at least as long as those predicates apply to them), or by saying that persons are like material bodies (i.e. most things other than persons to which M-predicates apply) in these ways. However, persons are distinguished from the other subjects of M-predicates by being characterizable also by what Strawson has called P-predicates, such as 'is smiling', 'is going for a walk', 'is in pain', 'thinks hard', etc. Not all P-predicates ascribe status of consciousness, although some (e.g. 'is in pain') do. However, the ascription of a P-predicate to an individual does imply that that individual is (at any rate intermittently) conscious. Persons are distinguished from inanimate things, on this account of Strawson's, as the subjects of P-predicates, that is as the sorts of occupants of space, which, unlike tables and chairs, are from time to time conscious. Now, as a number of writers have pointed out,[3] this is insufficient as an account of persons. For many P-predicates, as Strawson classifies them, can be ascribed to dogs and cats and monkeys, and we would not

---

[1] I shall, however, wish to suggest at a much later stage that the theist, in claiming that God is a 'person', does wish to understand this word in a *somewhat* extended sense. Yet his reasons for doing so are of a sophisticated kind which will emerge later.

[2] P. F. Strawson, *Individuals* (London, 1959), Ch. 3.

[3] e.g. B. A. O. Williams, 'Are Persons Bodies?' in S. Spicker (ed.), *The Philosophy of the Body* (Chicago, 1970); republ. in Williams's *Problems of the Self*, (Cambridge, 1973).

normally wish to say that these were persons. To be a person something must be characterizable by members of a special subclass of predicates within the class of P-predicates.

Various writers have drawn our attention to different attributes which distinguish persons from animals. Persons use language to communicate and for private thought. They use language to argue, putting forward one consideration as an objection to another. They have second-order wants; that is they can want not to have certain wants or aversions (e.g. a man may wish that he did not hate his brother). Animals show no evidence of having wants other than first-order wants—e.g. they want food or drink, but do not want not to want food or drink. Persons can form and state theories about things beyond observation (e.g. that observable things are made of particles too small to be seen). Avove all, they can form moral judgements—judgements that this or that action is morally obligatory, to be contrasted with judgements that the action is one which is to their advantage to do, or one which they would feel happy if they had done. Among the moral judgements which men are clearly capable of forming are judgements that a certain pattern of life is supremely worth while.[4]

If a thing is characterizable by all of the above predicates then it is a person; and if it is characterizable by none it is not. No doubt border-line cases are possible—things characterizable by some of the above predicates but not others; we need not go into the question of exactly which and how many predicates have to be applicable to a thing in order for it rightly to be called a person. Medievals following Aristotle would describe the difference which I have outlined between persons and animals by saying that persons have rational souls whereas animals have only sensitive souls. Some modern writers would describe it by saying simply that persons have souls whereas animals do not. Some writers, with Plato, have thought of such souls as parts of persons separable from their bodies; other writers, following Aristotle, have denied such separability.

Now it is plausible to suppose that the account which is given

---

[4] Quite a good list of such differences between men and animals may be found in St. Augustine's *De Trinitate* (12.2.2). Various modern philosophers have brought out the importance of several of the distinctions listed. Wittgenstein, for example, has stressed the importance of belonging to a language-using community as a distinguishing mark of persons. The point about second-order wants is due to

in the last paragraph but one is roughly correct—that we learn to apply the term 'person' to various individuals around us in virtue of their possession of the characteristics which I have outlined. The question arises whether the concept of 'person' which we have derived from seeing it applied to individuals with bodies is such that it could also be applied to an individual lacking a body. The question is of course not so much about the word 'person', but about whether there could be an individual to whom M-predicates did not apply, but to whom many P-predicates did apply, including the predicates listed in the last paragraph but one. If there were such an individual, it would, I suggest, be natural to call him a 'person'. So then could there be an individual who thought and perhaps talked, made moral judgements, wanted this and not that, knew things, favoured this suppliant and not that, etc., but had no body? Such an individual we may call a spirit.

What is it for there to be an Omnipresent Spirit?

We can begin to answer this question by asking what it is for a person to have a body; and we can answer that question by asking another—what is it that I am saying when I say that this body, the body behind the desk, is *my* body. This question has been well discussed by Jonathan Harrison in a paper 'The Embodiment of Mind, or What Use is Having a Body?'[5] Harrison suggests that there are five things which I am saying when I say that this body is my body. The first is that disturbances in it cause me pains, aches, tingles, etc.; whereas disturbances in the table or the body over there are unfelt by me. The second and related thing is that I feel the inside of this body. I feel the emptiness of this stomach and the position of these limbs. The third thing is that I can move directly many parts of this body—whereas I can only move parts of some other body or thing by moving parts of this body. To move the arm over there I have to grasp it with this arm, but I can move this arm straight off. Moving the limbs of this body is what Danto has called a basic action of mine. A basic action of an agent is

Harry G. Frankfurt, 'Freedom of the Will and the Concept of a Person', *Journal of Philosophy*, 1971, **68**, 5–20.

[5] *Proceedings of the Aristotelian Society*, 1973–4, **74**, 33–55.

one which he performs without having to perform some other action in order to do it. I signal by raising this arm. But there is nothing else which I do in order to raise this arm; I just raise it.[6] No doubt other things have to happen in order that I may move my arm—nervous impulses have to be propagated and muscles contract—but these are things that happen, not things which I consciously or intentionally do. The fourth thing is that I look out on the world from where this body is. It is things around this body which I see well, things further away which I see less well. I learn about other things in the world by their effects on this body (i.e. on the sense-organs of this body). The fifth thing is that my thoughts and feelings are affected by goings-on in this body. Getting alcohol into this body makes me see double.[7] Now clearly a person has a body if there is a material object to which he is related in all of the above five ways. And clearly a person does not have a body if there is no material object to which he is related in any of the above five ways. But what are we to say if a person is related to different material objects in each of these ways, or is related to a material object in only some of these ways? Presumably that he is embodied only to some degree.

Now what does the theist claim about God? Clearly God is not supposed to be embodied in either the first or fifth way. There is no material object, in which disturbances cause God pains; nor any material object whose state affects the way in which God thinks about the world. On the other hand, God is supposed to be able to move any part of the universe directly; he does not need to use one part of the universe to make another part move. He can make any part move as a basic action. There is no one place from which God looks out on the world, yet he knows without inference about any state of the world (whether he 'sees' it or 'feels' it we do not know). The traditional theistic view that God has no body has always been supposed to be compatible with the above limited embodiment. The claim that God has no body is the denial of more substantial embodiment, and above all the denial that God controls and knows about

---

[6] See Arthur C. Danto, 'Basic Actions', *American Philosophical Quarterly*, 1965, **2**, 141–8.

[7] I have some doubt to what extent the fifth thing is part of what is *meant* by saying that this body is my body, although it is no doubt normally true when this body is my body. However, there is no need to settle this issue here.

the material universe by controlling and getting information from one part directly, and controlling and getting information from other parts only by their being in causal interaction with the former part.

The claim that God controls *all* things directly and knows about *all* things without the information coming to him through some causal chain, e.g. without light rays from a distance needing to stimulate his eyes, has often been expressed as the doctrine of God's omnipresence. This doctrine has been expounded very clearly by Aquinas in *Summa Theologiae*, I.8, and I will outline briefly his exposition. God, writes Aquinas, exists everywhere in the first place because he acts everywhere. He does not act through intermediaries, but directly. He acts everywhere because he gives existence and power to things in all places. In Article 3 of the cited question Aquinas argues for the proposition that 'God is everywhere in substance, power, and presence'. 'God exists in everything by power inasmuch as everything is subject to his power, by presence inasmuch as everything is naked and open to his gaze, and by substance inasmuch as he exists in everything causing their existence.'[8] God being everywhere by power and substance is thus a matter of all things being subject to his direct control. God being everywhere by presence is a matter of him knowing goings on everywhere, without being dependent for his knowledge on such intermediaries as eyes and ears.[9]

So much for what is involved in God, as opposed to, say, a ghost or a poltergeist, lacking a body yet being a person. Is it a coherent supposition that there be such a being? Superficially, I suggest that it is. It is easy to spell out in more and more detail what such a supposition amounts to, and, as I argued in Part I, this more detailed spelling-out provides the only possible proof of coherence. Imagine yourself, for example, gradually ceasing to be affected by alcohol or drugs, your thinking being

---

[8] *Summa Theologiae*, vol. II (London, 1964; trans. Timothy McDermott, O.P.), Ia.8.3.

[9] The medievals were careful to rebut the suggestion that God had in any literal sense his dwelling in Heaven, a place which they supposed to lie beyond the outermost sphere of the stars. He might be in Heaven in a particular way, but he was present everywhere. See, e.g., Aquinas, *Summa contra Gentiles*, 3, 68, 7–8. For this view of course they could provide plenty of support in the form of quotations from the Old Testament, e.g. I Kings 8: 27; Jer. 23: 23 f.

equally coherent however men mess about with your brain. Imagine too that you cease to feel any pains, aches, and thrills, although you remain aware of what is going on in what has been called your body. You gradually find yourself aware of what is going on in bodies other than your own and other material objects at any place in space—at any rate to the extent of being able to give invariably true answers to questions about these things, an ability which proves unaffected by men interfering with lines of communication, e.g. turning off lights so that agents which rely on sight cannot see, shutting things in rooms so that agents which rely on hands to feel things cannot do so. You also come to see things from any point of view which you choose, possibly simultaneously, possibly not. You remain able to talk and wave your hands about, but find yourself able to move directly anything which you choose, including the hands of other people (although if you do move someone else's hands, he will normally himself deny responsibility for these movements). You also find yourself able to utter words which can be heard anywhere, without moving any material objects. However, although you find yourself gaining these strange powers, you remain otherwise the same—capable of thinking, reasoning, and wanting, hoping and fearing. It might be said that you would have nothing to want, hope, or fear—but that is false. You might hope that these strange powers would remain yours or fear that men would dislike you. Even if you could control their thoughts you might want them to like you spontaneously without being forced to do so by you, and you might fear that this want would not be fulfilled. Your hopes would be natural aspirations uttered to yourself, and shown by feelings of joy and relief when they were fulfilled, and sorrow when they were not realized. You would think and reason as men often do in words uttered to yourself. Surely anyone can thus conceive of himself becoming an omnipresent spirit. So it seems logically possible that there be such a being. If an opponent still cannot make sense of this description, it should be clear to many a proponent how it could be spelt out more fully.

Arguments against the Coherence of the Concept of a Spirit

There are current various positive arguments for the incoherence of the suggestion that there be a non-embodied person, a spirit, of any kind (whether or not an omnipresent spirit of the kind described above).

There are to start with various arguments which purport to show that it only makes sense to ascribe to a person such P-predicates as those considered above, e.g. 'hopes', 'thinks', or 'prefers' if that person has a body through which he can give natural expression to the properties ascribed by the predicates.

For example, it is suggested that predicates such as 'wants', 'hopes', and 'fears' can only be predicated correctly of a person who gives public expression to his wants, hopes, fears, etc. Only a person who sometimes runs away can rightly be said to fear things. Only a person who shows interest in things or takes steps to get things can rightly be said to want. Hence a person without a body can have no fears or wants, for he will be unable to run away or show interest.[10]

This kind of argument is, however, far too quick. For firstly, it seems that a person may have many wants or fears to which he never gives expression; and secondly, a spirit can give expression to wants and fears even though not through his body. To start with the first point, quite clearly a person may on occasion give no public expression to his mental states—he may want something which he takes no steps to get, fear something and yet show no signs of fear. This may be because he has no opportunity to give expression to his wants or fears (there may be not the slightest possibility of his getting what he wants, and so no point in his trying to get it) or because he inhibits the wants or fears. Why should it not always be the case for some person that for one or other of these reasons he does not ever give expression to his mental states?

However, whether or not this is a coherent suggestion, a spirit can give expression to his wants or fears, hopes, preferences, etc. even though he lacks a body. If he wants a certain man not to die of thirst, he may intervene in natural processes to cause rain. If he fears that a certain man will make a wrong choice, he may make marks on sand conveying a message to him. And so on. In the view of traditional theism not merely can the

[10] For argument of this kind see, e.g., Paul Edwards, 'Some Notes on Anthropomorphic Theology' in S. Hook (ed.), *Religious Experience and Truth* (New York, 1961), pp. 242 f.

omnipresent spirit who is God give public expression to his mental states but he often does—keeping the world in existence, controlling its destiny, interfering in what is going on in it, sending messages to its prophets. Likewise he is aware of and responds to goings-on in the public world. It is important in this connection not to overemphasize the extent of God's non-embodiment in the view of traditional theism. As we have seen, the view of traditional theism is that in many ways God is not related to a material object as a person is to his body, but in other ways he is so related.

The most substantial positive argument of recent years for the incoherence of any supposition that there exists any spirit (whether or not an omnipresent one) is an argument given by, among others, Terence Penelhum, which concerns the lack of identifying criteria for a non-embodied person, criteria for distinguishing one spirit from any other. In *Survival and Disembodied Existence* Penelhum examines the coherence of supposing that there exists a person without a body in more rigorous detail than any other recent writer. He investigates the possibility of such a being perceiving and acting on the world. He concludes that we can make sense of these descriptions—so long as we have criteria for the identity of such a person, so long, that is, as there are criteria for one such person at one time being the same person as or a different person from a certain other person at a different time. Penelhum thinks primarily of the case of disembodied persons, that is persons who formerly had bodies which now lie in graves or are decayed, but his conclusions apply generally to the case of non-embodied persons. He writes: 'We need some way of understanding the identity of the disembodied being through various post-mortem stages, and some way of understanding the statement that some such being is identical with one particular pre-mortem being rather than with another. We shall not be able to understand either unless we can also understand the notion of the numerical difference between one such disembodied being and another one.'[11]

Our normal criteria for one embodied person P_2 at a time t_2 being the same person as a person P_1 at an earlier time t_1 are the criteria of bodily continuity (that P_2 and P_1 have the the same body) and continuity of memory and character (viz. that P_2's

[11] Terence Penelhum, *Survival and Disembodied Existence* (London, 1970), p. 54.

memory claims include those of P_1 and that his character is similar to that of P_1). That P_2 and P_1 have the same body is something which we might come to know by keeping P_1's body under continuous observation. But we are more likely to come to know this is a more indirect way. Bodies of different persons normally look different (unlike e.g. pennies, which look much alike). We can see this by observing them simultaneously. That P_2's body looks much like P_1's body is evidence that it is P_1's body. Other evidence that two bodies are the same is provided by fingerprints, blood tests, etc. Now the bodily criterion is clearly not available to establish that two non-embodied persons are the same person, and so if there is sense in talking about two such persons being the same, this must, Penelhum claims, be a matter of their having similar memories and character. Penelhum asserts that the criterion of continuity of memory and character would by itself give no adequate answer to a question whether two persons were the same. Character would hardly suffice to distinguish between persons, since two persons often have the same character. Penelhum has various connected reasons for saying that memory would not help to provide the needed answer either. One is that a person's memory claims are only properly called 'memories' if it makes sense to suppose that we can check on them. If I claim to remember having been in London last month we can look for a witness who can testify to my presence. But if I have no body which could have been observed in London, Penelhum argues, this cannot be done. If what a man says he 'remembers' cannot be checked, it is not properly called a 'memory'. So the memory criterion does not work, Penelhum claims, to establish the identity of persons without help from the bodily criterion. Since the latter cannot be had for persons without bodies, 'we cannot give content' to the individuation of one incorporeal being from another',[12] for there would be no way of distinguishing between incorporeal beings. Penelhum suggests that the only escape-route for theism would be for it to claim that there was only one such being, any incorporeal being being of logical necessity the same as any other; in which case the need to individuate incorporeal beings, distinguish them from each other, would not arise. This is not to my mind a very attractive escape-route for theism, for many

[12] Ibid., p. 108.

theists have wished to claim that there were many incorporeal beings (e.g. angels, and spirits of the departed), only one of whom was God. In any case I believe the argument to be misguided and the conclusion to be false.

This argument seems to me misguided at more than one point, and once again adequate discussion would need very considerable space. Much recent philosophical writing has been devoted to this problem of wherein consists the identity of persons. I shall suggest one point very briefly and then argue for another at much greater length. The first point is that, at any rate for non-embodied persons of limited powers such as ghosts or Homeric gods, memory claims might be checkable. If a Homeric god claims to have been in London at a certain time, his claim can be disproved by showing that he was a long way away at the time or proved by showing that he was in London at the time. He cannot of course be *seen* in a place, but if each such being has sufficiently idiosyncratic ways of manifesting his presence (idiosyncratic voice, etc.) he can be known to have been there. We could have good evidence that each non-embodied person had an idiosyncratic voice—e.g. in the fact that the memory claims of each person with a certain voice included the previous claims of any person with that voice, and that these claims typically concerned goings-on in only one place at one time. True, non-embodied persons might not manifest their presence in idiosyncratic ways, and in that case we could not distinguish between them. But the fact that two persons lack bodies does not by itself ensure that we cannot distinguish between them. Of course we may make a mistake in our judgements in this matter—we may think that today's ghost is the same as yesterday's, and be wrong. But we may always make mistakes about the identity of embodied persons too. We may use bodily continuity to reach conclusions about personal identity. But how do we know that two bodies, B_1, the body we saw yesterday, and B_2, the body we see today, are continuous? Because they look alike? Maybe we are looking at the bodies of identical twins. Because we seem to remember having kept B_1 under continuous observation and seen it to be continuous with B_2? Maybe our memory is in error.

So memory (with character) could be used as a criterion of personal identity even in the absence of bodily continuity, because even here memory claims are checkable. Our results for Homeric gods can be extended to omnipresent spirits. If a voice of a spirit made claims about goings-on at all places and acknowledged that previous claims made in the same voice were his claims and if as a result of conversation with ourselves in which we asked the voice for certain things to be done they were done, we would, I suggest, have grounds for saying that the voice and the effects were the voice of and effects produced by the same omnipresent spirit. Along these lines with much filling-out of detail I suggest that an adequate defence can be made of the criterion of memory (with character) as a criterion for establishing the identity of non-embodied persons.

However, Penelhum's discussion, like so many other recent discussions of personal identity, seems to me to fail to keep distinct two very different questions about personal identity. The first is—what does it mean to say that a person P_2 at a time t_2 is the same person as a person P_1 at an earlier time t_1? The second is—what evidence can we have that a person P_2 at t_2 is the same person as a person P_1 at t_1 (and how are different pieces of evidence to be weighed against each other)? I shall argue for the rest of this chapter that the identity of a person over time is something ultimate, not analysable in terms of bodily continuity or continuity of memory and character. I shall reach this conclusion by considering the case of embodied persons only. The following pages thus constitute a considerable digression from the main topic, but the results are crucial for it. The conclusion of this digression will be that a person can be the same person as an earlier person even if none of the evidential tests is satisfied. Hence it will be coherent to claim that one non-embodied person is the same as an earlier one, even if no evidence can be produced to show that he is. The claim that a non-embodied person exists over time does not entail that any-one, even the agent himself, has or could obtain evidence that he is the same person as an earlier person. The claim that one spirit continues to exist over time is perfectly coherent even if no one is in any position to produce evidence of his con-tinued existence in the form of continuity of body, memory, or character, or other observable characteristics. So now for our degression into the nature of personal identity.[13]

[13] What follows is a shortened version of a paper of mine 'Personal Identity',

The Nature of Personal Identity

Let us begin by surveying at slightly greater length than we have done so far the kinds of solution given to the problem of personal identity, treating them for the moment as answers to our first question. The first kind of answer which derives ultimately from that given by Hume in the *Treatise* is that personal identity is a matter of similarity of memory[14] and character. P_2 at t_2 is the same person as P_1 at t_1 if and only if P_2's memories include most of those of P_1, and P_2 behaves in ways similar to P_1. If there is a considerable temporal interval between t_1 and t_2, then it suffices, for P_2 to be the same person as P_1, that there is a series of persons P_n at times t_n intermediate between t_1 and t_2, such that the memories of each person include almost all those of any person slightly earlier in the series, and each person is very similar in character to any member of the series existing at a temporally proximate moment. A clause may be added to this solution to deal with the case where two persons at t_2, P_2 and P_2*, both satisfy the stated criteria for being the same person as P_1. It may state that in such a case neither P_2 nor P_2* are the same person as P_1. While this and other qualifications may be added, the central idea of such a theory remains that personal identity is a matter of similarity of memory and character.

The second kind of solution claims that personal identity is a matter of bodily continuity. P_2 is the same person as P_1 if and only if he has the same body as P_1. A body B_1 is the same body as a body B_2 if they are spatio-temporally continuous, in the sense that they are connected by a continuous spatio-temporal path at each point of which there exists a body somewhat similar qualitatively (i.e. in appearance and construction) to its neighbours. This second solution is often amended in recent writing in a very important respect. Bodily continuity is not interpreted as continuity of all parts of the body, but only

published in *Proceedings of the Aristotelian Society*, 1973–4, **74**, 231–47. In a subsequent paper, 'Persons and Personal Identity' (published in H. D. Lewis (ed.), *Contemporary British Philosophy, Fourth Series*, London, 1976) I have developed, and discussed objections to, the argument of the earlier paper.

[14] I use 'memory' and cognate terms in the 'weak' sense in which a man's memories of what happened may or may not be correct. This is contrasted with the 'strong' sense in which necessarily if a man remembers p, then p.

of that part, i.e. the brain, which is responsible for a person's memory and character. On this view P_2 is the same person as P_1 if he has the same brain as P_1, even if it has been transplanted into P_2's body.

Neither of these solutions is especially plausible if taken in isolation from a solution of the other kind. The first one rules out as logically impossible that a man should lose his memory, something which we ordinarily suppose to be possible. The second solution rules out as logically impossible that a man should move from one place to another without passing through intervening space. Yet it seems far from obvious that it is *logically* impossible that I should pass through a brick wall without disturbing the bricks. For these and other reasons some sort of compromise theory tends to be favoured. Such a theory states how the various criteria to which I have referred work together. Thus a compromise theory may claim that satisfaction of either criterion by P_2 at t_2 makes P_2 the same person as P_1 at t_1, so long as there is no other person P_2^* at t_2 who satisfies the other criterion. The theory will then go on to tell us what to say under the latter circumstances, e.g. that neither person at t_2 is the same person as P_1 at t_1, or that the person who satisfies the bodily criterion is the same person as P_1; or the theory will provide some other solution. Or the theory may provide some other detailed account of how such criteria as bodily continuity, similarity of memory and character are to be understood and balanced against each other.

Now I see no objection to a theory of personal identity on these lines if it is regarded as an answer to my second question— what is the evidence that a person P_2 at t_2 is the same person as a person P_1 at t_1? Without doubt continuity of their bodies and especially of their brains is strong evidence that P_2 and P_1 are the same person, and lack of such continuity is strong evidence that they are not. Memory and character are, however, also relevant. If a woman turns up claiming to be Princess Anastasia and can tell us details of independently verifiable incidents in the Princess's life which would have been almost impossible for her to find out unless she were the Princess, that counts in favour of her being the Princess. Exactly how the different criteria are to be weighed against each other I do not propose to judge. What I am concerned to emphasize is that such an account is an account of what we would be justified in claiming about whether or not P_1 and P_2 are the same person on the basis of different kinds of evidence.

However, many recent philosophers seem to have wanted to put forward accounts on the lines which I have sketched above as accounts of what it is for P_2 to be the same person as P_1, and it is in these terms that I sketched above the pattern of such accounts. I wish to argue that such accounts are not at all on the right lines. I will call a theory which analyses personal identity as a matter of bodily continuity and continuity of memory and character an empiricist theory of personal identity.

I begin by drawing attention to the fact that an empiricist theory of personal identity has as an inevitable consequence that sometimes (it is logically possible) there will be no right answer to the question whether two persons are the same, and this will be so, whatever the detailed form of the empiricist theory. On an empiricist theory there are clear cases where P_2 and P_1 are the same person (I and the Swinburne whom you saw yesterday) and clear cases where P_2 and P_1 are different people (I and the Bloggs whom you saw yesterday), but it is easy to imagine a whole host of cases where the empiricist criteria give no clear verdict. This will be so whatever the details of how the different criteria are to be weighed against each other, simply because there will be cases where each criterion separately gives no clear result. There will be cases where P_2 has fairly similar memories and fairly similar character to P_1, so that P_2 lies on the border between satisfying and not satisfying the criterion of memory and character for being the same person as P_1. The same applies to the criterion of bodily continuity. How much of P_2's body (or brain) has to be continuous with P_1's in order for this criterion to be satisfied? If P_2 acquires only P_1's left arm, clearly the criterion is not satisfied, and if P_2 acquires all P_1's body except the left arm, clearly it is satisfied. But what about the case where P_2 acquires half of P_1's brain, or all his body except a quarter of the brain? However you interpret the criterion of bodily continuity it is easy to imagine circumstances in which P_2 lies on the border between satisfying and not satisfying this criterion. Because there are imaginable circumstances where any criterion gives no clear result, there are imaginable circumstances when any empiricist theory of personal identity would give no answer as to whether P_2 is the same person as an earlier P_1. In such circumstances on an empiricist theory it is the case that not merely are you or I unable to find out whether P_2 and P_1 are the same person, but there is no one right answer to the question. The answer that they are the same is as near to the truth as the answer that they are different. You can say which you like. The situation is similar to that of some other cases of identity such as the identity of a society or of an army. (Hume compares the identity of persons to the identity of 'a republic or commonwealth'[15].) When is army A_2 at time t_2 the same army as army A_1 at t_1? Clearly it is if A_2 has all the same soldiers in it as has A_1. Clearly it is not if all the soldiers of A_1 mutinied at an intermediate time and were replaced by new soldiers. But suppose that A_2 has a quarter of the soldiers who were in A_1 but that the other soldiers of A_1 have been gradually replaced by new soldiers. Are the two armies the same? Our criteria of 'same army' give no definite answer—you can say that the armies are the same or you can say that they are different. There is no right answer. Hume described the similar situation which he thought held with regard to the identity of persons by saying that 'the identity, which we ascribe to the mind of man, is only a fictitious one'.[16] That is a misleading way of putting the matter; the identity or lack of it is in *most* cases real enough—it is simply that in *some* cases there is no right answer as to whether two persons are the same—according to an empiricit theory.

Having outlined this important consequence of any empiricist theory of personal identity, I now propose to argue against all such theories. In order to do so it will be useful to classify them in a way different from the familiar classification which I adopted earlier, into three classes. I will then proceed to use a different pattern of argument against theories of each class. First we have theories which allow for duplication. Such a theory claims that P_2 at t_2 is the same person as P_1 at t_1 if P_2 satisfies some criterion, where it is logically possible that more than one person at t_2 satisfy that criterion. An obvious example of such a theory is of course the pure memory-and-character

---

[15] David Hume, *A Treatise of Human Nature*, p. 261.
[16] Ibid., p. 259. Hume goes on to say that the same applies to the identity 'which we ascribe to vegetables and animal bodies'.

theory, that P_2 at t_2 is the same person as P_1 at t_1 if and only if P_2 has similar character and memories to P_1. Now, as Bernard Williams pointed out in 1956,[17] it is logically possible that there be hundreds of persons at t_2 who have similar characters and memories to P_1 at t_1. If the fact that Charles's memories and character in 1956 are very similar to those of Guy Fawkes in 1604 *makes* him the same person as Guy Fawkes, then if Robert in 1956 also has very similar character and memories to Guy Fawkes in 1604, he would also *be* Guy Fawkes. Yet if P_2 at t_2 is the same person at P_1 at t_1, and so is P_2* at t_2, then P_2 and P_2* are the same person as each other. But that is absurd—for of logical necessity the same person cannot be (wholly) in two places at once. Any theory which allows duplication allows as a logical possibility that two persons at t_2 in different places be the same person as an earlier person, and that is clearly not a logical possibility. So any theory which allows duplication must be rejected.

Among theories which do not allow duplication, we must distinguish two further types. A theory of the second type of empiricist theory of personal identity is simply a theory of the first type with a clause added stating that a subsequent person at t_2 is not the same person as an earlier person if some other person at t_2 satisfies the criteria equally well. Thus the theory could have the following form: P_2 at t_2 is the same person as P_1 at t_1, if and only if P_2 has roughly the same memories and character as P_1, and no other person at t_2 has roughly the same memories and character as P_1. Another theory of this type, and one which incorporates a criterion of bodily continuity, is the following theory: P_2 at t_2 is the same person as P_1 at t_1 if and only if there is spatio-temporal continuity between some part of P_1's brain and some part of P_2's brain and there is not spatio-temporal continuity between any part of P_1's brain and any part of the brain of any person at t_2 other than P_2. By this theory if we remove P_1's brain, destroy half of it and successfully transplant the other half into P_2's body, P_2 will be the same person as P_1.

Now theories of the second type have an implausible consequence different from the absurd consequence derived from theories of the first type. This is that a man's identity (i.e. whether or not he is identical with a certain past person) could in certain circumstances, as a matter of logical necessity, depend on the success or failure of an operation to a brain and body other than his own. Who I am could depend on whether or not you exist. We can illustrate this with reference to the theory sketched at the end of the last paragraph, by telling a mad surgeon story.[18] A surgeon removes P_1's brain and divides it in half. He transplants the left half into one body from which the existing brain has been removed. The transplant succeeds. We will term the resulting person P_2. The surgeon also attempts to transplant P_1's right half-brain into another body from which the existing brain has been removed. Whether P_2 will be P_1 depends on whether this second transplant succeeds. If it does not, he will be; if it does, he will not, since there will then be two persons who satisfy equally well the criterion for being the same person as P_1. Yet how can who I am depend on what happens to you? A theory of personal identity which has this consequence does not seem to be analysing our ordinary concept of personal identity. Another absurd consequence of a theory of the second type is that the way for a man to ensure his own survival is to ensure the non-existence of future persons too similar to himself. Suppose the mad surgeon had told P_1 before the operation what he was intending to do, adding that while he felt confident that the left half-brain would transplant successfully, he had some doubt whether the right half-brain would take in the new body. P_1 is unable to escape from the clutches of the mad surgeon, but is nevertheless very anxious to survive the operation. If the empiricist theory in question is correct there is an obvious policy which will guarantee his survival. He can bribe one of the nurses to ensure that the right half-brain does *not* transplant successfully. Yet it seems absurd to suppose that as a matter of logic a man's survival can depend on the non-existence of some person. A concept of personal identity which has this conse-quence is not recognizably ours.

All theories, other than theories of the second type, which do not allow duplication I will call theories of the third type. A

---

[18] The value of such stories was brought out in the very important article by Bernard Williams, to which this chapter owes much, 'The Self and the Future', *Philosophical Review*, 1970, **79**, 161–80, also repub. in Williams's *Problem of the Self*.

theory of the third types rule out duplication as logically im-possible but it does not do so by having a clause forbidding duplication added to a theory of the first type. It is a more natural consequence of the theory that no more than one person at t_2 is the same person as P_1 at t_1. The obvious example of such a theory is the following: P_2 at t_2 is the same person as P_1 at t_1 if and only if the body of P_2 is spatio-temporally continuous with the body of P_1 in such a way that any body on the spatio-temporal chain joining them has almost all (e.g. 90 per cent) the same matter as any body at a temporally proxi-mate earlier moment (e.g. within one second earlier) on the chain. This chain cannot divide, for if a body is divided into two parts (e.g. a part is cut off), then no more than one of the resulting parts can have almost all the same matter as the previous body. Yet theories like this have an essential arbitrari-ness. Why 90 per cent? Perhaps 'over half' would be more natural. But then it would be a consequence of the theory that a man who lost half his body at a blow would no longer exist, whereas a man could lose half his body gradually over a few seconds and yet continue to survive.

The essential arbitrariness of such theories comes out as follows. Either the theory has rather demanding conditions for survival (e.g. continuity of 90 per cent of body matter) or it has less demanding conditions (e.g. continuity of 51 per cent of body matter). Yet in the former case, despite the theory, a man seems to have a coherent hope if he hopes to survive an operation even though the conditions are not fulfilled—e.g. if he has a brain tumour removed, consisting of 12 per cent of his brain, and the person with the rest of the brain lives. In the latter case, despite the theory, a man seems to have a coherent fear if he fears that he will not survive even though the conditions are fulfilled—e.g. if he has 40 per cent of his brain removed and the person with the rest of the brain lives. The obvious thing for you to say, if you are to undergo such an operation, is that its outcome would be a 'risk'.[19] Even if you can be sure that there will be a survivor of the operation (a person with much of your brain), it is still open to question whether that person will be you. A fashionable empiricist theory of the above kind may tell you whether that person will be you, but it could be wrong. You

[19] 'The Self and Future', 180.

might survive and you might not. But mere logic could hardly show you that hoping to survive such an operation (or fearing that you would not) would be hoping for (or fearing) something of which the description made no sense.

In hoping to survive (or fearing that you may not) you do not appear to be refusing to look logical facts in the face. In that case the claim of any such fashionable theory to state a logical truth is mistaken. Even if you do think that it is clear that a man does not survive if none of his brain survives alive in a body, and that he does survive if all of its does, you have to admit that what happens in intermediate cases is unknown. Mere reflection of the meanings of words would not appear to provide the answer. It appears to be an empirical matter whether or not a man survives a large-scale brain operation, yet not one which can be settled conclusively by observations which we can make. The person P_2 who has a certain fraction of P_1's brain will be expected to make some memory claims which P_1 would be expected to make and to have somewhat the same character. But how much suffices to make P_2 the same person as P_1? There seems no natural answer. And yet a man may hope to survive even if he does lose some of his memories and comes to react to circumstances in ways other than he used to react. But how can we say for certain when his hope has proved justified?

A further awkwardness for any such empiricist theory is that, as we have noted, there will inevitably be border-line cases for its satisfaction. Suppose that a theory that continuity of 90 per cent brain matter is necessary for survival is correct, and A is told that he is to have removed from his brain at a stroke a tumour which consists of approximately 10 per cent of the matter of the brain, so that the subsequent person will have approximately 90 per cent of the brain of A. Will A survive the operation? The answer given by the theory is that it is as true to say that he will as that he will not. A is told this answer, and is told that the subsequent person will then be tortured. Has he cause to fear? Presumably less cause than if the person to be tortured were fully himself, and more cause than if it were not at all himself. But how can an intermediate reaction be justified? Each subsequent person will either be tortured or not; no half-tortures will be laid on. An intermediate reaction would be justified if A did not know who would be tortured, i.e. whether it would be himself or someone else. But A has been told who will be tortured, i.e. someone who is equally well described as A or as not A. Yet how can any suffering affect A unless he suffers it all or suffers part of it?—and neither of these alternatives is what is being suggested here.

The arguments of the previous paragraphs, and especially the argument concerned with border-line cases, suggest an essential difference in the survival conditions for persons (and perhaps animals too) from the survival conditions for inanimate objects. There is (as I shall emphasize further in Chapter 13) nothing puzzling about a future car constructed from bits of my old car and other bits as well as being a border-line case for being my car. As cars do not have feelings or hope to survive the arguments of the previous paragraph cannot be deployed to argue against this possibility. But a conscious thing such as a person may wish to continue to be conscious, and there seems no intermediate possibility between a certain future conscious being being that person and not being that person.

So much for objections to empiricist theories. What can we put in their place? Wherein does the identity of persons consist? The identity does not consist solely in the continuity of one or more observable characteristics, for empiricist theories took all these into account. (If they left one out, an empiricist theory could easily be constructed which took account of it, and, there is every reason to suppose, would be found wanting for reasons of the kind which we have already considered.) The only alternative is to say that personal identity is something ultimate.[20] It is unanalysable into conjunctions or disjunctions of other observable properties. Bodily continuity, continuity of memory and character, are, however, the only evidence we have of its presence; it is observable only by observing these. In general there is plenty of evidence, normally overwhelming evidence, of bodily continuity, memory and character, as to whether or not two persons are the same, which gives very clear verdicts in the overwhelming majority of cases. Yet while evi-

[20] This was the view expressed in the eighteenth century by Butler, and, less explicitly, by Reid. See J. Butler, *Of Personal Identity* in his *The Analogy of Religion* (London, 1902), p. 328; and T. Reid, *Essays on the Intellectual Powers of Man*, ed. A. D. Woozley (London, 1941), III.4.

dence of continuity of body, memory, and character is evidence
of personal identity, personal identity is not constituted by
continuity of body, memory and character. Hence the evidence
may on occasion mislead, and two persons be the same,
although the best evidence which we have shows that they are
not, and conversely. Also on occasion the evidence of observable
characteristics may give no clear verdict as to whether P_2 is the
same person as P_1; but that does not mean that there is no
clear answer to this question, merely that we do not know and
cannot even make a reasonable guess at what it is. That evidence
of continuity of body, memory, and character is evidence of
personal identity cannot of course be something established
by enumerative induction; that is, by observing in the past
correlations between two independently observable things,
personal identity and continuity of body, memory, and character (i.e. observing that whenever two past persons were the
same person, there was continuity of body, memory, and
character between them). This is because personal identity
cannot be observed apart from observations of continuity of
body, memory, and character. Although it might in theory be
established by some more complex form of inductive inference
that the latter is evidence of the former, this is in fact, I suspect,[21]
either an analytic truth or some basic principle which we take as
intuitively obvious, like the basic principle of induction itself
that what has happened (described under some simple description) invariably in the past is evidence of what is going to
happen.

One comes to understand the meaning of 'same person', not
by being provided with a definition in terms of continuity of
body, character, and memory, but by being provided with clear
examples of pairs of persons who are and pairs of persons who
are not the same, and being shown the grounds on which judgements about personal identity are made. By being shown the
evidence and clear cases where the evidence points one way
rather than the other, we come to have an understanding of
what is at stake. But there is no reason to suppose that the
understanding is simply an understanding of the evidence (i.e.
that we mean no more by personal identity than some con-

[21] I have argued for this view in the paper 'Persons and Personal Identity',
referred to in fn. 13 on p. 110.

junction or disjunction of the kind of features which lead us to make judgements ascribing it) and the arguments of this chapter count against that supposition.

Because of the difficulty of what to say in puzzle situations about whether or not two persons are the same, one or two recent writers, and notably Derek Parfit,[22] have argued that our concept of personal identity is a confused one. The questions which I have posed assume all-or-nothing answers, that P_2 is or that P_2 is not the same person as the earlier P_1. Once we assume that, to give one or other answer in the puzzle situation seems unjustified, and that for some is worrying. So Parfit wishes to treat personal identity as a matter of degree, and instead of saying that two persons are or are not the same person, to say rather that they are exactly the same or almost exactly the same or pretty much the same or hardly at all the same. This is indeed a very natural development of the empiricist theory of personal identity. This is after all what we say of the identity of inanimate things. We say that Italy of 1972 is exactly the same country as the Italy of 1952 (its boundaries, constitution, etc. are the same) but only pretty much the same as the Italy of 1942 (which had somewhat different boundaries, and a very different constitution) and hardly at all the same as the Italy of 1862. If we started to talk in this way about people, then P_2 would be the same person as P_1 to the extent to which bodily continuity and similarity of memory and character existed. Then it would be clear how to describe the puzzle cases. The less and the less gradual was brain and other continuity, the more P_2 would be a different person from P_1.

However, the consequence of this way of talking is that we have to say of a man P_2 in his late fifties who does not remember most of the events of what we would ordinarily call 'his' childhood, has a very different character from the character which, we would ordinarily say, 'he' had when young, and has very few of the same brain cells as those which, we would ordinarily say, 'he' had fifty years before, that P_2 is only somewhat the same person as the boy he is ordinarily said to have been. Now if we do say this we are clearly using the word 'person' in a different way from the normal way. For on our normal under-

[22] See, e.g., his 'Personal Identity', *Philosophical Review*, 1971, **80**, 3–27 and 'On "The Importance of Self-Identity" ', *Journal of Philosophy*, 1971, **68**, 683–90.

standing the boy who had developed into a man in his late fifties without any brain operations, sudden losses of memory, or sudden changes of character, is not more or less the same person as the boy was; he is the same person *simpliciter*. That, given our normal concept of person, is at least a very well-evidenced judgement, if not an analytic truth. If Parfit makes a different claim, he is introducing a different concept of person, For on our normal concept of person he is not saying the right thing. But why should we scrap our normal concept of person which we find it natural to use in normal circumstances and even in abnormal circumstances (when a man wonders whether or not he will survive an operation)? Parfit's only reason for objecting to the normal concept seems to be the weak verificationist principle which I discussed in Chapter 2 that a proposition has no factual meaning if no evidence of observation can count for or against it.[23] No evidence of observation can count for or against the claim that in a puzzle situation (where on the criteria of bodily continuity and similarity of memory and character two persons P_1 and P_2 at different times are border-line cases for being the same person) P_1 and P_2 are the same person. Therefore, given the verificationist principle, it is not a factual claim to say that they are. Hence our concept of 'same person' does not apply in puzzle situations. We want a concept which does apply there. Hence, Parfit can argue, the need for a new concept.

If the arguments which I presented in Chapter 2 are accepted, it must be held that the weak verificationist principle is false and hence that Parfit has provided no good reason for holding that our normal concept of personal identity is confused.

The view which I have put forward that bodily continuity

[23] That Parfit uses the verificationist principle to establish his view can be seen on p. 5 of his article 'Personal Identity'. Here he considers a man's brain being split into two and each half transplanted into another body. He rejects the suggestion that one and only one of the resulting persons is the same person as the original person on the grounds that 'each half of my brain is exactly similar, and so, to start with, is each resulting person. So how can I survive as only one of the two people? What can make me one of them rather than the other?' The assumption here is that if one of the resulting persons is to be the original person he must differ from the other resulting person in some observable respect, which would be evidence for his being the original person; which assumption seems to derive from the principle that to be factually meaningful a claim must be confirmable, i.e. must be such that evidence of observation can count for or against it.

and similarity of memory and character are evidence of but do not constitute personal identity is, I believe, supported by other thoughts about personal identity which we have and judge to be coherent. Consider, to begin with, the resurrection of the dead (whose dead bodies have decayed). Most people, I suggest, uninfluenced by philosophical theory, would allow this to be a logical possibility. The affirmation that there is life after death in another world or reincarnation on earth is widespread. Perhaps equally widespread is the denial that these things happen. Yet most who deny that these things happen seem to allow that it makes sense to suppose that they do happen, while denying that in fact they do. Now an empiricist theory which allows life after death must claim that in such a case personal identity is a matter of similarity of memory and character. A man survives death if and only if there exists after his death a man with similar memory and character to his (subject, possibly, to the proviso that there is no more than one such man). We saw earlier that there are difficulties in such theories. But here is a further one. If it is logically possible that I should survive my death, I have a coherent hope if I hope to do so. On an empiricist theory, for me to hope for my resurrection is for me to hope for the future existence of a man with my memories and character, that is a man who will be able to remember the things which happened to me and will react to circumstances somewhat as I do. But that is not at all what I hope for in hoping for my resurrection. I do not hope that *there be* a man of that kind—I want it to be me. If it is not to be me, then despite my hope for my resurrection I am probably relatively indifferent to whether or not a man rises with my character and memories. And if I am to rise again, I probably should not mind *all* that much if I had lost many of my memories and much of my bad character. What matters is that *I* rise. So hoping for my resurrection is *not* analysable as hoping for the resurrection of a person in various ways like me. And so an empiricist theory which says that it is is false.

Another situation which an empiricist theory must rule out as not logically possible is that I should have your life and that you should have mine. Many people wish they had someone else's life in the sense that they wish they were in his shoes with his body, position, and relationships, appearance, memory, and character. Perhaps my body is withered, my own position and relationships are unsatisfactory, my looks are ugly, my memories give me no joy, and I am profoundly dissatisfied with my own character. You, on the other hand, seem very satisfactory in these ways. So I wish that I had your life. Is the wish coherent? that is, am I wishing for the existence of a logically possible state of affairs different from the present state? Superficially, yes. Many have wished wishes of this kind, and believed themselves to be wishing for such a state. Yet if it is logically possible that I should have your body, memory, character, etc., it is also logically possible that you should have mine. And if the former state of affairs differs from the present one, so does the latter one. And you acquiring my body, memory, and character seems to make a further difference from the present state from the difference which would be made by my acquiring your body, memory, and character. But if I acquired your body, memory, and character and you mine (or if I always had the former and you the latter) the world would be exactly the same as it is now in respect of the bodily continuity, memory, character, etc. of persons. If the possibility that I might have your life and you have mine can be coherently entertained, as appears to be the case, then any empiricist theory of personal identity is mistaken.

The purpose of this long digression into the topic of personal identity has been to show that personal identity is not constituted by such things as bodily continuity and continuity of memory and character, even though the latter are evidence for it. In the absence of the criterion of bodily continuity it may be difficult (perhaps even impossible) to *establish* whether or not two persons at different times are identical—although I have argued against this. Yet even if this were so it would still be coherent to claim that two persons are the same—even if there were no evidence that they were. Hence talk of distinct non-embodied persons is coherent—even if there could be no evidence that two such persons were or were not the same. Whether there could be such evidence is not central to our concerns here and so I have touched on it only fairly briefly. The main point being established, Penelhum's arguments fail. The attempt to show the incoherence of supposing that there is an omnipresent spirit by claiming that it was incoherent to suppose that there be non-embodied spirits at all because there would be no criteria of identity for them, fails. I therefore appeal to the superficial coherence of the supposition, which I have attempted to back up by spelling out in more detail what the supposition of the existence of an omnipresent spirit amounts to.

8

Free and Creator of the Universe

In this chapter I shall consider what it means and whether it is coherent to suppose that there exists an onnipresent spirit who has free will and is the creator of the universe; that is, I shall consider what it means and whether it is coherent to suppose that the omnipresent spirit postulated in Chapter 7 also has free will and is the creator of the universe. As in the last chapter, I shall conduct the argument for coherence simply by expanding, telling a story of how the claim could be true, and in the process rebutting arguments to show incoherence.

Creator of the Universe

Theists claim that God is the creator of all things. (In the Nicene Creed he is said to be 'Maker of Heaven and Earth, and of all things, visible and invisible'.) But initial restrictions must be put on this loose claim. Firstly, the theist does not normally claim that God is the creator of himself. That something should create itself is a difficult idea of which to attempt to make sense—to say the least; and the theist normally sees no need to make the attempt. (I shall argue in Chapter 14 that it would be incoherent to suppose that God is the cause of his own existence.) The theist's more usual claim is that God has no creator. The claim that there is an individual who is the creator of all things, is to be understood with the qualification 'apart from himself' or, more precisely, 'apart from anything the existence of which is entailed by his own existence'. Secondly, the theist is presumably not claiming that God is the creator of prime numbers, concepts, or logical relations. There are certain things which exist as a matter of logical necessity; that is, the statement that they exist is a logically necessary truth. It is a logically necessary truth that there exists a prime number between 16 and 18, or that there exists a relation of entailment between 'John is over 5 foot tall' and 'John is over 4 foot tall'. Such things which exist as a matter of logical necessity do not, we feel, exist in the hard real way in which tables, chairs, and people do. To say that they exist is not to give us any real information about how things are. That they exist cannot be due to the act of any creator; for they exist just because they are, because the propositions which assert their existence say what they do. For these reasons I suggest that the claim that there exists an omnipresent spirit who is the creator of all things is to be understood as the claim that there exists an omnipresent spirit who is the creator of all things which exist, the existence of which is neither a logically necessary truth nor entailed by his own existence. This we may phrase more briefly as the claim that there exists an omnipresent spirit who is the creator of all logically contingent things apart from himself.

How next is 'create' to be understood? We could understand it as 'bring about the existence of'. But if we understand it in that simple way, there is an obvious difficulty for the theist who claims that God creates all logically contingent things apart from himself. This is that, superficially, agents other than God bring about a lot of things. Men, not God, bring about the existence of tables and chairs. Sun and rain, not God, bring about the existence of healthy plants. One could say that really men, sun, and rain do not do these things—they only appear to, really it is God alone who does them. But most theists have not wished to deny that men, sun, and rain bring about things.[1]

[1] The view that God alone causes things is known as occasionalism. On this view other animate and inanimate agents and events merely provide the occasions on which God brings about the things which are normally called their effects. Striking of a match does not, on this view, bring about its ignition. It is simply that when matches are struck, God predictably makes them light up. Occasionalism is a view much more common among Islamic philosophers than among Christian ones. Among many who taught it were Algazel and Sanusi—see the well-expressed passage from the latter in A. Guillaume, *Islam* (2nd edn., Harmondsworth, 1956), pp. 141 f. The account which I have given of God as creator is compatible with occasionalism, though wider than it. It could easily be tightened up to give a pure 'occasionalist doctrine'.

The claim that God is the creator of all has been understood more subtly. By it the theist has wanted to make one main claim and sometimes also one subsidiary claim. The main claim is that God either himself brings about or makes or permits some other being to bring about (or permits to exist uncaused[2]) the existence of all things that exist (with the qualifications on this latter expression, stated above, being understood); that those things exist only because of God's action or permission. Other beings, that is, often bring about the existence of things, but when they do, they do so only because (in the case of beings without free will) God makes them do so, or because (in the case of beings with free will) God permits them to do so. Agents other than God act only because he makes or permits them to act.

The subsidiary claim which has often been made, e.g. by scholastic theologians, is that God alone brings about the existence of certain things, such as matter and human souls. I shall not consider this subsidiary claim further. I would need very careful and lengthy articulation to bring out what is meant by 'matter' and 'human soul' and the doctrine does not seem to be very central to theism. It would hardly seem to matter for theism if God on occasion permitted some other being to create matter. He would hardly be less worthy of worship if he did. I shall therefore understand the doctrine that God is the creator of all things as the doctrine that God himself either brings about or makes or permits some other being to bring about the existence of all logically contingent things that exist (i.e. have existed, exist, or will exist), apart from himself.

I could have set out the doctrine of God as creator as the doctrine that God brings about (or makes or permits others to bring about) the *beginnings* of the existence of all things which exist. But the theist believes that God's action (or permission) is needed not merely for things to begin to exist but also for them

---

[2] The point of the clause in brackets is that there may be indeterminacy in nature; things may happen without anything making them happen. If God is creator of the Universe this can only be because he keeps nature indeterministic. It is not incompatible with his being creator of the universe that he should allow the existence of an element of chance in nature. For the sake of simplicity of exposition I shall in general omit this clause in future expositions of the doctrine of God as creator except where it is necessary to refer to it. It should, however, be understood where it is not explicitly stated.

to continue in existence. We could phrase this point by describing God as the creator *and sustainer* of all things, but it is
simpler and in conformity with the usage of medieval theology
(though not perhaps of much modern writing) to make both
points by the use of the one word 'create', and this I shall do.
Aquinas held that natural reason was unable to prove either
that the universe (in either the wider or narrower senses to be
delineated below) was eternal or that it had a beginning of
existence.[3] Revelation alone (the Bible and the Church, that is)
showed us that it had a beginning of existence. Nevertheless,
natural reason could prove that it had a creator. Theists both
before and after Aquinas have usually held that the universe
(at any rate in the narrower sense to be delineated below) had a
beginning,[4] but for them, as for Aquinas, this doctrine can
hardly have the importance in their thought possessed by the
doctrine that God is responsible for the existence of the universe
at each moment of its existence. In the old legend Atlas holding
up the earth is responsible for it being in place—whether he has
been holding it for a few years or for ever. So on the theist's
view God keeps the universe in being, whether he has been
doing so for ever or only for a finite time.[5]

The theist claims that God is the creator of the world or the
universe. What is meant by 'the world' or 'the universe'?
Different men may well nean different things by these phrases.
For some 'the universe' or 'the world' may mean simply all that
there is. But the theist cannot give these phrases this meaning—
for the reasons given above. He may mean by them 'all logically
contingent things apart from God'. Or he may mean something
narrower. He may mean the system of all the physical things
which are spatially related to the earth. By physical things I
mean roughly material objects, such as stars and planets and
the tables, houses, and (embodied) persons on them and things
similar thereto (such as packets of energy, which, like material
objects, have mass and charge and can be converted into and

---

[3] See his *Summa contra Gentiles* 2.32–8.

[4] Aquinas held this about the universe both in the narrower and the wider sense.
See his *Summa Theologiae*, Ia.61.2–3.

[5] For discussion of what it means to say that the universe has existed for only a
finite time or alternatively for ever and of what kind of proof these propositions are
susceptible, see my 'The Beginning of the Universe', *Proceedings of the Aristotelian
Society*, Suppl. Vol., 1966, **40**, 125–38 (developed in Ch. 15 of my *Space and Time*).

obtained from matter). By 'spatially related' I mean 'in some direction at some distance' (e.g. a million miles along such-and-such a line). Planets, stars, and galaxies and the physical things between them and on them, however distant in whatever direction, form the universe. This definition, however, allows for the logical possibility of the existence of universes or worlds other than ours. For maybe there are planets and stars other than those which lie in some direction along some line from ourselves.[6] The theist who claims that God is the creator of the universe, will, if he uses the expression 'the universe' in this narrower sense, also claim that God is the creator of anything else logically contingent which exists. He claims, that is, that God is creator of the universe both in the narrower sense of 'all physical things spatially related to ourselves' and in the wider sense of 'all logically contingent things apart from God'. The latter class of things includes the movements of physical things, the way they behave. The theist claims that not merely does God bring about (or makes or permits others to bring about or permits to exist uncaused) the existence of tables and chairs, (embodied) persons and stars, but that he brings about (or makes or permits others to bring about) their moving and interacting in the way in which they do; and that their motion or interaction would not occur but for his action or permission. God's action (or permission) is needed, for example, not merely for the existence of the wind, but for it to blow this way rather than that. Theists may hold that the universe in the wider sense includes many other things beside physical things more naturally called 'things' than the movements and interactions of bodies. They may hold that as well as physical things spatially related to ourselves, there are angels and devils, disembodied spirits and other worlds—or they may not hold this. The doctrine that there is an omnipresent spirit who is the creator of the universe is therefore to be understood, in view of the tradition of theism, as follows. There is an omnipresent spirit who either himself brings about or makes or permits other beings to bring about (or permits to exist uncaused) the existence of all logically contingent things that exist (i.e. have existed, exist, or will exist), apart from anything, the existence of which is entailed

---

[6] Quinton has argued for this in his article 'Spaces and Times'. I develop his argument in Chs. 1 and 2 of *Space and Time*.

by his own existence. However, to understand what is being said more fully, we need to investigate what it is for a person to bring about or permit the existence of a state of affairs or to make or permit some other being to do so. To do this we must make a brief digression into the question of the nature of personal explanation.

Personal Explanation

Philosophers have distinguished two (superficially) distinct kinds of explanation of events—scientific explanation and personal explanation. A scientific explanation of an event or state cites two things—some previous event or state of the world, and a law or laws of nature (or other true generalizations about what always or usually happens) of which it is a consequence that the latter state is followed by the former. We explain a particular explosion by the ignition of a particular volume of gunpowder in certain conditions of temperature, pressure, and humidity and the generalization that always under such circumstances gunpowder explodes. We explain a particular piece of litmus paper turning red by its having been immersed in acid and the generalization that acid always turns litmus paper red. Sophisticated scientific explanations invoke many laws or generalizations and previous states described in some complexity, of which it is a somewhat remote consequence that the event or state to be explained occurs. It is a consequence of Newton's laws and arrangements of the sun and planets thousands of years ago that they are in the positions in which they are today. The previous state or event is often called the initial conditions. The initial conditions bring about the future event under the operation of the law.

We use the scientific pattern of explanation not only when engaged in science of any degree of sophistication but in much everyday explanation of happenings. We explain the cheese being mouldy by its having been left in a warm place two weeks ago and the generalization that almost always cheese turns mouldy within two weeks if it is left in a warm place. However, we also use in ordinary everyday explanation of happenings explanation of a very different pattern, which I shall call personal explanation. I will describe the structure of explanation of this type, and then show why it would be misguided to suppose it reducible to the scientific pattern.

In personal explanation the occurrence of an event E is explained as brought about by a rational agent or person P, having the intention J to bring about E. E is thus what we may term the 'result' of an intentional action A performed by P. (Henceforward, when I talk about 'actions' I understand thereby 'intentional actions'.) E may be the motion of my hand, P myself, J my intention to move my hand, and A my moving my hand. But E is not explained merely by our being told that P intentionally brought it about. We need to know how P was in a position to bring it about, how it was that P's intentions were efficacious. That leads us to the distinction between basic actions and mediated actions. As I wrote in the last chapter, a basic action is something which an agent just does, does not do by doing anything else. By contrast, a mediated action is an action which is not a basic action, one which an agent does by doing something else. I signal by moving my hand. I break the door down by giving it a kick. The former are mediated actions; the latter basic actions. Now an answer to the question how P brought about E may be *either* that bringing about E was a basic action and that the capacity to perform such basic actions is among P's capacities *or* that that E was an intended consequence of a basic action A^1 which P performed. Thus the answer to how P brought about the motion of his hand is that performing such actions is among his basic capacities. The answer to how P brought about the flattening of the door is that P kicked the door (a basic action) and that that kick caused the door to lie flat on the ground. In saying that E was an intended consequence of A^1, I use the word 'consequence' in a wide sense. E is a consequence of A^1 if E would not have happened if A^1 had not happened (but the occurrence of A^1 does not entail the occurrence of E).[7] This may be, as in the above example,

---

[7] I thus distinguish a consequence of an action from the 'result' of an action, in the sense of this term which I defined above E is the result of an action A of an agent P if his performing A consists in his bringing about E (where E is not an action of P's). Thus my action of opening my book consists in my bringing about the book being open. The book being open is the result of the action. The performance of an action entails bringing about its result, if it has a result. (Some actions do not have results. My action of trying to open my book does not consist in my bringing about any state of affairs other than my trying to open my book—which

because A^1 causes E (in a way in which can be explained by scientific explanation). It may also be because, given current circumstances C, the performance of A^1 constitutes bringing about E. Thus given the current conventions in motoring and banking, my writing my name in a certain place has as a consequence that a cheque bears my signature, and my putting my arm out of the window has as as a consequence that a signal indicating a turn to the right is made. E may also be a consequence of A_1 if the occurrence of E is physically necessary for (although not caused by) the performance of A_1.[8] It is in this way that the contraction of my arm muscles is a consequence of my moving my hand. E is an intended consequence of A_1 if P had the intention to bring about E and the belief B that performing A_1 would have E as a consequence.

So, to summarize, in personal explanation we explain an event E as brought about by a person P. If the bringing-about of E is a basic action A, we need to cite also an intention J of P to bring about E and to state that bringing about E is among the things which P is able to do at will, viz. among P's capacities X. P, J, and X function in the explanation of E. Of course we can often go further and explain how it is that P has intention J (viz. what his intention is in doing the basic action, why it is that he moves his hand) or how it is that P has those capacities (which nerves and muscles need to be operative for P to have these capacities). But P, J, and X suffice to explain E—whether or not we can explain how it is that J and X. If the bringing-about of E is a mediated action, things are more complicated. We cite P and his intention J to bring about E. But we need to say which basic action he did—say A^1 which consisted in bringing about some event S in virtue of intention J_2 and

---

is an action of mine.) By contrast, a consequence of an action is something which is brought about by the performance of the action, although its occurrence is not something which is entailed by the performance of the action. This distinction is due to G. H. Von Wright, (see *Norm and Action*, London, 1963, pp. 39 ff.).

[8] I understand by a state or event X being physically necessary for another one Y, that Y would not occur unless X had occurred—and that this is because of the bringing-about involved in personal or scientific explanation. To take my example in the text—I would not have moved my hand unless my arm muscles had contracted; and this because the contraction of my arm muscles brought about the motion of my hand. Of course this contraction would not have taken place unless I had had the intention to move my hand; and it is for this reason that both I and the contraction of my arm muscles bring about the motion of my hand.

capacities X—how S had E as a consequence (e.g. in virtue of natural law L) and that P had the belief B that S would have E as a consequence.

In both personal and scientific explanation we can distinguish the 'what', the object or state of affairs, which acted to bring about the effect E, from the 'why', whatever it was which allowed the 'what' to bring E about. The 'what' is the cause of E; the 'why' is the reason for the efficacy of the cause. In scientific explanation the reason is the natural laws or other generalizations which ensured that the cause had its effect. In personal explanation the person's intention and capacities (and the other factors involved when mediated actions are concerned) ensure that the person brought about the effect which he did. The intention explains why the person brought about E rather than some other effect, and his capacities explain the successful execution of the intention. I shall say that we have a full explanation of an event E if the explanation cites explanatory factors which brought about E, such that a statement of their occurrence entails the occurrence of E. (Thus in the explanation cited earlier of the litmus paper turning red, 'this piece of litmus paper is immersed in acid' and 'acid always turns litmus paper red' entails 'this litmus paper will turn red'.) Otherwise I shall say that we have only a partial explanation. If there is a full explanation of some effect, I shall say that the cause physically necessitated the effect; otherwise the cause merely makes the event (physically) probable. Unless the cause and the reason together deductively entail the occurrence of E, there is still something brute and ultimate, and so unexplained about the occurrence of E. It should be added that although there may exist a full explanation of some event E, since full explanations have a complicated structure, not all elements of the full explanation may be deployed explicitly when a man explains the occurrence of E.

Now superficially, personal explanation looks very different from scientific explanation. In scientific explanation, as we have seen, we explain an event E by past events or states C and natural laws L. In personal explanation we explain E as the result of an action A done by an agent P (not by an event) in order to realize intentions for the future. Despite the apparent difference it has, however, been argued by some philosophers, seminally by Donald Davidson[9] and at greater length by Alvin Goldman,[10] that really personal explanation conforms to the scientific pattern.

I shall confine discussion of this suggestion to the case of basic actions. Clearly if personal explanation of basic actions cannot be knocked into the scientific pattern, neither can personal explanation of mediated actions. The suggestion is that explanation of the occurrence of an event E in terms of the action of a person P with intention J (to bring about E) and capacities X is analysable in terms of initial conditions bringing about E in virtue of some generalization. Now talk about intentions is not talk about what always or usually happens, that is about generalizations. For a man may act on some intention which he has never acted upon before and will never act on again. So the most plausible way of attempting to analyse personal explanation in terms of scientific explanation is to regard intentions as initial conditions, and talk about capacities as talk about what always or usually happens. Then to say that P brought E about, having the intention J so to do, is just to say that P's intention, J, as one of the initial conditions, brought E about. To say that P had the capacity to bring E about is just to say that P's bodily conditions Y (brain states, muscle states, etc.) and the environmental conditions Z (e.g. no one having bound P's arm) and psychophysiological laws L are such that an intention such as J is followed by the event intended, E. So we have a scientific explanation of the occurrence of E in terms of initial conditions J, Y, and Z and generalization L. Proponents of this type of reduction of personal explanation to scientific sometimes use different words from those in which I have expounded the reduction. Originally, of course, instead of talking of 'intentions', they talked of 'volitions', where these were supposed to be something like decisions. Sometimes, now, instead, they talk of 'desires' or 'wants'. Now some of such terms denote actions or entail the occurrence of actions. A 'volition', for example, being something like a decision, denotes something which the agent brings about intentionally. If we are to reduce personal explanation to scientific explanation, we clearly cannot

[9] Donald Davidson, 'Actions, Reasons, and Causes', *Journal of Philosophy*, 1963, **60**, 685–700.
[10] Alvin I. Goldman, *A Theory of Human Action* (Englewood Cliffs, N.J., 1970).

allow such terms to appear unanalysed. For if we do, we should not have reduced personal bringing-about to scientific bringing-about. If reduction is to be affected, the initial conditions must be states of affairs other than intentional actions. They must be states of affairs which an agent finds himself having, not ones which he voluntarily adopts. 'Desires' and 'wants' are clearly like this; and 'intentions' will have to be construed as states which an agent finds himself having, if the reduction is to be affected.

But when we explain an event as brought about by the agent having the intention to bring it about, clearly we are doing more than to say that the agent's wants or desires caused the event. For a man's desire to raise his arm could have caused his arm to go up, even though he had no intention to raise his arm and so did not intentionally raise his arm. Men have desires and wants which they do not welcome and which they try to keep under control, try to stop having effects. A desire may nevertheless produce its effect, though the man in no way endorsed it. I might not have moved my arm intentionally at all, and yet might suddenly see or feel it going up, and a scientist might discover that my desire was the cause.

Now let us talk of 'intentions' instead of 'desires'. If P brings about E as a result of his intention J to bring about E, is this intention something which he may just find himself having or something which in some way he must choose to have? If the latter, then we are still left with personal bringing-about. If the former, it is possible that the intention might cause E without the agent having in any way intentionally (in the ordinary sense of this term) brought E about. Let E be the agent's arm going up. Now if an intention is something which an agent may find himself having, then an intention is like a desire, and P may find himself having an intention to raise his arm (say in order to attract attention),[11] but be too reluctant, hesitant, or shy to act on his intention. Nevertheless, the intention could suddenly cause E, to the agent's surprise without his intentionally having raised his arm. So bringing about an effect intentionally is not just a matter of an intention bringing about the effect (where an intention is a state which a man might find himself

[11] I take this example in a slightly modified form from R. Taylor, *Action and Purpose*, (Englewood Cliffs, N.J., 1966), pp. 248 f.

having). I conclude therefore that personal explanation is *sui generis*, and is not reducible to scientific explanation.

Now in order that a human agent's intentions may have the intended effects, often various states of affairs must hold and various laws must operate in the world. This is of course most evident where the actions are mediated actions. For my intention to kill Jones by shooting to be efficacious, there have to operate certain laws of ballistics and Jones has to be in a certain place, etc. etc. But even with the basic actions of humans, this holds. If my intention to move my arm is to be efficacious I have (of logical necessity) to have a certain capacity, and it is physically necessary that, if I am to have this capacity, I have certain nerves and muscles and there operate certain laws of nervous interaction. It is certainly physically possible that I should come to perform basic actions which needed less in the way of neural disturbances and laws. Perhaps I merely need to have certain brain cells in certain states, if I am to perform various mental actions—such as imagining, thinking about philosophy, or doing mental arithmetic. Maybe, too, men can learn to control goings-on in their brain as basic actions—to switch on their α-rhythm, not by performing some other action, but just like that. Maybe much less in the way of neural goings-on is physically necessary for a man to perform the action of switching on his α-rhythm, than is physically necessary for him to perform the action of moving his hand. And, moreover, it certainly seems *logically* possible that an agent perform certain basic actions without his having the capacity for so doing having any conditions physically (but not logically) necessary for its realization. Certainly for an agent P to perform a such basic action A, he has to have a certain capacity—and this is a matter of logical necessity. But there may be no brain states or bodily states or natural laws which have to operate for him to perform the basic action. His capacity to perform it might be an ultimate brute fact, not dependent on other distinct facts about the natural world. And personal explanation explains whether or not an agent's capacity to perform the act in question is dependent in the way stated on physical conditions. Men have given and accepted explanations, in terms of agent's intentions, of the actions which they have performed, for many millenniums without knowing anything about the physical conditions which are necessary for an agent to possess the capacity in question, and even without believing that there were any such conditions. You are not committed to any beliefs about bones, nerves, and muscles, if you accept that my intention to move my arm and my capacity for doing so explain the motion of my arm. Because I moved it intentionally explains why it moved. Again in these days of Uri Geller we may accept a man's intention to bend a fork at a distance from his body and his capacity for so doing as explaining why the fork bent without us having any idea of what his capacity depended on, and indeed while we possibly even deny that it depends on anything. Of course we may reject this explanation, but the point is that it is a possible explanation and we do not need to have a belief about something being physically (but not logically) necessary for the exercise of the capacity in order to accept the proposed explanation as explaining. Or again, we may explain a man's thoughts by his intentions without us having to believe that certain brain states and natural laws have to hold in order for a man to think or have intentions. (Mind–brain correlation is an—as yet—unestablished scientific hypothesis.)

So then, although scientific explanation often explains the occurrence and operation of the factors involved in personal explanation—it may explain our having the capacities we do or our having the intentions we do—nevertheless, personal explanation explains, whether or not it involves or is backed by scientific explanation. Clearly the theist, in claiming that there is an omnipresent spirit, God, who makes or brings about (or permits the bringing-about of) all logically contingent things apart from himself, is using personal explanation. He is claiming that physical and other objects existing and exercising the powers which they do are the results of actions of an omnipresent spirit, God. Clearly the theist holds that in this case (with a partial exception to be noted at the end of this paragraph) there is no scientific explanation (or any explanation in terms of the agency of some other person) of the existence and operation of the factors involved in the personal explanation. These factors are the person, God, his intentions, capacities, beliefs, and the fact that his basic actions have the consequences which they do. That God has the capacities which he does is a consequence of his omnipotence; that he has the beliefs which he does is a consequence of his omniscience. I shall discuss omnipotence and omniscience in the next two chapters. They are properties which belong to God's nature, and we shall see in a later chapter how the theist holds that the existence and nature of God have no further explanation. We shall see later in this chapter how the theist holds that God is free in a sense in which no other causal factor, such as a state of the world or natural law, in any way influences the intentions on which God acts. That God's basic actions have the consequences which they do is either a matter of logic or a matter of the factual connections which hold in the world. That the latter hold, the theist may admit, does have a scientific explanation; but this in turn is explicable by the agency of God. For, as I shall emphasize shortly, the theist holds that the operation of natural laws is a result of a basic action of God.

The theist claims that God brings about some things himself and makes (i.e. brings it about that) other beings bring about other things, and permits other beings to bring about yet other things. An example of the first class might be the physical universe (that is, the universe in the narrow sense) at the first moment of its existence (if it had one). Creating the universe *e nihilo* (not, that is, out of any pre-existing matter) would be a basic action of God. Human beings do not have the power to bring matter into existence (given that we construe 'matter' in a wide sense which includes energy). It is, however, fairly easy to picture what it would be like for them to have such a power. If I could just by so choosing produce a sixth finger or a new fountain-pen (not made out of pre-existing matter) I would have the power to bring matter into existence. Others could see that I had this power by asking me to perform the acts in question. It seems coherent to suppose that an omnipresent spirit have and exercise far more extensive such powers.

An example of God making some things to bring about others would be his bringing about the operation of natural laws. In the natural world things bring about other things. Gunpowder, being ignited, brings about an explosion. The sun brings about the acceleration of the earth towards it. The laws of chemistry and mechanics describe these processes. The theist holds that these processes only happen because God makes them do so.

God makes the ignited gunpowder produce its explosion, makes the sun bring about the attraction of the earth. And, more generally, God makes the universe continue in existence by making its past states bring about subsequent states. Now human beings often enough make things produce effects. A man may by releasing the clutch make his car move forward, or make a billiard-cue push a ball, or a hammer crush a nut. Thus—to put things clumsily but truly—the man brings it about that the car brings about its moving forward, the billiard-cue brings about the ball's motion, the hammer brings about the flattening of the nut. But the theist who thinks about the matter will wish to add that there is an important difference between the divine and human agency in these cases. When a human being makes X bring about Y, he relies on the operation of natural laws over which he has no control to produce the effect. He does something which by the operation of natural laws brings it about that X brings about Y. He releases the clutch which brings it about (because of the arrangement of parts in the car and the operation of natural laws) that the car moves forward. The theist holds that any natural laws only operate because God brings it about that they do. That things have the effects in accord with natural laws which they do is, for the theist, itself an act of God. We saw earlier how scientific explanation often explains the occurrence and operation of the factors involved in personal explanation. If this is coherent, it seems equally coherent to suppose that things may on occasion work the other way round—there may be a personal explanation of the occurrence and operation of the factors involved in scientific explanation. This is the theist's claim here. That things have the powers to bring about the effects which they do bring about (of physical necessity or at any rate with high probability), that is the operation of laws of nature, is due to the action of a person, an omnipresent spirit, having the intention and capacity so to do.

Permitting or allowing is a species of bringing-about. As I shall use these terms, God 'permits' or 'allows' a state of affairs S to occur if he brings it about that nothing stops S from occurring. In particular he 'permits' or 'allows' an agent Q to bring about S if he brings it about that nothing stops Q from bringing about S. This involves his bringing it about that Q

has the power to bring about S and is free to do so. An example of God permitting some things to bring about others might be his permitting one man to kill another. The theist holds that such things only happen because God permits them to do so. Humans often enough allow some thing to bring about some effect. I may allow the rain to make the car wet because I cannot be bothered to put the car away in the garage. But the theist will wish to claim a difference between divine and human agency. It will only be true of me that I permitted the car to get wet if I could have stopped it getting wet. But I would only have been able to stop it getting wet if I could have moved it into the garage, and I need natural laws to operate in order to do that. (If natural laws ceased to operate, my pushing the car, or pulling the starter and releasing the clutch, would not have made it move.) Natural laws independent of man must operate for man to permit things to happen. God is not, in the theist's view, dependent in this way on the operation of natural laws independent of himself. Things happen just because he allows them—nothing independent of himself need operate for his permission to be efficacious.

Some of the actions ascribed by the theist to God will be basic actions, others will be mediated actions. That the particular laws of nature operate which do operate is presumably the result of a basic action of God. He just brings it about that material objects behave in the way they do without bringing it about by doing something else. On the other hand, by making the particular laws of nature operate which do operate he brings about many further results. For example, he may bring about a drought in Egypt by bringing it about that the laws of nature which operate are such as to keep clouds away from Egypt.

Free Action

The theist believes that everything which God brings about he brings about intentionally; everything which he does, that is, is an action, as I have used the term. There are no unforeseen consequences of God's actions. The theist also normally[12]

---

[12] I write 'normally' because there have been Islamic philosophers following Avicenna, who claimed that God acts of necessity. This, however, set them at odds with Islamic orthodoxy.

holds that all God's actions are free. All that the omnipresent spirit who is God does, he does because he chooses to do. Nothing makes him do what he does. He did not, for example, have to create the world; nor does he have to keep the laws of nature operative.

What does it mean to say of God that he acts freely or of his own free will? This question is best approached by asking what it means to say of a man that he acts freely. We may use expressions like 'acts freely', 'is free to', 'can choose whether to' in a variety of contexts. We may be talking of legal freedom, and then talk of what men are free to do will be talk about what is allowed by the law. Or we may be talking of what we may term practical freedom; that is, of what others will not use force to stop men doing. In that context we may say of me that I am free to run a three-minute mile, though of course it is entirely outside my physical powers to do so. However, when we use the expression 'free will' as well as the other expressions referred to above, we are often talking of what we may term metaphysical freedom. In this sense, if a man P does A freely, then no cause makes him do A. He is ultimately responsible for A being done; for nothing makes him make A be done. He is properly praised for doing A, if A is a good action; and properly blamed for doing A, if A is a bad action.

This is the kind of freedom which philosophers discuss (or ought to be discussing) when they discuss the freedom of the will. Let us try to give a somewhat fuller account of it. What is it to say of a man that he does some action, such as put jam on his bread or get married, go into the army or walk down the corridor, of his own free will?

We are concerned with free action. An action, as we have understood the term, is something which an agent does intentionally, does meaning to do it, does because he chooses to do it. If P brings about the knocking of a cup off a shelf because someone holds his arm and pushes it against the cup, then knocking the cup off the shelf is no action of P's. The same applies to any events which an agent brings about because his brain states make him do so, whatever he chooses. Such events are events which happen irrespective of a man's intentions. For them he is indeed not to praise or blame. When an agent does something because he so intends, then personal explanation has application. He is the cause of the action which he does for some purpose which he believes that the action will realize.

An action, I suggest, is a free action if and only if the agent's choosing to do that action, that is having the intention to produce the result of that action, has no full explanation—of any kind, whether of the kind described by scientific explanation or of the kind described by personal explanation. If P's choice to do action A is fully explained by a brain state, or by his genetic make-up, or by his upbringing, affecting him in accord with natural laws, then, given the brain state or the genetic make-up or the upbringing, P could not but have chosen as he did—as a matter of physical necessity. In that case he is hardly to blame or praise for doing it. For the ultimate responsibility for what P did is not P's but goes back much further in time. If P is not responsible for his choosing to do action A (since the choice is caused by factors over which he has no control), he can hardly be held responsible for doing the action A itself, for his only contribution towards its being done was to choose to do it. The same applies if P's choosing, that is having the intention, to do action A is fully explained by the action of some other agent Q. If Q makes P choose to do A, and P's doing A is fully explained by Q's action, then P did not do A freely. He is hardly to praise or blame for doing A. Yet if nothing else makes P perform the action A, which being an action is something which he does intentionally, does because he chooses to do it, then surely praise and blame are in place.

A long tradition of philosophy developed from Hume and even earlier has denied the necessity of the requirement described in the last paragraph. According to Hume,[13] a man acts freely if he does what he wants even if what he wants is predetermined by his brain state or upbringing. This tradition seems mistaken for the reasons just given. A man acts freely in the sense of 'free' which we are considering if and only if it is appropriate to blame him for doing what he believed to be wrong and praise him for doing what he believed to be right. But a man is only to be blamed for his actions if in the circumstances he could have done otherwise, if he was the ultimate source of things happening as they did. But if a man's choice was fully caused by his brain state and environment, and happened

[13] See his *Enquiry Concerning Human Understanding*, Sect. 8.

as it did ultimately because of the state of the world long before he was born, then his choice was predetermined, he was not the ultimate source of things happening as they did. In the circumstances (of his brain and environment being as they were) he could not (as a matter of physical necessity) have done other than he did do. Blame and praise then seem inappropriate. Men generally find blame and praise of some man inappropriate if they do come to see that the man could not in his circumstances have done other than he did. A man may perform actions because he has been hypnotized or brain-washed. They are actions because he brings about effects in virtue of his intentions. Yet if X is hypnotized to do action A and then does A we are very hesitant to blame or praise him for doing A. If X is 'brain-washed' into doing A, the same applies. This suggests that normally we praise or blame only because we think (rightly or wrongly) that people are more in control of their actions than they would be, had they been hypnotized or brain-washed. It also suggests that our doubts about whether even in cases of hypnosis or brain-washing some little praise or blame are appropriate arise from doubts about whether in these cases there is still some slight room for an agent affecting what happens in spite of the causes which have affected him.

There is fortunately no need to consider here the controversial question of whether man does act freely. All that I have been doing is to analyse what is meant by saying that he does. To say that of God that he acts freely would seem to be to say at least the same as of man—that God's actions result from his choice and that his choosing has no full explanation.

However, the theist wishes to say something more about God. He wishes to say that while men are quite obviously influenced, although perhaps not fully determined, by precedent causes, God is quite uninfluenced by such factors. Human choices are obviously influenced by many causal factors (as opposed to reasons) over which we have no control, factors which act upon us as it were from without. The state of our body makes us tired or hungry, and so strongly influences us towards making choices which will allow us to rest or eat. The tired prisoner, told that he will be allowed to sleep if he confesses to a crime, is obviously much more likely to confess than he would otherwise be. Such causal factors incline or 'pull' us towards doing one action rather than another. It is in such situations that men suffer temptation. Their reason tells them that A is the right action to do, but their body 'pulls' them as it were towards not doing A. Yet on our normal understanding of God, no causal factors over which he has no control act from without on God. His freedom is unimpaired by sensual desire or nervous impulses. A person who is not influenced in his choices by any causal factors I will call a perfectly free person. Although our normal understanding of God involves thinking of him as perfectly free, this characteristic is not always mentioned explicitly in definitions of God.[14] When God is said to be 'free' this word seems to be understood in this stronger sense of perfectly free.

So, then, the theist's claim that there is an omnipresent spirit who has free will and is the creator of the universe is to be understood as follows: (a) there is an individual X who is an omnipresent spirit and the creator of the universe, (b) everything that X does, X does intentionally, (c) no agent or natural law or state of the world or other causal factor in any way influences X to have the intentions on which he acts, that is to choose to act as he does.

Freedom and Reason

Now, to do an action, as we have used the term, is to do something, meaning to do it. If an agent does something meaning to do it, he must have an intention or purpose or reason for doing the action. For clearly if P does A meaning to do it, either he does A to forward some further purpose or he does not do A to forward some further purpose. In the latter case since he means to do A but does not do A to forward some further purpose, he must be doing A for its own sake. An agent has always to have a reason for doing an action, even if it is only the minimal reason that the agent wanted to do it. If a man says that he did something 'for no reason at all', the natural interpretation is that he did the action merely for the sake of doing it, not for any further reason. The suggestion that a man performed an action, without having any reason at all for doing it, is

[14] But see, e.g., Paul Tillich, *Systematic Theology*, vol. i, (London, 1953), p. 275, for one statement of this characteristic.

incoherent. Now having a reason for an action consists in regarding some state of affairs as a good thing and the doing of the action as a means to forwarding that state, and hence itself a good thing. If my reason for going to London is to meet Jones, I must regard it as in some way a good thing that I should meet Jones, and so in some way a good thing that I go to London. If I regard it as in no way a good thing that I should meet Jones, if I regard my meeting Jones as an event which would serve no useful function at all, meeting Jones cannot be my reason for going to London. The point that to do an action I must (of logical necessity) see my performance of it as in some way a good thing is a very old one due to Aristotle, emphasized by Aquinas, and re-emphasized in our day by, among others, Stuart Hampshire.[15] God, like man, cannot just act. He must act for a purpose and see his action as in some way a good thing. Hence he cannot do what he does not regard as in some way a good thing. This is not a physical constraint, but a logical limit. Nothing would count as an action of God unless God in some way saw the doing of it as a good thing.

So an agent has to have some reason if he is to do an action A. Can an agent still do action A even if he judges that he has an overriding reason for refraining from doing A? What are we to make of the suggestion that a man might see doing A as a good thing in one way (e.g. by its giving sensual pleasure to himself), refraining from doing A as a good thing in another way (e.g. by its contributing to the lifelong peace of mind of someone else), see refraining from doing A as over all a better thing than doing A, but nevertheless do A? When it is suggested that a case is of this sort, we may well suspect that it is not, that the agent did not really see refraining from doing A as over all a better thing than doing A. Yet we are sometimes prepared to allow that the situation is as suggested. We do seem to allow the possibility that a man might do an action which he regarded as a good thing only in some respect but on balance a bad thing. But although we allow this possibility, we do feel that some further explanation is called for. If a man really does accept

---

[15] 'A man cannot be sincere in accepting the conclusion that some course of action is entirely mistaken, if he at the same time deliberately commits himself to this course of action'—Stuart Hampshire, *Freedom of the Individual*, (London, 1965), p. 7.

that to refrain from doing A would be on balance better than to do A, and so accepts that he has overriding reason for refraining from doing A, he judges that he has adequate reason for refraining from doing A but totally inadequate reason for doing A. Rational considerations point clearly in one direction, and yet the agent goes in the other direction. Yet to say that someone judges that he has a reason for doing something is to say that if there are no equally good reasons for not doing that thing and if no factors other than reasons influence him, he will do that thing. We could not understand an agent who claimed to acknowledge 'overriding reason' for refraining from doing A rather than doing A and also claimed to be uninfluenced by anything other than the reasons which he acknowledged, and yet did A. For if the latter claim is taken at its face value, what on earth can the agent have meant when he said that he acknowledged 'overriding reasons' for refraining from doing A? Not what we normally mean, for normally to acknowledge a reason for doing something is to acknowledge an inclination, *ceteris paribus*, to do that thing. So to say of someone that he acknowledges that he has overriding reason for refraining from doing (or for doing) action A is to say that in so far as no factors other than reasons influence him, he will refrain from A (or do A, as the case may be). If you said that you recognized that over all it would be better for you to go home rather than to go to the cinema, and then you went to the cinema, we should have to suppose either that you were lying or had changed your mind, or that factors other than reasons influenced what you did. An explanation of your behaviour is needed, not only in terms of what you judged about the relative merits of the actions, in terms that is of reasons; but also in terms of other factors such as sensual desires and neurological impulses which led you to do what you did not recognize adequate reason for doing. If a man has strong sensual desires, it makes sense to suppose that he judges that over all it would be better to refrain from doing A than to do A but nevertheless intentionally does A. Such non-rational factors over which the agent does not have control explain 'weakness of will', a man acting 'against his better judgement'. But the suggestion that a man might see refraining from A as over all better than doing A, be subject to no non-rational influences inclining him in the direction of doing A and nevertheless do A, is incoherent.[16]

It follows that a perfectly free agent will never do an action if he judges that over all it would be worse to do the action than to refrain from it; he will never do an action if he acknowledges overriding reasons for refraining from doing it. Similarly, he will always do an action if he acknowledges overriding reasons for doing it rather than for refraining from doing it, if he judges that doing it would be over all better than refraining from doing it.[17] His freedom of choice only operates for choice whether to do an action A when he does not acknowledge overriding reasons for doing A rather than refraining, or for refraining rather than doing A. (Of course, he may not acknowledge the existence of overriding reasons in most or even in any cases.) This is a logical limit on the freedom of a perfectly free agent. If an agent's actions are uninfluenced by non-rational factors, rational considerations can alone influence them.

[16] The extreme position on this issue of R. M. Hare as represented in Ch. 5 of *Freedom and Reason* (London, 1963) seems to be that necessarily if a man judges that A is the better action, he will do A unless it is psychologically impossible for him to do A. Many writers have opposed this position. Steven Lukes has pointed out that ordinarily we describe situations in ways which conflict with this principle. We describe men as tempted and yielding to temptation when there is no *irresistible* temptation for them to yield to. Irving Thalberg points out that 'ought' implies might-not'. In Hare's account of moral action it would never be appropriate to blame a man for not living up to his principles. See the contributions of Hare, Lukes, Thalberg and others published in Geoffrey Mortimore (ed.), *Weakness of Will* (London, 1971).

[17] It should not be inferred from this without further argument that a perfectly free creator who creates a universe, will necessarily create the best of all logically possible universes which he is able to create. It is not necessarily over all a less good action to create a less good universe than the best which the agent is able to create. For interesting argument relevant to this issue, see R. M. Adams, 'Must God Create the Best?', *Philosophical Review*, 1972, **81**, 317–32.

9

Omnipotent

Theists have often wished to claim that God is omnipotent, that is, literally, can do anything. Can a coherent account be provided of what it is for a person (who is also an omnipresent spirit, perfectly free, and creator of the universe) to be omnipotent which brings out what theists have wanted to say when they claim that God is omnipotent?

A Coherent Account of Omnipotence

The analysis of omnipotence which initially suggests itself consists in taking literally the account given above and qualifying it by the obvious qualification that to be omnipotent a person need not be able to do the logically impossible. Thus we get what I shall term analysis [A]—that a person is omnipotent if and only if he is able to do any logically possible action, any action, that is, of which the description is coherent. It may be objected that in order to be truly omnipotent, a person should be able to do not merely the logically possible, but the logically impossible as well. This objection is, however, misguided. It arises from regarding a logically impossible action as an action of one kind on a par with an action of another kind, the logically possible. But it is not. A logically impossible action is not an action. It is what is described by a form of words which purport to describe an action, but do not describe anything which it is coherent to suppose could be done. It is no objection to A's omnipotence that he cannot make a square circle. This is because 'making a square circle' does not describe anything which it is coherent to suppose could be done.[1]

---

[1] This point was recognized by Aquinas. He wrote that 'it is incompatible with

However, [A] runs immediately into the difficulty that certain actions are such as (logically) can only be performed by beings of certain kinds, and a being *S* cannot (logically) be a being of all these kinds at the same time. Thus 'getting divorced' is an action that can be performed only by a married person; 'committing adultery with an unmarried man' is an action that can be performed only by a married woman; 'entering into a monogamous marriage' is an action that can be performed only by an unmarried person. Sitting down can only be done by an embodied being; becoming incarnate can only be done by a non-embodied being; and haunting (in the literal sense) can only be done by a ghost. Yet we should hardly regard the fact that an unmarried spirit could not get divorced as showing that he was not omnipotent.

An alternative line of approach, in the face of this difficulty, is to regard omnipotence, not as an ability to do any (logically possible) action, but as an ability to bring about any (logical possible) state of affairs. We shall see shortly how this line of approach avoids the difficulty.

So, as a second analysis, which I shall term [B], I suggest that a person *P* is omnipotent if and only if he is able to bring about any (logically possible) state of affairs. However, [B] will not do as it stands since it requires that to be omnipotent, *P* be able to bring about any logically possible state of affairs *x*, even though the act of bringing about *x* is logically impossible for any being or, in particular, for *S*. One case of a logically possible state of affairs which it is logically impossible for anyone to bring about arises where the state of affairs is a state of the universe before the time at which abilities to bring it about are being assessed. Most writers would hold that it is logically impossible for an agent or other cause to bring about a past state, and I will make this reasonable assumption.[2,3] To deal with this point we

---

the meaning of the absolutely possible that anything involving the contradiction of simultaneously being and not being should fall under divine omnipotence. Such a contradiction is not subject to it, not from any impotence in God, but simply because it does not have the nature of being feasible or possible. Whatever does not involve a contradiction is in that realm of the possible with respect to which God is called omnipotent.' (*Summa Theologiae*, vol. v (London, 1967; trans. Thomas Gilby, O.P.), Ia.25.3.) Descartes, however, seems to have held otherwise. See the quotations in Harry G. Frankfurt, 'The Logic of Omnipotence', *Philosophical Review*, 1964, **73**, 262 n. 3.

[2] For argument on this see, e.g., Richard M. Gale, 'Why a cause cannot be later

must introduce temporal considerations into our account of omnipotence, and so we reach what I shall term analysis [C]: a person P is omnipotent at a time t if and only if he is able to bring about any (logically possible) state of affairs after t.[4]

We must understand here by a state of affairs x being a logically possible state of affairs after t that x be not merely logically possible and after t but also that x be a state of affairs logically compatible with all that has happened at and before t. Thus 'The Prime Minister of 1974 being the son of Albert Jones who died in 1935' might seem to be a logically possible state of affairs after 1973, and so to be within the capacity of an omnipotent being to bring about in 1973. But clearly it will not be within the power of any being in 1973 to bring about if Albert Jones did not die in 1935. Nor should we regard it as counting against a being's omnipotence if he could not in 1973 bring about the state described, because Albert Jones did not die in 1935. We can deal with this point by pointing out that the state described is not a state logically compatible with all that has happened before 1973 and so not a logically possible state of affairs after 1973. This point allows us to cope with the difficulty that certain kinds of action are only (logically) possible for certain kinds of agent. An unmarried spirit P cannot get divorced (here and now, that is). For P to get divorced he would have to bring it about that P be a divorced person. But that state of affairs is not logically compatible with all that has happened up to the present time, for the story of the world up to the present time does not include P being

---

than its effect', *Review of Metaphysics*, 1965, **19**, 209–34, or Ch. 8 of my *Space and Time*. In the next chapter I shall discuss a point about how the claim that it is logically impossible for an agent to bring about a past state is to be understood.

[3] Aquinas held that God, although omnipotent, could not change the past, that is by any action make both p and $\sim p$ true of a past instant. ('As we have seen, anything that implies a contradiction does not fall under God's omnipotence. For the past not to have been implies a contradiction', op. cit., vol. v, Ia.25.4.) The possibility of God bringing about a past state (yet not so as to change it) by later action did not arise for Aquinas for, as we shall see in a later chapter, Aquinas held that God's acting could not be dated on the human time scale, although its effects could.

[4] I pass by the difficult question of whether it is logically possible that an agent bring about a state of affairs simultaneous with his action of bringing it about. If the reader thinks that it is, he should read in [C] and the subsequent analyses [D] and [E], instead of 'after', 'simultaneous with or after'; and if he thinks that it is not he should leave the analyses as they stand.

married; and only if it did, could it, immediately afterward, include P being divorced. Hence it does not, on analysis [C], count against the omnipotence of an unmarried spirit that he cannot immediately get divorced.

However, analysis [C] is not fully satisfactory—for two further reasons. First, it requires of an omnipotent being that he be able to bring about logically necessary states. To be omnipotent a person P has to be able to bring it about that all red objects tomorrow are coloured. But no being can bring it about that all the red objects in the world tomorrow are coloured. This is because (of logical necessity) all the red objects in the world tomorrow will be coloured, whatever any agent does. It is not coherent to suppose that red objects could be other than coloured. Yet we hardly regard it as showing that a being is not omnipotent if we show that he cannot make red objects coloured. The states of affairs after *t* must be confined to logically contingent ones, that is states of affairs of which both the existence and non-existence are coherent suppositions.

[C] is, however, still unsatisfactory because it requires that for P to be omnipotent in 1976, P must be able to bring about a completely uncaused state of affairs in 1977 or a state of affairs in 1977 not brought about by P. For these states are logically contingent states of affairs after 1976. Again, we hardly require it of a person P that he should be able to bring about such states in order to be omnipotent, since the bringing-about of them is logically impossible for P. We can allow for this difficulty by modifying [C] to the following [D]: a person P is omnipotent at a time *t* if and only if he is able to bring about any logically contingent state of affairs after *t*, the description of which does not entail that P did not bring it about at *t*.

The Paradox of the Stone

Having got this far, let us test the coherence of this account of omnipotence by facing it with the paradox of the stone which has been discussed in the journals recently. The discussions take for granted my analysis [A] of omnipotence. I shall show how the paradox can be avoided on analysis [D]. The paradox arises when we ask whether God, allegedly an omnipotent being, can make a stone too heavy for himself to lift. If he cannot, the argument goes, then there is an action which God cannot perform, viz. make such a stone. If he can, then there will be a different action which he cannot perform, viz. lift the stone. Either way, the argument goes, there is an action which God cannot perform, and so (given account [A]) he is not omnipotent. What applies to God applies to any other being and so, the argument goes, it is not coherent to suppose that there be an omnipotent being.

The example of an action which God might or might not be able to perform, lifting a certain stone, is not perhaps a very happy one. One may wonder whether it makes sense to talk of a non-embodied agent, such as God, lifting things. However, a paradox in all essentials the same can be constructed with different examples in which there is no question but that the action is of a kind appropriate to a non-embodied being. We can, for example, ask whether God can make a planet too massive for him to split apart, or a universe too independent for him to annihilate. Nevertheless, I will continue with the stone example, since so much of the discussion in the journals has used this, and, to meet the difficulty, understand by 'lift' 'cause to rise'. When I rephrase the paradox in terms of analysis [D] this difficulty will disappear.

There are two distinct kinds of solution to this paradox current, to show that it provides no objection to the coherence of the concept of omnipotence. The first has been put forward by Mayo,[5] Mavrodes,[6] and Plantinga.[7] Let us take Mavrodes. He argues that God is omnipotent, presumably by definition. But 'on the assumption that God is omnipotent, the phrase "a stone too heavy for God to lift" becomes self-contradictory'.[8] Since it is no objection to the omnipotence of a being that he cannot do self-contradictory things, it is no objection to his omnipotence that he cannot do this self-contradictory thing.

But Mavrodes, like Mayo and Plantinga in their similar solutions, misses the point of the paradox. As Wade Savage[9]

[5] Bernard Mayo, 'Mr. Keene on Omnipotence', *Mind*, 1961, **70**, 249 f.

[6] George I. Mavrodes, 'Some Puzzles Concerning Omnipotence, *Philosophical Review*, 1963, **72**, 221–3.

[7] Alvin Plantinga, *God and Other Minds* (Ithaca, N.Y., 1967), pp. 168–73.

[8] Op. cit., p. 222.

[9] C. Wade Savage, 'The Paradox of the Stone', *Philosophical Review*, 1967, **76**, 74–9.

pointed out, the point of the paradox is to show that the concept of omnipotence is incoherent. It is therefore begging the question to assume that a certain person, if he exists, has that property, whether by definition or not. A more satisfactory formulation of the paradox is given by Wade Savage as follows: (I replace his 'x' by P to conform to my notation):

Where P is any being

(1) Either P can create a stone which P cannot lift, or P cannot create a stone which P cannot lift.

(2) If P can create a stone which P cannot lift, then, necessarily, there is at least one task which P cannot perform (namely, lift the stone in question).

(3) If P cannot create a stone which P cannot lift, then, necessarily, there is at least one task which P cannot perform (namely create the stone in question).

(4) Hence there is at least one task which P cannot perform.

(5) If P is an omnipotent being, then P can perform any task.

(6) Therefore P is not omnipotent.

Since P is any being, this argument proves that the existence of an omnipotent being, God or any other, is logically impossible.[10]

The solution adopted by Wade Savage, which has some similarity to that adopted by Keene,[11] is to deny that (3) is a necessary truth. Wade Savage claims that 'P cannot create a stone which P cannot lift' does not entail that 'there is at least one task which P cannot perform'. It might seem that it does. But, it is claimed, this illusion vanishes on analysis. "P cannot create a stone which P cannot lift" can only mean "If P can create a stone, then P can lift it". It is obvious that the latter statement does not entail that P is limited in power.'[12]

Now it seems to me that each of these logically equivalent propositions does entail that P is limited in power. We can see this as follows. Clearly one can only lift something once it has come into existence. So what (1) is presumably claiming is 'Either P can create a stone which P cannot subsequently lift or P cannot create a stone which P cannot subsequently lift'. So (3) is to be understood as 'If P cannot create a stone which

---

[10] Op. cit., 76.

[11] G. B. Keene, 'A Simpler Solution to the Paradox of Omnipotence', *Mind*, 1960, **69**, 74 f.   [12] Op. cit., 77.

P cannot subsequently lift, then there is at least one task which P cannot perform'. Now certainly 'P cannot create a stone which P cannot subsequently lift' is logically equivalent to 'If P can create a stone, then P can subsequently lift it'. The former proposition says that P cannot create a stone and endow it with such properties as to make it impossible for P subsequently to lift it. It is logically equivalent to 'necessarily, P does not create a stone which P cannot subsequently lift'. This is logically equivalent to 'Necessarily, if P creates a stone, then P can subsequently lift it', which is to say 'If P can create a stone, then P can subsequently lift it'. What these propositions say is that if P creates a stone it *must* be the case that he is subsequently able to lift it. That means that P cannot give to any stone which he creates the power to resist subsequent lifting by P: indeed, that if P does create a stone, he cannot then or thereafter limit his stone-lifting powers so as not to be able lift that stone, and that he cannot commit suicide. So there is a task which P cannot perform—to make a stone to which he gives the power to resist subsequent lifting by himself. That is clearly a task which many ordinary beings can perform. As Cowan put it, 'there is a perfectly simple, straightforward, entirely non-self-contradictory task which I, who am fairly skilful at making things but not much on muscles, can do. I can make something too heavy for the maker to lift.'[13] I conclude that, despite Savage, (3) is a necessary truth.[14]

Savage backs up the argument cited by bringing in the notion of poundage. He claims that P would be limited in power if he was unable to make stones of some poundage, say, ones of more than seventy pounds; but that being unable to make stones which he (or anyone else) cannot lift is as such no limitation on his power. 'If P can create stones of any poundage and Y can lift stones of any poundage, then P cannot create a stone which Y cannot lift, and yet P is not thereby limited in power. Now

[13] J. L. Cowan, 'The Paradox of Omnipotence', *Analysis*, 1965, **25**, 102–8.
[14] A man might well feel it to be a limitation on his powers to be unable to make something which he could not subsequently lift, because he might wish to feel the power of forces too strong for him. Mayo imagined a being soliloquizing 'I do wish there were things that I couldn't control. It would be so interesting to find out what they would do. I often wish I could make some. In fact, I sometimes try. But alas, I always find that, no matter how hard I try, I just can't.' (Op. cit., 250).

it is easy to see that precisely parallel considerations obtain where P is both stone creator and stone lifter.'[15]

This new argument takes for granted that Y's inability to lift a stone must arise solely from its having a weight greater than some finite amount. But this need not be so at all. Y might be able to lift most stones of any weight, but only stones of up to seventy pounds which had some other property, e.g. great bulk, or a slithery surface. So the claim that P cannot create a stone which Y cannot lift is the claim that he cannot give to a stone any property which will defeat Y's lifting powers, and that means Y's future lifting powers; that P cannot endow matter with the power of resisting Y's strength. P might be able to make some stone of any poundage, but not a stone with that property. In that case P would be limited in power. And, further, P might have the ability to make a stone with the required property, even though at the present instant Y could lift any stone at all. Hence Savage's further argument fails.

I conclude that neither of the two attempted solutions of the paradox, current in philosophical literature, work. However, the paradox has been generated by adopting my analysis [A] of omnipotence. Savage's (5) says in other words the same as my [A]. However, we have seen good reason for rejecting [A]. Let us attempt to reformulate Savage's statement of the paradox using [D].

Where P is any being

(1) Either P can at t bring about the existence of a stone of which P cannot subsequently bring about the rising, or P cannot at t bring about the existence of a stone of which P cannot subsequently bring about the rising.

(2) If at t, P can bring about the existence of a stone of which P cannot subsequently bring about the rising, then necessarily there is at least one logically contingent state of affairs after t, the description of which does not entail that P did not bring it about at t, which P is unable at t to bring about (namely, the rising of the stone in question).

(3) If at t, P cannot bring about the existence of a stone of which P cannot subsequently bring about the rising, then necessarily there is at least one logically contingent state of affairs after t, the description of which does not entail that P did not bring

[15] Op. cit., 78.

it about at t, which P is unable at t to bring about (namely, the existence of such a stone.)

(4) Hence there is at least one logically contingent state of affairs after t, the description of which does not entail that P did not bring it about at t, which P is unable at t to bring about.

(5) If P is an omnipotent being, then P is able to bring about any logically contingent state of affairs after t, the description of which does not entail that P did not bring it about at t.

(6) Therefore P is not omnipotent.

Once the paradox is rephrased in terms of [D], we can see where the fallacy lies. It lies in (2). We have no reason to suppose (2) to be true for all P. We suppose that P is able to bring about the existence of a stone endowed with such properties that he cannot subsequently cause it to rise. What then is the state of affairs which P is unable to bring about? The rising of the stone 'in question'. But this needs filling out—the stone needs to be described more fully. Of which stone is P unable to bring about the rising? 'A stone too heavy for P to bring about its rising'? But the rising of that stone is a state of affairs of which the description entails that P did not bring it about after t. 'The next stone created by P'? There is no reason to suppose that P will create any more stones, but if he does there is no reason to suppose that P will be unable to make them rise. 'The stone created by P which is too heavy for P to bring about its rising'? There is no reason to suppose that P will bring about the existence of such a stone; that he can does not entail that he will. But anyway once again, the rising of that stone is a state of affairs of which the description entails that P did not bring it about after t. Any attempt to describe the state of affairs which P is allegedly unable to bring about will either lead to the description of a state which there is no reason to suppose P unable to bring about, or to the description of a state which entails that he did not bring it about. I conclude that the paradox fails because there is no reason for believing (2) to be true for all P. The paradox provides no ground for believing the concept of omnipotence delineated by [D] to be incoherent.

True, if an omnipotent being actually exercises (as opposed to merely possessing) his ability to bring about the existence of a stone too heavy for him subsequently to bring about its rising, then he will cease to be omnipotent. [D] states what it is for a person to be omnipotent at a certain time. But the omnipotence of a person at a certain time includes the ability to make himself no longer omnipotent, an ability which he may or may not choose to exercise. A person may remain omnipotent for ever[16] because he never exercises his power to create stones too heavy to lift, forces too strong to resist, or universes too wayward to control.

A Modified Account of Omnipotence

So I would claim that there is a concept of omnipotence [D] which appears to withstand current objections to the coherence of such concepts. To say that God is omnipotent in sense [D] seems to me to be to ascribe to him an omnipotence in no way narrower than the kind of omnipotence which theists have traditionally wished to ascribe to God. There seems no reason for denying that it is coherent to suppose that there is an omnipresent spirit who is creator of the universe and is omnipotent in this sense. In creating the universe he is merely exercising his omnipotence, yet not in a way so as to limit his future exercise of it. It follows from a spirit's being omnipotent that he is omnipresent in respect of his power—he is able to act directly on any part of the universe. But there does seem to be an incompatibility between a person being perfectly free in the sense which I distinguished in the last chapter, and his being omnipotent.

For, we saw at the end of Chapter 8, a perfectly free person

---

[16] This despite Mackie ('Evil and Omnipotence', *Mind*, 1955, **64**, 200–12). Mackie, who began the recent discussion of omnipotence in the journals, alone of those who contributed to it emphasized temporal considerations. He distinguished 'first order omnipotence (omnipotence (1)), that is unlimited power to act, and second-order omnipotence (omnipotence (2)), that is unlimited power to determine what powers to act things will have'. This distinction would need to be made more precise, but it can be seen roughly what Mackie has in mind. He continues: 'Then we could consistently say that God all the time has omnipotence (1), but if so no beings at any time have powers to act independently of God. Or we could say that God at one time had omnipotence (2), and used it to assign independent powers to act to certain things, so that God did not thereafter have omnipotence (1). But what the paradox shows is that we cannot consistently ascribe to any continuing being omnipotence in any inclusive sense' (p. 212). That does not follow at all. A being can have omnipotence (1) and omnipotence (2) at all times, so long as he does not use his omnipotence (2) to give to other beings irretractable powers. But why should he?

can only perform an action if he believes that there is no over-riding reason for refraining from doing it. A perfectly free person cannot do an action if he believes that it would be over all better to refrain from doing it. So a perfectly free person cannot be omnipotent in sense [D]. If we understand by a morally wrong action one for refraining from doing which there are overriding reasons (as I shall urge in Chapter 11 that we should) it will follow that if God is perfectly free, he cannot do actions which he believes to be wrong. Theists normally claim that God cannot do wrong actions. If God also knows which actions are wrong (a claim which I shall discuss in Chapters 10 and 11) and so holds true beliefs about which actions are wrong, the latter claim follows from the former one.

Aquinas argues that 'since God is a voluntary agent, that which he cannot will he cannot do';[17] that 'the object of the will is the apprehended good'; that 'the will cannot aim at evil unless in some way it is proposed to it as a good; and this cannot take place without error. But in the divine knowledge there cannot be error . . . God's will cannot therefore tend towards evil,'[18] and from all this Aquinas concludes that God cannot sin. Aquinas thus accepts the claim which I have made that God cannot do actions which he believes to be evil. But he regards this as quite compatible with God being 'omnipotent'. That 'God cannot sin' is included in a long list of things which God cannot do in a chapter headed 'How the omnipotent God is said to be incapable of certain things'.[19] The things which God is said not to be able to do seem to fall into two groups. In the first group are things which it is logically impossible for any being to do. God cannot, we are told, make 'the three angles of a rectilinear triangle not to be equal to two right angles' or 'the past not to have been'. We saw that any coherent account of omnipotence must rule out such possibilities. In the second group are things which although it is logically possible that some being do them, God cannot do them while retaining his nature (i.e. his other essential properties). God cannot, we are told, repent or be angry or make a thing equal to himself—or will

[17] *Summa contra Gentiles*, 2.25.20 (Bk. II trans. under the title *On the Truth of the Catholic Faith*, Book II, by James F. Anderson, New York, 1956).

[18] *Summa contra Gentiles*, 1.95.3.

[19] Op. cit., 2.25.

anything evil. Clearly Aquinas has a much narrower understanding of the power of God than is provided by my account
[D]. I suggest that theists generally would wish to restrict God's
power further, although they might disagree with Aquinas
about whether God can do some of the particular things which
Aquinas declares him unable to do. At any rate a further
restriction is required, as we have seen, if the theist is to continue to assert, as he surely must, that God is perfectly free.

So to knock theism into a coherent shape, we are faced with
the choice of providing a narrower definition of 'omnipotence'
on which being 'omnipotent' is compatible with being perfectly
free, or choosing another word to describe the extent of divine
power, to denote a property of which the possession is compatible with being perfectly free. There seems to me not much
to choose between these alternatives. Traditional theological
use favours the former. Many theologians down the centuries,
including Aquinas, have declared God to be 'omnipotent'
while also declaring that he 'cannot do evil'. Yet modern
secular understanding of the natural meaning of 'omnipotent'
suggests that being 'omnipotent' is incompatible with being
'unable to do evil' and so suggests that we ought to describe
the power of a perfectly free being by some other word than
'omnipotent'. The latter alternative has been taken recently
by Professor P. T. Geach who prefers the word 'almighty' to
the word 'omnipotent' to describe how powerful God is.[20]

However, aware of disadvantages but conscious of history,
I shall take the former alternative. I suggest that theism quite
often understands 'omnipotent' in this way; and if it wants the
power of God to be compatible with his being perfectly free, it
can in any case say no more of him than that he is omnipotent
in the following sense [E]: a person P is omnipotent at a time t
if and only if he is able to bring about the existence of any
logically contingent state of affairs x after t, the description
of the occurrence of which does not entail that P did not bring
it about at t, given that he does not believe that he has overriding reason for refraining from bringing about x.

Does this limitation on God's omnipotence make him less
worthy of worship? Why should it? Being perfectly free hardly
makes a being less worthy of worship. His being perfectly free

[20] See his 'Omnipotence', *Philosophy*, 1973, **48**, 7–20.

means that he cannot exercise his power in ways which he regards as irrational. Why should the fact that his intentions cannot fail to be realized through interference from causal influences make him any less worthy of worship? That a being's power cannot be exercised in ways which he judges to be on balance irrational surely does not detract from his dignity.[21]

There seems no good objection to the coherence of the supposition that there exists now an omnipresent spirit, who is a perfectly free creator of the universe and omnipotent in sense [E]. Any difference which he chose to make to the world at a future time (so long as the description of it is a coherent one) he could make—so long as he viewed the making of such a difference as on balance a good thing, a better thing than refraining from making the difference or doing some other action incompatible with the former. A man could imagine himself coming to find that he could make any difference which he chose to the world; yet also finding himself free from pressures which influenced him to act irrationally, so that he does only that for which he believes himself to have good reason.

[21] Thus Anselm argues that the more God possesses 'the power of doing or experiencing what is not for his good, or what he ought not to do . . . the more powerful are adversity and perversity against him': *Proslogion*, 7 (trans. S. N. Deane, Chicago, 1903).

10

Omniscient

TRADITIONALLY, God is said to be omniscient, to know all things. What does it mean to say of a person that he knows all things? Omniscience, like omnipotence, apparently belongs to persons at this or that time.[1] So it would appear that to say of a person P that he is at time t omniscient is to say that at t P knows of every true proposition that it is true.

A Coherent Account of Omniscience

Is it coherent to suppose that a person be omniscient in this sense? Superficially, yes. Persons obviously can know much. Why cannot a person know all? That a person knew everything would be shown by his ability to answer any question correctly. Against this, however, comes a substantial objection which I develop from arguments of Prior and Kretzmann.[2] The objection alleges that the supposition that there is an omniscient being conflicts with certain evident truths. One of these (that if there is one instant of time, there is more than one instant of time) is almost certainly a logical truth, and so the objection amounts to a claim that the supposition that there be an omniscient person is incoherent.

[1] I shall consider in Ch. 12 the suggestion that omniscience might belong to a person timelessly.

[2] A. N. Prior, 'The Formalities of Omniscience', *Philosophy*, 1962, **37**, 114–29. Norman Kretzmann, 'Omniscience and Immutability', *Journal of Philosophy*, 1966, **63**, 409–21. Kretzmann claims in his paper that certain items of knowledge can only be had at certain times and so if God is to have a certain item of knowledge, he must acquire it at a time and so change. But it follows from that that God cannot at any one time know all true propositions. Kretzmann goes on to argue that only certain persons can know certain things, and so that if God knows all things, he cannot be a person distinct from others. The conclusions which I draw above seem to follow immediately from all this.

Kretzmann argues that there are some propositions which can be known only at certain times or by certain persons. Kretzmann claims that the proposition that 'it is now t_1' (e.g. 2 October) can only be known at t_1 (viz. on 2 October). This proposition, Kretzmann claims, is not the same proposition as the proposition that at t_1 it is t_1 (e.g. that on 2 October it is 2 October), which can of course be known at any time. But if there is an instant of time t_1, there must (logically) be some instant of time before t_1—for before t_1 either there was something or there was nothing, and so there was a time at which there was something or nothing. Hence there must be a time at which no person could have had the knowledge, expressed at t_1 by the proposition that 'it is now t_1'. So, generally, since for any instant of time there is at least one other, at each instant any agent will be necessarily ignorant of a truth expressible at another instant by stating that it is 'now' that instant. So at any instant an agent must be ignorant of something. My claim that of logical necessity there is more than one instant of time might be disputed, and in that case the above argument becomes no longer an argument against the coherence of the concept of omniscience, but an argument to show that the claim that there is an omniscient person conflicts with an evident truth that there is more than one instant of time. It will be appropriate to consider Kretzmann's other claim in this context—that some propositions can only be known by certain persons, even though it would not tend to show the concept of omniscience incoherent, but only to show the claim that there is an omniscient person to be incompatible with the evident truth that there is more than one person. I shall consider the latter claim because of its similarity in style of argument to the first claim. Kretzmann claims that 'every person knows certain propositions that no other person can know'. Suppose that Jones is an amnesia case in hospital. He knows that he is in hospital. What he knows is not that Jones is in hospital. Being an amnesia case he may well not know the latter. Other people may know that Jones is in hospital. But what they cannot know is what Jones knows.

Let us now examine Kretzmann's first claim in more detail. Suppose that on 2 October A knows that 'it is now 2 October'. Cannot B know on 3 October what A knows on 2 October? Let us call A's item of knowledge the proposition p. Certainly if *B* does know this on 3 October, he will not and indeed cannot express the knowledge, state the proposition, in the same words, by the same sentence, as *B* used on 2 October. But this, we shall shortly see, does not by itself ensure that *B* cannot know *p*.

It is characteristic of the propositions which Kretzmann discusses that they are expressed in sentences containing indexical or quasi-indexical expressions. These are words such as 'I', 'you', 'now', 'yesterday', 'tomorrow', 'here', 'five miles to the east of here'. When these words are used as indexical expressions they pick out places, times, people, etc. by their spatial or temporal relations to the speaker. 'Now' is the instant contemporaneous with the speaker's utterance, 'you' is the person to whom the speaker is speaking, and so on. When I say 'you are ill', I am predicating the property of being ill of an individual picked out as the individual to whom I am talking. When I say 'it is Tuesday today' I am predicating the property of being Tuesday of the day picked out as the day on which I am talking. The use of such expressions as indexical expressions is to be contrasted with their use as what Castañeda calls quasi-indexical expressions.[3] The expressions are used as quasi-indexical expressons when they pick out objects by their relation to the subject of the sentence (or subordinate clause) in which they occur. When John says 'Jones knows that he is ill' the 'he' refers not to the speaker, John, but to the subject of the sentence, Jones. In 'John knew that it was then too late', the 'then' refers to the time of John's knowing.

Now quite clearly two people can often possess the same item of knowledge, can know the same thing. Both you and I can know that Germany won the World Cup in 1974. Further, two people can often know the same thing even if they must use different words in which to express their knowledge. If I know that 'your house has four bedrooms' and you know that 'my house has four bedrooms' what we know is the same. The same proposition is expressed by different sentences. The mere fact that one thing which you know cannot be expressed by you in the same words as anything which I know can be expressed

[3] See Hector-Neri Castañeda, 'Omniscience and Indexical Reference', *Journal of Philosophy*, 1967, **64**, 203–10. Much of my argument of the next few paragraphs derives from this valuable paper.

by me does not by itself guarantee that I cannot know the thing which you know.

Now Castañeda urges against Kretzmann's examples the following principle:

(P) If a sentence of the form 'X knows that a person Y knows that...' formulates a true statement, the person X knows the statement formulated by the clause filling the blank '...'

(P) seems plausible enough. If John knows that Mary knows that $2 + 2 = 4$ or that George is ill, then John knows that $2 + 2 = 4$ or that George is ill. If the clause '...' of (P) contains quasi-indicators, then when the clause is shifted from the first sentence to the second, the quasi-indicators may have to be replaced by other indexical devices in view of the fact that the subject of the sentence is now different, in order for the clause to 'formulate', i.e. express the same statement. If 'John knows that Mary knows that her own house has four bedrooms', it does not follow that 'John knows that her own house has four bedrooms', which is an unclear claim of dubious grammar, but rather that 'John knows that Mary's house has four bedrooms.'

If P is correct, Kretzmann's claims seem false. A knows on 2 October the proposition 'it is now 2 October'. Surely B on 3 October can know that A knew what he did on 2 October. How can B report his knowledge? By words such as 'I know that A knew yesterday that it was then 2 October'. How can we report B's knowledge? As follows: B knew on 3 October that on the previous day A knew that it was then 2 October. Hence, by (P), B knows on 3 October what A knew on 2 October, although B will use different words to express the latter knowledge. In reporting B's knowledge of this item, we need a different referring expression to pick out the day of which being 2 October is predicated; but what is known is the same. B's second piece of knowledge would be unsatisfactorily reported as the knowledge that '2 October is 2 October'. For that looks like (although it need not be) the tautology that 'if any day is 2 October, it is 2 October', which is clearly NOT the item of knowledge about which we have been talking. What A knows on 2 October and B knows on 3 October is that a certain day which can be picked out in many and various ways, according to our location in time as 'today' or 'yesterday' or 'the day on which *A* thought that it was 2 October' (or even as '2 October') is 2 October.

Similar considerations apply to Kretzmann's other example. Jones knows that he is in hospital. Clearly Smith can know that Jones knows that he is in hospital. Hence by (P) Smith can know what Jones knows. If Smith knows what Jones knows, how do we express his knowledge? Presumably by 'Smith knows that Jones is in hospital'. But this, Kretzmann says, is not what Jones knows. For Jones may know that he is in hospital without knowing that Jones is in hospital. Kretzmann's claim here seems mistaken. If Jones knows that he is in hospital, Jones knows that Jones is in hospital. Of course, Jones may not describe himself as 'Jones' or even know that he is called 'Jones'. He may well not know that someone called 'Jones' is in hospital. But what 'Jones knows that Jones is in hospital' is claiming is that Jones knows in respect of the man who is Jones (whether or not known by Jones so to be) that he is in hospital. This piece of knowledge can be possessed both by Jones and by Smith.

I conclude that the objection fails. In default of it I suggest that it is coherent to suppose that there is an omniscient person. There would be no reason why it is incoherent to suppose that a spirit, omnipresent and creator of the universe, is omniscient. Such a spirit, if asked, could give you the answer to any question, if he chose to do so. The state of the universe in the past and future would be so clearly known to him—maybe its whole history would be seen by him at glance and be held in his mind —that he would not need to conduct an investigation to find out how things had been years ago or would be in years to come. Just as a man does not need to conduct an investigation to know what he is now looking at, no more does God, in the theist's view, need to conduct an investigation in order to know anything about the world's history.

Of course in the theist's view God does not need sense-organs in order to see things. Sir Isaac Newton brought out this point and the vivid immediacy of God's perception by describing space as God's 'sensorium'. Newton accepted an extreme representative theory of perception, according to which when men look at things, the images of those things are conveyed by sensory nerves from the eyes to a kind of internal cinema screen, the sensorium. Men perceive directly the images on the sensorium, but only indirectly the external objects. God, however, Newton says, perceives directly what we perceive only indirectly.[4]

The Incompatibility of Omniscience and Free Will

However, to the suggestion that it is coherent to suppose that a spirit is perfectly free and is also omniscient, there is a plausible objection. This objection is very similar to the claim that there is an incompatibility between God's omniscience and human free will. But that claim does not tend to show that theism is incoherent or even false. For even if the claim is true, the theist could just say that all that it shows is that man does not have free will, and a significant number of theists have—largely for other reasons—said just that. However, an argument can be put forward on just the same lines to show an incompatibility between God's omniscience and his own free will and so, if valid, the objection would show that a person could not be both omniscient and perfectly free. However, in view of the similarity of the two arguments and the considerable literature on the alleged incompatibility between divine omniscience and human free will, I will discuss this first. I will then quickly transfer my conclusions to the problem of the relation between divine omniscience and divine free will.

To phrase it loosely to begin with, the argument purporting to show an incompatibility between divine omniscience and human free will runs as follows. If God is omniscient then he foreknows all future human actions. If God foreknows anything, then it will necessarily come to pass. But if a human action will necessarily come to pass, then it cannot be free. Augustine discusses this objection in Book III of *De Libero Arbitrio*. His solution is that human actions may be free even if they come to pass by necessity.[5] We saw reason in Chapter 8 for denying that view. An alternative approach of rejecting the claim that

[4] I. Newton, *Optics*, Query 28. This claim of Newton's was misunderstood by Leibniz and led to some controversy in the Leibniz–Clarke correspondence.

[5] For exposition and commentary see William L. Rowe, 'Augustine on Foreknowledge and Freewill', *Review of Metaphysics*, 1964, **18**, 356–63; repub. in Baruch A. Brody (ed.), *Readings in the Philosophy of Religion* (Englewood Cliffs, N.J., 1974).

if God foreknows anything, then it must necessarily come
to pass, is considered by Aquinas:

The proposition 'All that God knows must necessarily be' is usually
distinguished: it can apply either to the thing or to the statement.
Understood of the thing, the proposition is taken independently of
the fact of God's knowing, and false, giving the sense, 'Everything
that God knows is a necessary thing'. Or it can be understood of the
statement, and thus it is taken in conjunction with the fact of God's
knowing, and true, giving the sense, 'The statement *a thing known
by God is*, is necessary.'[6]

What Aquinas is saying here is that although it is true that
'necessarily, if God foreknows anything, it will come to pass',
it is false that 'If God foreknows anything, it will necessarily
come to pass'. Only the latter yields the conclusion that man
does not have free will. But one may argue as does Aquinas in
the cited paragraph and as do Rowe[7] and Kenny,[8] that all that
theism needs is the former, not the latter. All that theism says
is that the only things which God can rightly be said to foreknow are those which in fact come to pass. It may be argued,
as by Rowe and Kenny, that it does not follow from that that
they must, or will necessarily, come to pass, and so human
freedom is unendangered.

However, things are by no means so simple. Not merely of
God is it true that necessarily, if he foreknows anything, that
thing will come to pass. It is true of any body at all—you can
only foreknow something if it is true. 'Necessarily, if God
foreknows anything, it will come to pass', is hardly an interesting
theological truth. It is in fact from neither of the propositions
considered by Aquinas that the difficulty arises for those who
affirm both divine omniscience and human freedom. The
difficulty arises not from the fact that whatever God knows must
be, but from the fact that whatever is, God must know it. That
is true only of an omniscient person, not of other persons. The
difficulty, to phrase it more precisely, is as follows.

    [6] *Summa Theologiae*, vol. iv, 1a.14.ad.3.
    [7] Op. cit.
    [8] Anthony Kenny, 'Divine Foreknowledge and Human Freedom' in A. Kenny
(ed.), *Aquinas: A Collection of Critical Essays* (New York, 1969); repub. in Baruch A.
Brody, op. cit.

If P knows x, various other things must be. One is that x is true. A man would be incorrectly said to know something if that something was not the case. Another is that P has a certain cognitive attitude towards x which we may describe as believing x.[9] Another is that P is justified in believing x, has the right to believe x. A man who believed x but was not justified in believing x (e.g. because he had insufficient evidence as to whether or not x) would incorrectly be said to know x.[10] Now if a person is omniscient, in the sense which I have analysed, he knows all true propositions. It follows that he believes all true propositions. Of logical necessity, if P is omniscient at t, he believes at t all true propositions. It follows too that he has beliefs about everything describable by a true proposition. Now consider the free action of an agent S performed at a time t_1, later than t. We saw earlier that if S acts freely, which action he performs at t_1 is ultimately determined by his choice at t_1 and not necessitated by earlier states. Now consider any person P at t who has beliefs about what S will do at t_1. By his choice S has it in his power at t_1 to make the beliefs held by P at t true or false. S does not, however, have it in his power at t_1 to make it the case that P has a certain belief at t. For if S did have the power, he would be able to bring about a past state, and affecting the past seems to be a logical impossibility, as I suggested in the last chapter.

Admittedly I can make it the case that some statements about the past are true. For example, by an action in 1976 I could make it the case that in 1974 Jones had only two more

[9] It is normally supposed that 'P knows x' entails 'P believes x'. Some have argued, however, that some of the things we are said to know we can hardly be said to believe. 'I know that $2+2 = 4$, I don't believe it', it is often said. If we believe x, the argument goes, there is still some doubt in our minds about whether or not x. I propose to use the word 'believe' so that we may be said to believe both those propositions which we are ordinarily said to believe and also those propositions about the truth of which we are convinced or have no doubt.

[10] We cannot analyse knowledge simply as justified true belief. For one thing, mere belief is perhaps insufficient; a belief has to be strong before it can be classified as knowledge. Further, one's justification for believing x has to be of a certain kind before the resultant belief can be called knowledge. This was brought out by a well-known objection of Edmund L. Gettier (see his 'Is Justified True Belief Knowledge?' *Analysis*, 1963, **23**, 121-3). There have been many attempts to specify the extra element needed to turn justified true belief into knowledge. (See, e.g., K. Lehrer, 'Knowledge, Truth and Evidence', *Analysis*, 1964-5, **24**, 168-75.) Assuming that the extra element can be specified, we may perhaps analyse 'P knows x' as 'x is true, P strongly believes x, and P has the right justification for believing x'.

years to live. Or, most relevantly, by my doing A in 1976 I can make it the case that the belief which Jones had that I would do A was a true belief. But, one is inclined to say, statements to the effect that in 1974 Jones had only two more years to live or that in 1974 Jones's belief about what I would do in 1976 was a true one are not statements totally about the state of the world in 1974. Although they are really about the world in 1974, they also have a covert future reference. The principle that agents cannot bring about past states means only that they cannot make it the case that statements which are totally about the past are true.[11] The statement that a person has a certain belief at t does seem to be a statement totally about t. On the other hand, the statement that a person at t has a true belief about things at t_1 seems to be a statement with a covert future reference which can have its true value affected by an agent's action at t_1.

All this being so, it follows that S does not have it in his power at t_1 to bring about which beliefs a person has at t (nobody can influence that after t), but that S does have it in his power at t_1 to bring it about that a belief that a person has at t about what S will do at t_1 is a false belief. Hence if S is a free agent at t_1 and P is a person at t with beliefs about everything describable by a true proposition, P will be in danger of having one of his beliefs made false by the action of S at t_1. The more free agents there are and the more their free actions, the greater the risk that in the course of time at least one of P's beliefs at t will be made false.

All the same it could happen that there was a person P having beliefs about all the future actions of free men, all of whose beliefs turned out to be true. But P could only be omniscient if in fact no man ever chose to make P's beliefs false. Yet, since the free actions of men, although influenced, are not necessitated by other agents or prior states of the world, if

[11] I shall not attempt here a rigorous account of when statements superficially about the past really are totally about the past. I have attempted to do this in Ch. 8 of my *Space and Time*. Here I merely appeal to the intuitive obviousness of the particular claims made; that a statement that P has a certain belief at a time t is a statement totally about that time, and carries no implications about how things will be in future, whereas a statement that P has a true belief at t about how things will be subsequently is not a statement totally about t, but is one which contains a covert future reference.

nevertheless all of P's beliefs turned out to be true that would be a very fortunate coincidence, to say the least. Surely a theist does not want to claim that God is omniscient in this very precarious way.[12,13] Furthermore, it seems very doubtful if P would be justified in holding all the beliefs which he did about the future free actions of men. One might suppose that because men are much influenced in the choices which they make, by other agents or prior states of the world, P knowing these circumstances would be justified in his predictions about the choices which agents would make, and so would hold justified beliefs about their future free actions. But it seems clear that P could not hold justified true beliefs about the future actions of a perfectly free agent A (in the sense of 'perfectly free' which I defined in Chapter 8). For if P's beliefs are true, they must include a belief that A is a perfectly free agent. If P is to be justified in supposing that his beliefs about A's actions are true, he must be justified in believing that there are correlations between P's beliefs about them and A's future actions. But given

[12] The treatment of the last few paragraphs owes much to Nelson Pike, 'Divine Omniscience and Voluntary Action', *Philosophical Review*, 1965, **74**, 27–46. Pike, however, wishes to claim that God could not be omniscient in such a precarious way, since 'it is a conceptual truth that God's beliefs are true. Thus we cannot claim . . . that Jones in fact acted in accordance with God's beliefs but had the ability to refrain from doing so'. Pike argues that it is analytic that whatever God believes is true; hence no agent can act so as to make God have a false belief. However, to put it more carefully, what Pike wishes to say is analytic is that if a person P is God (and so omniscient in the sense in queston), all P's beliefs are true. But for any person P, who has a belief at t about a man's future free actions, the man can so act as to make that belief false. What he would then be doing is to make it the case, not that God had a false belief, but that P was no God. That an agent should have such powers, even if permitted by God to do so, is surely not something which a theist would wish to affirm. This point comes out in these articles commenting on Pike's, and especially in the last one: John Turk Saunders, 'Of God and Freedom', *Philosophical Review*, 1966, **75**, 219–25; Nelson Pike, 'Of God and Freedom: A Rejoinder', *Philosophical Review*, 1966, **75**, 369–79; and Margaret McCord Adams, 'Is the Existence of God a "Hard Fact"?' *Philosophical Review*. 1967, **76**, 492–503.

[13] The theist in wishing to claim that God is not omniscient by fortunate chance must claim, given the original definition of omniscience, that in some sense future events such as the free actions of men *could* not make God have false beliefs. For his claim is that God is necessarily or incorrigibly omniscient. Clearly even if by fortunate chance free agents did not ever make God's beliefs false, they could have done so, and so, on the original definition, could have made God not omniscient. This constitutes a further objection to the original definition. God's being necessarily omniscient is one thing involved in his being necessarily the kind of being which he is. I shall consider in Ch. 14 the theist's claim that God is necessarily the kind of being which he is.

that nothing in the past in any way influences what *A* does (and *P* knows this), *P* could only be justified in supposing that there was a correlation between his beliefs and *P*'s actions if he were justified in supposing that *P*'s actions made a difference to his beliefs; that his beliefs about them were caused (or largely influenced by) *P*'s actions. But to make this supposition is to allow backward causation, which as I have suggested, is apparently something logically impossible. Hence I conclude that *P* could not be justified in holding beliefs about the future actions of a perfectly free agent. Hence he cannot himself be both omniscient and perfectly free—for he would not be justified in holding beliefs about his own future free actions.[14] I conclude that it seems doubtful whether it is logically possible that there be both an omniscient person and also free men; but that it is definitely logically impossible that there be an omniscient person who is himself perfectly free—all this given the natural sense of 'omniscient' which I delineated at the beginning of this chapter.

A Modified Account of Omniscience

Although Aquinas discusses the solution which I mentioned a few pages back, he seems ultimately to rely on a different one.[15] It will be recalled that Aquinas distinguished between 'Necessarily, if God foreknows anything, it will come to pass' and 'If God foreknows anything, it will necessarily come to pass', and claimed initially that theology needed only the former. But he then reflected that such a statement as 'God foreknew yesterday that I will philosophize tomorrow' appears to be a statement about the past, and as such necessary. For Aquinas all statements about the past are necessary since no one can by any action now affect their truth value. It follows that 'God foreknew yesterday that I will philosophize tomorrow' is necessary, and so too therefore is what follows from it—'I will

---

[14] Or, rather, about most of them. For, as we saw in Ch. 8, a perfectly free agent must do any action for doing which he judges that there are overriding reasons. If he is omniscient he will make correct judgements about this, given that such judgements have truth values. (I shall argue that they do in Ch. 11.) Hence he will do any action for doing which there are overriding reasons. But it is implausible to suppose that this greatly limits his future choice.

[15] See Kenny, op. cit., for discussion of Aquinas's treatment of the issue.

philosophize tomorrow'. So, generally, God's past foreknowledge of x (where x is a future state of affairs) being past, necessitates the occurrence of x which is entailed by it. So apparently all that God foreknows is necessary, after all, and divine foreknowledge seems incompatible with human free will. Now in talking of statements about the past being necessary, we are of course talking about necessity of a different kind from logical necessity, a necessity more akin to physical or causal necessity; and that perhaps makes complications for the argument.[16] But the main error in Aquinas's argument seems to be one which I have discussed already—his assumption that 'God foreknew x' (where x is a proposition about the future) is a proposition totally about the past. It is not, however, a proposition totally about the past, since it depends for its truth or falsity in part on things yet to happen. Hence the proposition x is not altogether necessary, even on Aquinas's understanding of necessity. It is concerned with the future—and, Aquinas holds, such propositions are indeed contingent.

Aquinas's own solution is also to deny what appeared to him initially to be the case, that 'God foreknew x' is a statement about the past, but his denial is on grounds far different from the mundane ones given above. For Aquinas held that statements about God acting or having properties are not really about the past or the future, but are about a divine present moment. God, Aquinas held, is outside time. He lives in a timeless eternity. Everything which he knows is simultaneous with his knowing it, for the divine present moment is simultaneous with moments which we call present, past, and future. Strictly speaking, God does not *fore*know anything. He knows it as it happens, but there is no moment at which he does not know it. Hence he is omniscient in the sense which I have been considering, because all things are present to him (simultaneously, at his own divine moment) as they happen. If this is what God's knowledge really amounts to, the earlier objections do not get off the ground. For there is no question of God first believing something and then, later, there occurring that which makes his belief true or false. That someone P knows what someone else S is now doing in no way makes what S is now doing necessary.

[16] In Ch. 13 I distinguish different kinds of necessity and call the kind of necessity being discussed here type [C].

The idea of God existing timelessly and yet being aware of things as they happen has very considerable difficulties, and I shall explore these in Chapter 12. For the present we continue to think of God as a person doing now this, now that, as a person existing in time. Can there be an omniscient person, in the sense of 'omniscient' defined earlier, existing in time, who is also perfectly free? The arguments set out above show that that is not logically possible. For a perfectly free person could not hold justified beliefs about his future free actions (apart from any for doing which he would have overriding reasons). Hence he could not have knowledge of his future free actions.

There seems to be one way in which the theist might avoid this conclusion. He could coherently assert that there was a perfectly free and omniscient person, if it were the case that all (or certain particular) propositions about the future were neither true nor false. An omniscient person knows of every true proposition that it is true. But if propositions about the future actions of agents are neither true nor false until the agents do the actions, then to be omniscient a person will not have to know them. A person will be omniscient in 1974 if he knows all propositions which are true in 1974. All propositions which correctly report what happened in earlier years—e.g. that I moved house in 1972 or that my grandfather died in 1963 —were true in 1974, and a being omniscient in 1974 must know them. But if you maintain that propositions which correctly predict what will happen in later years (at any rate propositions which correctly report the future actions of free agents) are not true until that which they report occurs, then you allow that a being may be omniscient without knowing them. A number of philosophers from Greek times onwards have maintained that many propositions about the future are neither true nor false until the time to which they refer. Aristotle[17] seems to have claimed that 'either there will be or there will not be a sea-battle tomorrow' may be true without either 'there will be a sea-battle tomorrow' or 'there will not be a sea-battle tomorrow' being true.

This way out seems to me to depend on using 'true' in a way different from the way in which it is ordinarily used. Ordinarily we speak of claims about the future (including claims about

[17] *De Interpretatione*, 9.

any future free actions) being true or false. I may say on Tuesday 'Jones will go to London tomorrow', and you may comment 'What you say is true'. Suppose Jones does go to London on Wednesday. Then, on Thursday, looking back, someone may say to me 'What you said on Tuesday was true'. In normal use, propositions about a named future time (including claims about any future free actions) are true or false—timelessly. We may not *know* them to be true or false, until the occurrence of that of which they speak. That which makes them true or false may also lie in the future. But what I claim may be true, even if I do not know it to be true, and even if what I claim has yet to occur.

We could of course insist on a special use of 'true' in our analysis of omniscience, but it would be less misleading to use such an ordinary word as 'true' in its normal sense. If the theist is to maintain that there is a 'perfectly free' person, omnipresent, omnipotent, creator of the universe, who is also 'omniscient', he has to understand either 'perfectly free' or 'omniscient' in more restricted ways than those which I have outlined. It seems to me clear that he would prefer a restriction on 'omniscient'. For this there is precedent. As we saw in the last chapter, theologians, such as Aquinas, have been careful to explain omnipotence, not as the ability to do anything, but (roughly) as the ability to do anything logically possible. The last chapter was devoted to spelling out the latter notion more rigorously. It would be natural to develop an account of omniscience along similar lines, not as knowledge of everything true, but (very roughly) as knowledge of everything true which it is logically possible to know. I therefore suggest the following understanding of omniscience. A person P is omniscient at a time t if and only if he knows of every true proposition about t or an earlier time that it is true *and* also he knows of every true proposition about a time later than t, such that what it reports is physically necessitated by some cause at t or earlier, that it is true. On this understanding of omniscience, P is omniscient if he knows about everything except those future states and their consequences which are not physically necessitated by anything in the past; and if he knows that he does not know about those future states. If there is any future state which is not physically necessitated by goings-on in the past or present, then, of logical necessity, no person can know now that it will happen—without the possibility of error. There may of course not be any such future state. In that case any person omniscient on this account would be omniscient on the earlier account also. But if there are men who have free will, as many theists have claimed, there will be at some time such future states. And further if God has free will, as almost all theists have claimed, there will be at some time such future states. Omniscience in the earlier sense is not compatible with God's freedom, but omniscience in this sense is compatible. A being may be perfectly free and know everything—except which free choices he will make and what will result from the choices which he will make.

That God is omniscient only in the attenuated sense would of course—given that he is perfectly free and omnipotent—have resulted from his own choice. In choosing to preserve his own freedom (and to give others freedom), he limits his own knowledge of what is to come. He continually limits himself in this way by not curtailing his or men's future freedom. As regards men, their choices are much influenced by circumstances and this makes it possible for a being who knows all the circumstances to predict human behaviour correctly most of the time, but always with the possibility that men may falsify those predictions.[18]

We must note, however, that Christian theologians have normally[19] wished to attribute to God a much stricter omniscience (especially with regard to future human actions) than the limited omniscience which we have found to be compatible with his other properties. They have in general either said that God foreknows future human actions or they have followed Aquinas in claiming that God is outside time and that all human actions are simultaneously present to his view. The former view is obviously acceptable to those who claim explicitly that men's actions are not free or who implicitly deny that

[18] That this is the right way to understand divine omniscience is well argued in J. R. Lucas, *The Freedom of the Will* (Oxford, 1970), Ch. 14.

[19] But not always. Paley writes that God's omniscience would seem to involve 'a foreknowledge of the action [of created things] upon one another, and of their changes', but he then qualifies this by adding 'at least, so far as the same result from trains of physical and necessary causes'. In effect therefore he claims that God is omniscient only in our attenuated sense. See W. Paley, *Natural Theology* (London, 1802), Ch. 24.

freedom. Those who, like Aquinas, have wished to affirm human freedom have been driven to the second view. There is no need for them to be thus driven if we treat omniscience in the way in which theologians have traditionally treated omnipotence. It seems to me also that the Bible, or at any rate the Old Testament, contains implicitly the view that God is omniscient only in the attenuated sense.

Typically in the Old Testament God has certain plans for men and at their intercession changes them. Consider Abraham's intercession for Sodom (Gen. 18), or the intercession of Moses for the children of Israel (Exod. 32). Or God may change his plans because men change their behaviour (the Book of Jonah tells how God spared Nineveh because it repented). But if God changes his mind he cannot have foreknown his own future actions, and so his knowledge cannot be unlimited. Again in the Old Testament God often makes, as well as absolute promises (that he will do so-and-so), conditional promises (that he will do so-and-so if men do such-and-such). Yet there would be no need for a conditional promise if God already knew how men would act. Jeremiah is told by the Lord to make a certain proclamation in the Lord's house to the people of Judah. The Lord comments that 'it *may* be they will hearken and turn every man from his evil way' (Jer. 26:3; my italics). Jeremiah is told to tell the people that *if* they continue in their evil way then the Lord will destroy Jerusalem and the Temple. The natural interpretation of the passage is that the Lord does not know whether the people will repent. By contrast, the New Testament talks a great deal of God's 'foreknowledge', but, at any rate sometimes, it does not seem to regard this as absolute. Man can upset God's plans. God indeed has a book of life in which his plans are written. But the contents of the book can be changed as men's behaviour changes. In the Book of Revelation the angel is told to tell the church of Sardis that those who overcome will not have their names blotted out of the book of life (Rev. 3: 5), and the implication seems to be that if they do not overcome, they will have their names blotted out.

If a theist is not satisfied with saying that God is omniscient in the attenuated sense which I have delineated, he would—in order to avoid the apparent incompatibility between divine freedom and divine omniscience—have to say that God is 'omniscient' in an analogical sense such that a definition of this term in ordinary words with mundane senses cannot be provided. He could say, for example, that an omniscient being is one who 'knows' everything—but that 'knows' has less strict syntactic and semantic rules for use than the normal use. He would thus have to proceed along the lines sketched in Chapter 4. But, as I urged there, although it may be necessary for a theist to plead 'analogical senses' of words, this is not something to be done unless it is really necessary; and for the reasons which I have given it does not seem to me that this is here really necessary. The attenuated sense of 'omniscient' which I have set out seems quite adequate for the theist's claim. For a person would not be less worthy of worship if he voluntarily limited his knowledge in order to allow himself and some of his creatures to determine their own destiny.

The theist's claim then, if it is to be coherent, is, I suggest, a claim that there exists (now) an omnipresent spirit, perfectly free, creator of the universe, omnipotent and omniscient (in the attenuated sense). The God thus postulated brings about all things which exist (or permits them to exist) and in so doing knows what he brings about and what that will lead to, in so far as he has brought about things which physically necessitate certain effects. Yet to maintain his freedom, he limits his knowledge of his own future choices.

II

Perfectly Good and a Source of Moral Obligation

A THEIST normally holds that God is by nature morally perfectly good and also that men have a duty to obey the commands of God—that the commands of God create moral obligations.

Perfect Goodness

In claiming that God is by nature morally perfectly good, the theist means that God is so constituted that he never does actions which are morally wrong. I understand by an action being wrong that it is a bad action, one which the agent ought not to do, has a duty or obligation not to do. I understand by an action being right that it is a good action, one which the agent has no obligation or duty not to do, one of which it is not the case that he ought not to do it. An action which an agent ought to do, or has a duty or obligation to do, is one which it would be wrong for him to refrain from doing.[1] Refraining from doing an action is to be counted as itself an action; and so it will be true of a perfectly good being that he does any actions which he ought to do. A wicked or evil action is one which is morally very wrong.

But what is it to judge that an action is morally good or bad, as opposed to being good or bad in other respects? We often contrast moral goodness with goodness of other kinds. We may allow that some action is good in some respects (e.g. in respect

---

[1] I shall mention later a more restricted sense in which 'ought', 'obligation', and 'duty' may be taken.

of the pleasure which it gives to the agent), while denying that it is morally good. Or, conversely, we may hold that what a man did was in various ways not a good action—it was poorly executed, perhaps, or aesthetically unpleasing—while allowing that morally it was a good action. So what is it to judge that some action is morally good? I suggest that to judge that an action ought morally to be done is to judge that it is on balance, over all, a better action than alternative actions; that it is of overriding importance to do it, that it matters that it should be done, that the reasons for doing it override any reasons for not doing it. A morally bad or wrong action is then one which an agent ought morally to refrain from doing; and a morally good action is one which he has no moral obligation not to do. In saying that God never does actions which are morally wrong, the theist is surely saying that in choosing between alternative actions, although God may do actions which are perhaps ugly or lead to the possibility of men suffering, he never does an action which is on balance worse than any alternative action which he might have done instead. He does whatever it is of overriding importance that he should do, he does whatever it matters that he should do.

Some philosophers have given different accounts of what moral goodness consists in.[2] According to one school, for example, to judge that an action is morally good is to judge that it is good in the respect that good (i.e. well-being, pleasure, or something of that kind) for humans (or, perhaps, other sentient beings) results from the action. Moral judgements about actions are those which assess actions in respect of the good or harm for humans (or other sentient beings) which result from them. Feeding the starving or showing friendship to the lonely would be fairly evident cases of morally good actions. But keeping promises to the dying or refraining from lying (when to lie would lead to the saving of life) would not, on this account, be cases of morally good actions—unless in some complicated way human well-being resulted from them. Of course this definition of the moral which we are discussing is a rather vague one, and

---

[2] See the collection edited by G. Wallace and A. D. M. Walker, *The Definition of Morality* (London, 1970). The introduction to this collection describes different philosophical theories about when a judgement is a moral judgement, and there are articles in the collection illustrating the different theories.

it would need to be made much more precise if it was to be
treated at length, but it seems to me fairly evident that it is an
odd definition, and not the one which we require for our
purposes.

It is an odd definition in that it does not do justice to the
way in which the word 'moral' is often used in ordinary
language. This can be seen as follows. There is, superficially,
nothing incoherent in supposing that it is more important to
tell the truth in all circumstances than to make men (or other
sentient beings) happy. This moral judgement might be
wrong (and perhaps contain a deeply buried incoherence), but
there is nothing *obviously* incoherent about it. Yet it follows
from the cited judgement that it is sometimes more important
to do an action which is not morally good than to do one which
is morally good. But this does seem a very odd thing to say.
On a very natural use of 'moral' nothing could be more important than morality. Or again, the man who says 'it matters
more that I should paint pictures than that I should do my
moral duty' says something paradoxical in a way in which the
man who says 'my moral duty is to paint pictures rather than
to bring happiness to men' does not. The latter judgement may
be false, but it does not have the evident appearance of being
a self-contradiction which the former has. This suggests that at
any rate often in ordinary language 'morally' good actions are
those which it is of overriding importance to do, which are
over all better than other ones, etc.[3]

This definition too is surely the one which we require for
our purposes. In saying that God is morally perfectly good,
the theist does commit himself to the view that God does
whatever it is of overriding importance that he should do,
including any actions, if there are any such, which are of
overriding importance although they bring no happiness to
humans or other sentient beings. (Of course there may not be
any such actions, but the theist surely holds that if there are
any, God does them.) Similar criticisms apply to any other
rival definitions of the moral which might be offered. In saying
that God is morally perfectly good, the theist holds that God
does whatever it is of overriding importance that he should do,

[3] Neil Cooper commends this sense of 'moral' in his 'Morality and Importance',
in Wallace and Walker, op. cit.

even if this were to involve doing what is not 'morally' good on some other definition of morality.

Sometimes of course theists have denied that God is 'morally' good or at all concerned with 'morality', but a little examination of what they are saying will, I suggest, reveal that they, unlike other theists, do not construe 'moral' in a way in which the 'moral' is what matters. The man who says 'God is above morality' means only that God is concerned with things more important than human good or harm, or with things other than those which men think will bring them happiness. He does not mean that God does not do what is of ultimate importance. I suggest that in our sense of 'moral' all theists hold that God is perfectly good, and that this is a central claim of theism.

That there can be a person who is by nature morally perfectly good in our sense seems evidently a coherent claim. It seems coherent to suppose that there be a person who is so constituted that he always does what there is overriding reason to do, and always refrains from doing what there is overriding reason for not doing. He always does the good because that is how he is made. But is perfect goodness compatible with perfect freedom? For surely a free agent may choose good or evil; his choice cannot be predetermined.

We have already seen in earlier chapters the outlines of the answer to this difficulty. I propose to argue that not merely is perfect goodness compatible with perfect freedom,[14] but that it is logically necessary that an omniscient and perfectly free being be perfectly good. We saw in Chapter 8 that a perfectly free being will always do an action if he judges that there is overriding reason for doing it rather than for refraining from doing it. But what is it to judge that there is overriding reason for doing an action? Is it merely to take up an attitude towards that action, an attitude which does not stand in need of rational justification? Or is it rather to believe a statement about how things are which could be true or false, to judge that an action has the property of being supported by an overriding reason, of being over all better to do than to refrain from doing? If the latter, if 'judgement' really means judgement, then an

---

[4] I do not wish to deny that there is an incoherence in supposing that a free agent subject to non-rational influences (and so to temptations) be so constituted as always to choose the good. But that is not what is at issue here.

omniscient being will—of logical necessity—make those judgements about overriding reasons for doing actions which are true
judgements. Hence if he is perfectly free he will do those actions
which there is overriding reason to do and refrain from those
actions from which there is overriding reason to refrain.

So, to prove my point, I need to show that judgements about
overriding reasons for doing actions, about one action being
over all better than another, are statements which are true or
false.

The Objectivity of Moral Judgements—(1) The Issue

The issue then is whether the moral goodness of actions in
the sense defined is an objective matter, and much of the rest
of this chapter will be devoted to tackling this. Is it either true
or false that abortion or euthanasia are always wrong actions,
that truth-telling is always right, that this or that or the other
particular actions are morally good or bad? If I say 'we are
now living in England' or 'grass is green in summer' or 'the
cat is on the mat' what I say will normally be true or false—the
statements are true if they correctly report how things are, or
correspond to the facts; and if they do not do these things, they
are false. Such a statement will only fail to have a truth value
if its referring expressions fail to refer (e.g. there is no object to
which 'the cat' can properly be taken to refer), or if it lies on the
border between truth and falsity (e.g. the grass is blue-green)
so that it is as true to say that the statement is true as to say
that it is false. Are moral judgements normally true or false
in the way in which the above statements are true or false?
I will term the view that they are objectivism and the view that
they are not subjectivism. The objectivist maintains that it is as
much a fact about an action that it is right or wrong as that it
causes pain or takes a long time to perform. The subjectivist
maintains that saying that an action is right or wrong is not
stating a fact about it but merely expressing approval of it or
commending it or doing some such similar thing. I shall attempt
firstly to show that all arguments for subjectivism manifestly
fail, and secondly to produce a strong argument for objectivism.
Inevitably my discussion will be more brief than the topic and
the vast amount of current philosophical writing about it

deserve. However, I can only plead the excuse which I made in the introduction to this book that there are considerable advantages in discussing within the compass of one book all the philosophical issues relevant to the coherence of theism.

The objectivist holds that a sentence such as 'capital punishment is always wrong', which expresses a moral judgement, expresses a proposition which is true or false. It ascribes a property to all actions of a certain type. Rightness, wrongness, goodness, badness are, he holds, moral properties. The objectivist may claim for his moral properties either that they are logically distinct from the 'natural' properties of things or that possession of the former is entailed by possession of certain of the latter. The former view I will term anti-naturalism, the latter naturalism. By natural properties I mean such properties as being square, yellow, magnetically charged, causing pain, or making someone happy, properties which those who do not think that morality is objective are content to suppose to belong to things; properties which we ascribe to things when not overtly engaged in moral discourse. Most predicates denote natural properties. The naturalist claims that if something has a moral property such as goodness or rightness, its possession of this property is entailed by its possession of a natural property. The naturalist position may be subdivided further. A naturalist may claim that possession of a moral property just is possession of a certain natural property—e.g. he might claim that right actions just are those actions which forward the greatest happiness of the greatest number. The claim is that the moral word just is the name of a natural property—'right' just means 'forwarding the greatest happiness of the greatest number'. Alternatively, the naturalist may claim that moral properties are properties distinct from natural properties, although possession of the former is entailed by possession of certain of the latter. Clearly one statement may entail another which makes a claim very different from the claim made by the former. Thus 'he has eleven cars' entails 'the number of cars which he owns is equal to the next prime number greater than 7'; but the latter says something very different from the former. The relation between statements ascribing natural properties and statements ascribing moral properties is of this kind, according to the second type of naturalist theory. On theories of this latter type, as on anti-naturalist theories to be described below, moral properties being properties distinct from natural properties may be termed non-natural properties.

On the anti-naturalist view possession of natural properties never entails possession of moral properties. Moral properties are logically distinct from natural properties, and so it is logically possible that any moral property be possessed by an object with any combination of natural properties. Various versions of anti-naturalism are possible, according to what view is taken about how one gets to know that a certain moral property belongs to a certain object. The view that this is something one just 'sees' is intuitionism. One could develop an alternative view that one gets to know that an object possesses some moral property by means of a non-deductive inference from its possession of certain natural properties.

Any anti-naturalist view seems to me implausible because of the problem of supervenience.[5] The anti-naturalist allows the logical possibility of two objects being exactly alike in their natural properties but differing in their moral properties— e.g. two actions of killing a man in exactly the same circumstances differing only in that the one action is right and the other wrong. But this does seem incoherent. An action cannot be just wrong—it must be wrong because of some natural feature which it possesses, e.g. because it causes pain or is forbidden by the government. An action being right or wrong is thus said to be supervenient on its possession of natural properties. Now if it is the possession of certain natural features which makes the action wrong, then any other action which had just those natural features would also be wrong. In this sense all moral judgements are universalizable. If certain men or actions or states of affairs are good, any other man, action, or state of affairs which are qualitatively similar in their natural properties would also be good. Since two objects which agree in their natural properties must agree in their moral properties, anti-naturalism is false.

The first form of naturalism also seems implausible. If 'good' or 'right' were *definable* in natural terms, then if you and I agree about the natural properties of an action but disagree about whether it is 'right', either we are using words in different

[5] See R. M. Hare, *The Language of Morals* (Oxford, 1952), pp. 80 f.

senses, or one or other of us does not know English. Yet that seems implausible. The fact that you say that capital punishment is always 'wrong' and I say that it is not always 'wrong' does not guarantee that we are talking about different things.[6] Surely moral disagreement is a genuine phenomenon! I conclude that the objectivist must retreat to the second form of naturalism, and in defending objectivism this is the form of it which I will henceforward adopt.[7,8]

The naturalist must claim that there are two kinds of moral truth—(logically) necessary moral truths and contingent moral truths. The naturalist claims that when an object a has a certain moral property, say M, its possession of it is entailed by it possessing certain natural properties, say A, B, and C. Then it is a necessary truth that anything which is A, B, and C is M; but a contingent truth that a is M or that there is an object which is A and M. Contingent moral truths hold because

[6] It is the first form of naturalism which is open to Hare's well-known objection. 'If it were true that a good A meant the same as an A which is C (when "C" is a "descriptive" term) then it would be impossible to use the sentence "An A which is C is good" in order to commend A's which are C; for this sentence would be analytic and equivalent to "an A which is C is C". Now it seem clear that we do use sentences of the form "an A which is C is good" in order to commend A's which are C; and that when we do so, we are not doing the same sort of thing as when we say "A puppy is a young dog", that is to say, commending is not the same sort of linguistic activity as defining' (ibid., pp. 90 f.) The second form of naturalism does not assert that 'good' means 'C' (where 'C' is some descriptive term). However, even naturalists who subscribe to a naturalistic theory of the first form have a defence. They can point out that some statements which ascribe natural properties to objects are on occasion 'used to commend'. One may commend by saying 'He is an extremely persevering student', 'He will certainly get a first', 'This is real leather' etc. etc. So the fact that moral judgements are often used to commend does not show that they do not ascribe properties of any kind.

[7] Hume's well-known objection to naturalism (see *Treatise of Human Nature*, 3.1.1) does not tell against the second form. Hume rightly comments that when we pass from propositions containing 'is' and 'is not' to propositions containing 'ought' and 'ought not', the latter express 'some new relation or affirmation'. He goes on to claim that it 'seems altogether inconceivable' that 'this new relation can be a deduction from others, which are entirely different from it'. Contrary to Hume, as the example on p. 184 should bear out, this is not at all inconceivable. Deducing new relations from old is the life-blood of philosophy and mathematics.

[8] The naturalist must hold that all, not merely some, true moral judgements about particular objects are propositions entailed by propositions correctly reporting their possession of natural properties. If he claims that there are some true moral judgements of which the latter is not true the principle of supervenience makes his position very implausible, as has been well argued by S. W. Blackburn (see 'Moral Realism' in John Casey (ed.), *Morality and Moral Reasoning*, London, 1971).

of the contingent feature of the world that certain objects have certain natural properties. Thus among contingent moral truths are such statements as 'I ought now to pay £10 to the bookshop' or 'I ought to give Smith a fail mark on his ethics paper'. These moral truths are contingent, because, although the cited actions are obligatory on me, they are obligatory only because things have the natural properties which they do. Why I ought to pay the bookshop £10 is because I bought £10 of books from them and they have sent me a bill for the books. If such contingent circumstances did not hold, I would have no obligation to pay the bookshop £10. Contingent moral truths hold because the world is as it is in respect of natural properties. But that those moral truths hold under those circumstances is itself a necessary moral truth. For if we state fully the natural features of the world which make a contingent moral truth to hold, it cannot be a contingent matter that it does hold under those circumstances. Yet it is a moral truth that it does, and hence a necessary moral truth. It is a necessary moral truth that when I have bought £10 of books from the bookshop and they send me a bill for this, I ought to pay the bill. No doubt this moral truth holds because a much more general moral truth holds—that men ought to pay their debts—of which the specific truth is a consequence. Among the necessary moral truths one would expect to find general principles of conduct such as that one ought to care for one's children, not punish the innocent, not tell lies (subject to whatever qualifications are needed).

The Objectivity of Moral Judgements—(2) The Failure of Arguments Against Objectivism

Now that I have clarified the form of objectivism which I wish to defend, let us turn to arguments against it. I know of four initially plausible objections to the position which I have described. The first, which may be found in very many writers, is that 'argument fails us when we come to deal with pure questions of value, as distinct from questions of fact'.[9] According to this objection dispute about a moral matter may have two elements—a 'factual' element and a 'moral' element. If I say that *a* is wrong and you say that it is right, then our dispute

[9] A. J. Ayer, *Language, Truth, and Logic*, p. 111.

may arise because we have different factual beliefs about *a*. If I say that capital punishment is right and you say that it is wrong, our disagreement may arise because we have differing views about the deterrent effects of capital punishment. I may think that the existence of capital punishment as a penalty for some crime deters men from committing that crime and you may think that it does not. This factual disagreement is in principle settlable, and settling it may lead to moral agreement. But we may still disagree about whether capital punishment is wrong when we have come to agree about the 'facts'—e.g. that it is an effective deterrent. If we do, our disagreement is a pure moral one, and then, the objection goes, our disagreement is not resoluble by argument. This shows, it is claimed, that factual premisses do not entail moral conclusions —because if they did, one could prove a moral conclusion to someone by deducing it from the 'facts', and thus cases of pure moral disagreement could be resolved.

This objection is often stated rather loosely. Let us try to state it more carefully. To do so, I will talk not about facts', but about 'natural facts', and thus avoid begging the question whether morality is a factual matter. I define pure moral disagreement as disagreement about whether things are right, wrong, good, bad, etc. which remains or would remain after agreement has been reached about relevant natural facts. Pure moral judgements are judgements about what kinds of thing are right, wrong, etc. which do not depend for their truth on any claims about natural facts. (I will call moral judgements which are not pure ones, impure ones.) The objection has the form of an argument from a premiss to the conclusion (C) 'premisses stating natural facts do not entail moral conclusions'. What is the premiss from which the objector seeks to infer (C)? It may be one of three premisses:

(P1): Seldom does any one change his pure moral views as a result of argument.

(P2): Never does any one change his pure moral views as a result of argument.

(P3): Nobody knows how to go about producing arguments to settle pure moral disagreements.

We now have three different forms of the first objection to

objectivism, according to which premiss we use in attempting to prove (C). I now proceed to argue that the objection does not work in any of its three forms. (P1), though true, does not yield (C); and (P2) and (P3) are false, and so whether or not (C) follows from them does not matter.

(P1) is undoubtedly true. But then a statistical survey of arguments of all kinds would, I suggest, show that most of them do not end in agreement. Arguments about whether a man or his wife left the door open, whether the reintroduction of capital punishment would lead to a decrease in the number of murders, or increases in tax rates will lead to people working less hard, typically do not end in agreement. Yet even on a subjectivist account of morals the arguments surely concern facts. The mere fact that arguments in a certain field often do not end in agreement does not show that they cannot or would not if men were rational and persevering enough. And in the case of moral argument, there is a good explanation of why agreement is even less likely to be found here than in other fields. This is that the temptations to irrationality and lack of perseverance are greater here than in other fields. This is because of the close connection of morality with behaviour. Suppose I change my mind about a purely moral matter and come to see action of a certain kind as wrong instead of right. Then I come to see it as an action of a type which it is important to avoid, which any man has an overriding reason for avoiding. Hence if I am to be rational, to act in accordance with my beliefs, to 'live up to my principles', I shall have to change my behaviour. If I come to agree that corporal punishment is wrong, then I shall have to stop beating my children. Men often do not wish to change their pattern of behaviour, yet wish to 'live up to their principles'. Hence the temptation to irrationality and lack of perseverance in moral argument. Changing my mind about natural facts, such as details of history or chemistry, however, seldom has such consequences for my behaviour. Yet on occasion there may be such consequences. I may believe that I ought to do actions of kind A, and yet naturally avoid doing actions of kind B. x may be an action of kind B and hence one which I naturally avoid. Yet you may persuade me that x is really also of kind A. This will have the consequence that, if I am to live up to my principles, I ought to do x. I may believe that I ought to give up murderers to the police, yet naturally avoid giving up my son to the police. If I come to agree that my son is a murderer, this will have unpleasant consequences for my behaviour. It is indeed just in such cases of arguments about natural facts that men are at their most irrational in argument about natural facts. This bears out my point that there is a ready explanation of why arguments about purely moral matters do not very often end in agreement.

However, (P1), as we saw, does not yield (C). (P2), however, is false, and we can ignore the question whether or not it yields (C). Argument sometimes does settle pure moral disagreements. A says that capital punishment is wrong; B says that it is right. Their disagreement, we may suppose, does not result from any disagreement about natural facts, such the extent of the deterrent effect. A then points out to B various considerations—ones of which B was aware but to which he had not given weight—that the judge may make a mistake, imprisonment can reform men whereas capital punishment does not, etc. etc.; and in the end B comes to agree with A and to say that he made a mistake before. Such procedures do occur. A man may say that this procedure is not argument about how things are; it is persuasion to adopt a stance. But, let us suppose, B gradually admits that the various considerations tend to show his view 'wrong', 'mistaken', 'in error', 'untrue', and tend to 'establish' a 'conclusion' different from his original view. In a like situation, where A and B are discussing history and A has one opinion and B a different one, and A adduces considerations which, B admits, tend to show his view false, we would say that A and B are arguing. Why not in this case? Settling disputes by the sort of procedure just described is what we mean by settling disputes by argument.

(P3) is also false and so we can ignore also the question of whether it yields (C). Most of us know how to go about producing arguments to settle pure moral disagreements. To start with, a disputant may draw an opponent's attention to his own moral principles, and to the fact that they have consequences other than those which the opponent has appreciated. You and I may both agree that an action a has natural properties A, B, C, and D. Yet your moral principles may have as a consequence that A-type actions are wrong. You may not have appreciated this. I point out the consequence and this resolves the disagreement. Thus I might believe that signing a false statement on an income-tax form is a case of lying and also believe that men ought not to lie. Yet I may not have drawn the obvious conclusion from this that I ought not to sign a false statement on the tax form. Secondly, a disputant may endeavour to show a man that his moral principles are incorrect. He will typically do this by pointing out some counter-intuitive consequence which they have. I may describe in detail, and if possible actually show you, the nature and consequences of some action which by your principles is morally justifiable, and then ask if you really agree with this consequence of your principles. You may then see this consequence as obviously unacceptable, and so have to reject the principles. Professor Hare has described this process in *Freedom and Reason*.[10] He shows how, often, a man can be made to give up the view that Jews ought to be exterminated when some of its consequences are delineated (e.g. that if he was a Jew, he ought to be exterminated). Or we may show a man the orphaned children of someone killed in battle and ask him if he still wants to say that war is sometimes morally justified. In turn he can show us some of the horrible things which governments do and ask us if we are really going to allow such things to go on without trying to stop them by force. Cases such as these make men think that their principles are wrong and they then modify them so that they yield what seems to them the correct judgement about the awkward cases. Instead of saying 'war is wrong', I may say instead 'war is wrong unless it is trying to prevent extermination of peoples'. We look for the moral principle which most naturally fits the particular judgements we make. The process of getting people to change their moral principles by describing counter-intuitive consequences of them will be aided if we can point out to an opponent that one of his moral principles yields different judgements about particular cases from some other of his own principles, and therefore one or other must be wrong. In turn certain moral principles which we develop may seem so obviously right that we have to change our judgements about particular cases. It may have seemed obvious to a man that the British were right to fight the Second World War; but it may

---

[10] See esp. Chs. 6 and 11.

now seem to him, as a result of considering other wars, that war is never justified; and so he may come to change his judgement about the Second World War. In the course of argument others may lead us along such a path.

Now argument on the above lines certainly goes on and most of us know how to argue on those lines. So (P_3) is false. Whatever a man's initial moral position, argument is relevant to changing it. Argument will start from some principles, showing that others conflict with them, or from particular cases where, an opponent claims, some action is obviously right or wrong. A disputant encourages his opponent to extrapolate correct moral principles from particular cases. x is obviously wrong, he says, and that is purely because it is A, and so surely A-things are wrong, he suggests. In order for moral argument between two persons to get off the ground, two disputants have to agree about some moral principles or some judgements about the morality of particular cases. People in general do have that kind of community of agreement. You and I may differ over all sorts of well-publicized moral issues—abortion, capital punishment, taxation, and war. But typically we share moral judgements over all sorts of particular cases, most of which are so obvious that the moralist does not bother to comment on them. Which are the moral judgements which I share with you will depend on who you are, but typically I may agree with others—that people ought not to write poison-pen letters, that Florence Nightingale did better actions than Hitler, than men ought not to lie in courts of law on oath, that I ought not to break your arm just because I dislike you, etc. etc. Although I have discussed moral matters with many and various people over many years, I do not recall ever having discussed them with someone with whom I found myself sharing no moral judgements at all. From particular moral judgements we draw out moral principles. Normally the rebel does *not* throw out all the morality with which he has been born. What happens is that he draws out what he thinks to be the principles implicit in certain moral judgements to which his society is committed, and those principles have consequences which conflict with other judgements which his society makes. Thus the first-century Jew judged that you ought to help your neighbour if he gets into real trouble. He then began to reflect what was it about your neighbour which made it your duty to help him. He might then see as the natural answer the answer suggested by Christ's parable of the Good Samaritan that it was the fact that that neighbour was human being. A consequence of this is that you ought to help the Gentile too if he was in real trouble, a judgement which some of Christ's contemporaries opposed. Generalization of principles which are supposed to apply within a nation or a family to worldwide application is indeed typical of moral development.

I am not claiming that moral disagreements are always readily settled. As I have admitted, this does not often happen. But this may be because argument does not go on long enough or because men are irrational. All that I am claiming is that there are recognized ways of going about settling a moral disagreement, and most of us know how to use them.

I turn now to the second objection to the objectivity of moral judgements. This says that however fully we describe an action in natural terms, as 'φ' (e.g. 'killing a man not in self-defence, nor in execution of a judicial process, nor in war . . . '), it always makes sense for one man to say 'φ is always a right action' and for another man to say 'φ is not always a right action'. Both of these remarks are intelligible. Yet if an action being φ entailed it being right or entailed it being not always right, one or other of these remarks would be incoherent, which they are not.[11]

The conclusion that one or other remark must be incoherent is certainly one which the naturalist must accept. But incoherence is typically not always visible on the surface—if it was, most philosophers would be out of business. 'There is more than one space', 'time has many dimensions', 'men survive their death' may or may not be incoherent claims, but if they are it needs books of argument to show them to be so. There may be a similar incoherence buried in 'capital punishment

[11] For this objection see, among others, C. L. Stevenson and R. M. Hare. Thus Stevenson: 'Persons who make opposed ethical judgments may (so far as theoretical possibility is concerned) continue to do in the face of all manner of reasons that their argument includes, even though neither makes any logical or empirical error' (*Ethics and Language*, New Haven, 1944, pp. 30 f.). And Hare: 'it is possible for two people without logical absurdity to agree about the description but disagree about the evaluation' ('Descriptivism', repub. in W. D. Hudson (ed.), *The Is/Ought Question*, London, 1969. See p. 246).

is always wrong', or in 'capital punishment is sometimes right', and generally in one or other of all statements of the form 'φ is always a right action' and 'φ is not always a right action' (where 'φ' gives as full a description as you like of an action in natural terms). The fact that one or other of these may ultimately be incoherent is not touched by the suggestion that statements of both forms are always 'intelligible'. We can understand what is being said by the negation of most analytic statements (other than very trivial tautologies). We can understand what is being said by 'π is greater than 3.2' and by 'π is less than 3.2', but a little argument will show that there is an incoherence buried in the first claim. It may well be like this with moral judgements for anything that the second objections had shown. The incoherence would have to lie buried fairly deep in the case of one or other of some pairs of moral judgements. But some incoherences are buried very deep. Consider again Goldbach's famous conjecture, put forward in the eighteenth century, that 'every even number is the sum of two prime numbers'. This has been proved to hold for many million even numbers, but no one has yet proved either that it holds universally or that there is an exception to it. Yet given the definitions of the terms codified in the axioms of arithmetic, there is presumably an incoherence either in 'every even number is the sum of two primes' or in 'not every even number is the sum of two primes'; that is, a contradiction can be derived from one or other claim. Yet after two hundred years of hard work no one has yet proved which claim is incoherent.

I pass now to the two objections which concern the connections of moral judgements with attitudes and actions respectively. The third objection claims that (to put the matter in our terminology) agreement on natural facts does not entail agreement in attitude whereas agreement about moral matters does entail agreement in attitude. This suggests a strong disanalogy between agreement about natural facts and agreement about morals, suggesting that agreement of the latter kind is not agreement about any kind of fact at all. Thus Stevenson: 'Supporting reasons have only to do with beliefs, and in so far as they in turn are proved by demonstrative or empirical methods, only agreement in belief will, in the first instance, be secured. Ethical agreement, however, requires more than agreement in belief; it requires agreement in attitude.'[12]

The difficulty with this objection concerns what is meant by an 'attitude'. In one sense of 'attitude' agreement about natural facts seems to require agreement in attitude. To believe that a is φ involves thinking of a as φ and thus, if taking an attitude is a mere cognitive stance, taking an attitude towards a as towards a φ-thing. 'There are beliefs such as the belief that something is alive which may also entail the possession of an attitude, even if all that can be said about the attitude is that it is one which one feels towards things which are alive, but not towards other things.'[13] Yet if taking an attitude is a matter of emotive stance, moral agreement does not necessarily involve community of attitude. I may judge that some action is my duty, without liking to do it or wanting to do it. The only hope for this objection seems to be to spell out 'agreement in attitude' as 'agreement in commitment to action' and thus the third objection turns into what I term the fourth objection—the objection concerned with the close connection between moral judgements and actions.[14]

This objection brings to our notice the fact that which moral judgements I accept makes a difference to what I do, and the fact that the connection between moral judgement and action does not appear to be a merely contingent one. Yet the connection between beliefs about natural facts and actions does appear to be contingent. This suggests a strong disanalogy between beliefs about natural facts and moral judgements, suggesting that the latter are not beliefs about facts at all. The connection between moral judgement and action has been described in various ways. Some writers hold the connection to be rather tighter than do others. For Hare moral judgements entail self-addressed imperatives; and to accept an imperative is to obey it. Thus 'X is wrong' entails 'let me not do X'; and I

---

[12] Op. cit., p. 31.

[13] Blackburn, op. cit. 103. Blackburn seems to consider that this entailment only holds for some beliefs; but that claim suffices for our purposes.

[14] Stevenson explains 'opposition of attitudes' as being 'opposition of purposes, aspirations, wants, preferences, desires, and so on' (op. cit., p. 3). But this is very vague, and confuses things which need to be kept distinct if any clear account of morality is to be given. For one can have agreement of 'purposes' but opposition of 'wants'. Does one then have moral agreement?

accept the latter if and only if I do not do X. I accept a moral judgement, according to Hare, only if I act in accordance with it. There are well-known difficulties in asserting so tight a connection. Cannot a man believe that X is wrong, and yet do X—through weakness of will? Yet surely there does exist a rather looser connection between moral judgements and actions, and the following account of it, developed at the end of Chapter 8, follows from the definition of morality with which we are working. Moral judgements provide overriding reasons for doing things. If I accept that morally I ought to do X rather than Y, I have to agree that doing X rather than Y would be doing the action which is over all the better; that there is stronger reason for doing X rather than Y. I may not of course conform to reason. I may give in to pressures or inclinations and do Y. Yet in so far as I act on reason, I will do X. The fourth objection can now be expressed in the light of this account of the connection between moral judgements and action as follows: claims about natural facts do not entail the existence of reasons for doing things, whereas moral judgements do. Such claim about natural facts as that there is food in the larder may provide a reason for doing something, e.g. going to the larder, but it only does so under certain contingent circumstances—e.g. if I am hungry, or want to ensure that there is no food left for anyone else—and it need not do so even then; there is no entailment from claims about natural facts to the existence of reasons for actions.

Yet the objection seems mistaken. There are claims about natural facts which do entail the existence of reasons for doing things. These are claims about a man's wants, desires, purposes, and intentions. My wanting to eat the food in the larder does seem to entail the existence of a reason for my going to the larder. The reason is not necessarily an overriding one—I may well have reasons for not going to the larder, e.g. if I wish to slim or if I have promised to fast. But surely my wanting to eat the food in the larder entails the existence of a reason for my going to the larder. Although there might be other reasons for not going to the larder which overrode the reason for going, circumstances could hardly be such as to make my wanting the food no reason at all for going to get it. Or, more generally, circumstances could hardly be such as to make my wants no reason at all for doing anything. It does seem incoherent to say of me 'although he knows that there is food in the larder, and wants the food, he has no reason for going to the larder'. That being so, claims about natural facts do entail the existence of reasons for doing things. True, only moral judgements (or any statements about natural facts which entail moral judgements) entail the existence of overriding reasons fcr actions. But since it is the defining characteristic of moral judgements that they are concerned with over-all goodness and overriding reasons, it is hardly surprising that they (together with any statements about natural facts which entail moral judgements) alone carry such entailment. Yet pointing out that some claims about natural facts do entail the existence of reasons for action breaks down the suggested strong disanalogy between claims about natural facts, and moral judgements.

The Objectivity of Moral Judgements—(3) An Argument for Objectivism

If objections to objectivism fail, what can be said more positively in its favour?

One might of course just say that surely nothing needs to be said. 'Good', 'right', etc. are adjectives of our language which qualify nouns. To call things 'square' or 'red' or 'unpopular' or to apply almost any other adjective to a thing is to attribute a property to it, such that (with the qualifications mentioned on p. 183) it is either true or false to say that the thing possesses that property. If anybody claims that 'good' and 'right' do not function in this way like other adjectives the onus is on him to show the difference; and, as I have shown, attempts to do so fail.

However, a more positive argument is perhaps called for in view of the widespread scepticism about the objectivity of moral judgements. Before I provide one, however, it would be useful to develop more fully how the naturalist will interpret the account of moral argument given earlier. For I argued that if morality is an objective discipline, the naturalist account of it is to be preferred to others. In the naturalist's view the moralist in trying to establish a corpus of pure moral judgements is trying to establish a set of analytic truths. We saw earlier that argument about pure moral judgements consists of trying to show that they are entailed by or alternatively are incompatible with other moral judgements agreed by the disputants to be obviously true. The naturalist claims that in accepting the moral judgement as true a disputant is accepting a claim about what is the case. The naturalist believes that pure moral judgements—that actions of types A, B, and C are wrong; actions of types D, E, and F are right—are either logically necessary propositions or ultimately incoherent ones. True pure moral judgements are logically necessary and false ones are ultimately incoherent. Other judgements that particular actions or kinds of action are morally right or wrong, i.e. impure moral judgements, are contingent propositions—they depend for their truth value on factual propositions about which natural properties the action or kind of action has, as well as on the necessary propositions connecting the natural and moral properties of actions. There are recognized ways of showing of factual components of moral judgements whether they are true or false. The other component, the pure moral judgement, is in the naturalist's view either a necessarily false (i.e. incoherent) proposition, or a necessarily true one (i.e. one which is coherent, but has an incoherent negation). Now we saw in Chapter 3 that the only way to prove a proposition to be incoherent is to show that it entails a contradiction; and since judging that p entails q involves judging that p-and-not-q is incoherent, proving one proposition to be incoherent is only possible if you assume another one to be incoherent. We also saw in Chapter 3 that the only way to prove a proposition coherent is to show that it is entailed by another coherent proposition; and so proving one proposition to be coherent is only possible if you assume another one to be coherent (and that the latter entails the former). Hence arguments about morality, in assuming certain moral judgements to be true for the purpose of proving others, make (as well, maybe, as factual assumptions) assumptions of the kind which philosophers must make in proving propositions to be coherent. In both cases we assume what is more obviously so for the purpose of proving what is less obviously so. But on another occasion what is assumed on this occasion can be *shown* to be so or not to be so from what is even more obvious. Moral argument can take place and make progress, so long as there is consensus about some moral truths, just as philosophical argument can take place and make progress, so long as there is some consensus about what is coherent and what is not.

Having thus developed how the naturalist will interpret the account of moral argument given earlier, I return to the question of producing a positive argument for the objectivity of moral judgements. We saw in Chapter 3 that it is a sufficient condition (though not a necessary condition) of a sentence expressing a statement, in other words of a judgement being true or false, that there are established ways of arguing for or against what it expresses. Now we know how to go about showing whether a thing is square or yellow or sour; and though we cannot always in practice reach a definite conclusion, we know what procedures would settle the matter. Ultimately agreement depends on agreement in observation—reports and agreement about which observation reports render which other claims probable. We know too in general how to reach conclusions in theoretical physics and in history—though here procedures are often somewhat lengthier and less sure. The same applies to mathematics. Yet in all these cases we must admit that quite often disagreement may persist after a substantial amount of argument; that we are only fairly well agreed as to how to go about resolving it; and that to some extent criteria for assessing arguments are not precise enough to make all issues settlable. Nevertheless, the procedures are sufficiently well agreed for us to say that physics, history, and mathematics are objective disciplines, the 'conclusions' of which are true or false.

Now I argued earlier that if morality is objective, the naturalistic account of it is to be preferred to others. On that account, as we saw above, morality is a deductive discipline seeking to establish a core of analytic truths. In that case (after any factual issues have been disposed of) moral argument would clearly be of a kind with argument in philosophy or mathematics. If we can find that agreement on procedures and results is as easy or hard to get in one of these clearly objective disciplines as in morals, that will indicate that there is enough agreement on procedures and results in morals for us to term it an objective discipline. I suggest that the required parallel for morals exists in philosophy, and in particular in philosophical argument about what sorts of thing are and are not logically possible. Philosophers try to prove such things as that it is not logically possible for an event to precede its cause, for there to be more than one space, for there to be uncaused events, etc. etc. Philosophy looks like an objective discipline; looks as if, like history or physics, it is concerned to establish results which are true or false. Yet of course it is notorious that after years of argument philosophers often continue to disagree. Why then should we call it an objective discipline?

Surely for the following reason. There is quite substantial agreement between most people with respect to many sentences as to whether they express logically possible suppositions. 'He is older than his elder brother' does not, and 'Mr. Heath is no longer Prime Minister' does, express a logically possible supposition, most would agree. Further, as we saw in detail in Chapter 3, there are agreed ways of proving whether or not other suppositions are logically possible. You can prove that a supposition is logically possible if you can prove that it is a consequence of something else that is logically possible. Thus you can prove that 'there is more than one space' is logically possible if you can describe a logically possible state of affairs in which, you can deduce, there is more than one space. You can prove that a supposition is not logically possible, if you can deduce from it a consequence which is not logically possible, e.g. a self-contradictory statement. Further, people are often brought to change their mind about philosophical issues by application of the above techniques. And if agreement is not reached in a finite time disputants normally know how to locate the area of disagreement and know the kinds of arguments which would have relevance in that area.

Now the situation with regard to morals is altogether parallel, as we saw earlier in this chapter. Most people share quite an area of moral agreement. They start from their common basis to try to settle disagreement by the recognized routes which I sketched earlier in the chapter. This procedure may not always produce agreement within a finite time, but there is no obvious stopping-point. There are always ways of going on. We can adduce new cases, argue further about consistency, etc. Since philosophy is just like morals in the extent of ready agreement that can be reached, there is an obvious conclusion—that if philosophy is an objective discipline, so is morals. You may say that I have exaggerated the extent of the parallels between philosophy and morals, and that agreement is easier to come by in philosophy. I do not think that I have exaggerated; but even if agreement is easier to come by in philosophy, there are explanations of this which are very plausible and have nothing to do with philosophy being a more objective kind of discipline. These are the temptations to irrationality in morals—which we saw earlier—and the great skill which philosophers possess in argument.

So my argument in summary is as follows. If morality is objective, the naturalistic account of it is correct and morality is based on a set of logically necessary truths. In one discipline concerned with logically necessary truths, viz. philosophy, it is as easy or difficult to reach agreed results as it is in morals. Yet there is a sufficient amount and kind of agreement over methods and results in philosophy for it to be termed an objective discipline, and its results termed true or false. Therefore morals is also properly accounted an objective discipline and moral judgements correctly termed true or false. The extent to which agreement on moral judgements is possible when men are determined to reach conclusions to which they can honestly assent is emphasized by Hare in *Freedom and Reason*. But he does not draw the conclusion which seems to me to follow—that morality is a discipline which yields results which are true or false. Of course morality has its 'fanatics', unconvertible to the majority view in a lifetime; but philosophy has its fair share of those too. Their existence is not seen to cast a serious doubt on the objectivity of philosophy. Why take them more seriously in morals?

I conclude that moral judgements such as that an action x is a right action or that it is morally better than y, or that actions of type A are never morally good, are statements which are true or false. To say this is, however, not to deny that actions are often morally on a level. I do not wish to deny that often there are no overriding reasons for doing some one action rather than some other action or rather than refraining from any action at all. Nor do I wish to deny that various life-styles are often morally on a level—your way of living may be very different from mine, and yet there be no overriding reason for pursuing my life-style rather than yours. All that I am claiming is that sometimes it is not like this—some actions, some life-styles are morally better or worse than others. And judgements which affirm that this is so, as also judgements which affirm that it is not morally better to do a certain action than not to do it, are statements which are true or false. We have good reason for saying that judgements about the moral goodness or badness of actions are true or false. That being so, an omniscient person (one 'omniscient' in the attenuated sense delinated at the end of Chapter 10) will know of any action, the characteristics of which are fully set out (e.g. that it is done by a person of such-and-such a kind in such-and-such circumstances), whether or not that action is morally good or bad. While we have rather cloudy feelings that abortion and euthanasia are evils, he will know the truth about these matters (whatever it is) with crystal clarity. He will in consequence know at any time of the actions which it is logically possible that he do at that time whether or not they are good or bad. An omniscient person who is also perfectly free will necessarily do right actions and avoid wrong ones—since, we saw in Chapter 8, being perfectly free, he will necessarily do those actions which he believes right and avoid those which he believes wrong, and, we have now seen, being omniscient, he will hold true beliefs in this field.[15] A man may fail to do his duty because he does not recognize what his duty is or because he yields to non-rational influences outside his control. But neither of these possibilities is a possibility for a perfectly free and omniscient person. It is logically necessary that a perfectly free and omniscient person be perfectly good.

While I have argued in this chapter that moral judgements are true or false, I have not argued for the truth or falsity of any particular moral judgement. Where the issue is in dispute, an attempt to show in any way conclusively that some particular moral judgement is true can be a lengthy business. However, two of my subsequent results depend for their correctness on the truth or falsity of some particular moral judgement. I shall produce arguments for the judgement in question. I regard these arguments as good arguments and I hope that they will convince many. Some readers, however, will find them too brief. I can only plead considerations as to what is a desirable

[15] Kant describes the moral situation of such a being in his *Groundwork of the Metaphysic of Morals*, Ch. II (see p. 81 in the translation by H. J. Paton of this work under the title *The Moral Law*, London, 1953).

length of this book as my excuse. Adequate argument in favour of these moral judgements could only be given in the context of a book about morality, and this book is not primarily about morality.

A Source of Moral Obligation

The second claim of theism to be analysed in this chapter is the claim that if God issues commands they create moral obligations; that actions become our duty or become wrong, when commanded or forbidden, as the case may be, by God; that man's duty is to conform to the announced will of God. Is it coherent to suppose that man's duty is to conform to the announced will of a certain perfectly free and omnipresent spirit who is the creator of the universe, omnipotent, and omniscient?

A theist who makes this claim about duty is faced with a traditional dilemma first stated in Plato's *Euthyphro*[16]—are actions which are obligatory, obligatory because God makes them so (e.g. by commanding men to do them), or does God urge us to do them because they are obligatory anyway? To take the first horn of this dilemma is to claim that God can of his free choice make actions obligatory or non-obligatory (or make it obligatory not to do some action). Yet the critic may rightly object that torturing children or genocide are immoral, whether or not God commands them. God's command could not make such actions right. To take the second horn of the dilemma is to claim that actions are good or bad in themselves and remain so whatever choices God makes. This horn has seemed an uncomfortable one for the theist for three reasons. The first is that it seems to place a restriction on God's power if he cannot make any action which he chooses good. Our answer to this objection is clear. It is no restriction on God's power that he cannot do the logically impossible. *If* it is logically necessary, as we have claimed, that *certain* actions, e.g. genocide, are wrong, then God can no more make them right than he can make a man both married and a bachelor at the same time. The second objection to taking the second horn is that it seems to limit what God can command us to do. God, if he is to be

16 *Euthyphro*, 9e.

God, cannot command us to do what, independently of his will, is wrong—since, it is plausible to suppose, it is morally wrong to command a man to do what is morally wrong. Our answer to this objection is similar to our answer to the first objection. An omniscient and perfectly free being can—for logical reasons—do no wrong. Hence he cannot command wrong-doing. This in a way limits his power but makes him, for reasons considered earlier, no less worthy of worship. The third objection to taking the second horn is that traditionally God has been believed to have the right at will to command men to do at any rate many things, and men to have an obligation to do those things merely because he commanded them.

To meet this third objection to taking the second horn and also the earlier objection to taking the first horn, it seems to me that the most plausible course for the theist to take is to take different horns for different actions, and to say that *some* actions are right or wrong independently of what anyone commands, and that *some* actions are made right or wrong by divine command. Genocide and torturing children are wrong and would remain so whatever commands any person issued. It would follow, as we have seen that no omniscient and perfectly free person could command us to do them.[17] However, the theist may claim that *many* actions are such that if God commands them we have an obligation to do them. It would be because it is an analytic truth that if anyone with certain properties commanded us to do such and such actions, we would have an obligation to do them. For example, it may be suggested that a man has an obligation to attend Mass on Sundays or to care for the sick in Africa, if God commands, but not otherwise.

A powerful argument against this position is that we know perfectly well how to decide moral issues without bringing in the commands of God. Suppose we debate the rightness or wrongness of capital punishment. We know the kind of considerations which count for or against the wrongness of capital punishment as a penalty for murder. For is the consideration that if you find out that you have wrongly executed a man, you

---

[17] That the rightness or wrongness of certain actions is unalterable by divine command is the view of Aquinas. See his *Summa Theologiae*, II.2ae. 100.8 ad 2 and also II.2ae.94.5. For Aquinas the first principles of natural law are completely unalterable.

cannot remit any of his penalty or make amends. Against is the horror of murder and the need for an adequate punishment. Statistics of the deterrent effect of capital punishment or the lack of it are also relevant to one or other side of the controversy. We know how to settle the matter without bringing God in. Rightness or wrongness being establishable independently of God, his command cannot alter things.

This argument, though it seems initially powerful, is confused. Certainly we know how to decide moral issues if we ignore divine commands by supposing that there are none. But that does not mean that divine commands, if there are any, are irrelevant to moral issues; any more than the fact (if it is a fact) that we can show the wrongness of capital punishment, if we ignore any possible deterrent effect (i.e. suppose there to be none), means that deterrent effects, if they exist, are irrelevant to its rightness or wrongness. Maybe divine commands, if they exist, are relevant, possibly decisively relevant, even though we can settle moral issues on the assumption that divine commands do not exist. I shall now proceed to argue that if God has issued commands, they do have moral relevance.

Their relevance is nothing to do with the power of God.[18] Power does not give the right to command, even if it is infinite power and even if it is benevolent power. There seem to me at least two different characteristics among those traditionally ascribed to God which make his commands impose moral obligations on a man which would not otherwise exist. The first is that he is that man's creator and sustainer. Men depend for their existence at each instant on his will. Now many would hold that men have an obligation to please their benefactors. A man who makes no effort to please those who have done much for him is generally felt to be behaving in a morally bad way. A consequence of the general principle that men have an obligation to please their benefactors is that children have an obligation to please parents, who brought them into the world and keep them alive, clothe, and feed them. The obligation to please parents would be fulfilled by conforming to the parents' wishes (which may be expressed by commands), e.g. that the child should do the shopping or the washing-up, go

[18] Contrary to what Peter Geach seems to claim. See his *God and the Soul* (London 1969), p. 127. For criticism of this see D. Z. Phillips, *Death and Immortality*, Ch. 2.

to bed at a certain time or shut the door. There might be no special reason why the child ought or ought not to go to bed at the time in question other than that the parent has commanded it. But the parent's command makes what was otherwise not a duty a duty for the child. The child owes something to the parent in view of the parent's status. It is not that children have a duty to pay something back to the parent, but that because in an important respect the parent is the source of their being he is entitled to their consideration.

The moral views expressed in the last paragraph are by no means universal, but they are, I suspect, held by a considerable majority of the human race. A morality which did not think the worse of a man for making no effort to please those who had done him much good would seem a pretty poor morality. If the moral views of the last paragraph are correct then men are under a great obligation to obey the commands of God—a great obligation because, if God is our creator and sustainer, our dependence as the children of God on God is so much greater than the dependence of the children of men on men. We depend to a large extent on our parents for our initial existence and to some extent for our subsequent existence—they provide food, shelter, etc. But we depend on other persons too for our subsequent existence—the police, our parents' employers, the state's welfare officers, etc. And our parents are only able to bring us into existence and sustain us because of the operation of various natural laws (e.g. the laws of genetics and embryology), the operation of which, is, on the theistic hypothesis, due to God. However, our dependence on God, the author of nature, is, if he exists, far greater. He gave to our parents the power and inclination to bring us into being, and to them and to others the power to keep us alive. He keeps operative natural laws, as a result of which we have food and drink and health. Our obligation to God must be correspondingly very much greater than to our parents.

The other characteristic among those traditionally ascribed to God which makes his commands impose moral obligations which would not otherwise exist is that he is the creator of the rest of the universe other than men; he brought it into existence and keeps it in existence, and so is properly adjudged its owner. What greater claim could one have to property than having created it *e nihilo*, and kept it in being by one's free choice, unaided? The owner of property has the right to tell those to whom he has loaned it what they are allowed to do with it. Consequently God has a right to lay down how that property, the inanimate world, shall be used and by whom. If God has made the earth, he can say which of his children can use which part. The Bible is full of claims that God has given to persons various possessions (and thereby commanded other persons to leave them alone). Thus the Lord is said to have declared to Joshua that he gave to the Israelites the land of Canaan (Joshua 1:2 ff.). The right of God to dispose of the material objects of the world as he wishes is affirmed by Aquinas: 'What is taken by God's command, who is the owner of the universe, is not against the owner's will, and this is the essence of theft'.[19] It follows from this that it is logically impossible for God to command a man to steal—for whatever God commands a man to take thereby becomes that man's and so his taking it is not stealing.

Again, the moral principle about property to which I have appealed would not be universally accepted, but, possibly with qualifications, it would, I believe, be very generally accepted, and for those who do accept it the conclusion about God follows directly. So appealing to widely accepted moral principles,[20] I have argued that, if God is the creator of man and of the inanimate world, his commands can impose obligations which did not exist before. By parity of argument the commands of the creator can add to the obligation to do an action which is obligatory anyway. An action of a child which is wrong anyway becomes wrong in a new way if the parent forbids it.

Still, there are surely limits to the obligations which a divine command could create. Exactly where they are to be put men will differ. There are certainly limits to the obligations which a human parent's command can create, and to the obligations to obey a human owner of property in respect of its use. If a parent commands a child to kill his neighbour, the command

---

[19] *Summa Theologiae*, vol. xxviii (London, 1966; trans. Thomas Gilby, O.P.), Ia.2ae.94.5.ad 2.

[20] In his paper 'Morality and Religion Reconsidered' (pub. in Baruch A. Brody (ed.), *Readings in the Philosophy of Religion*) Baruch A. Brody argues along similar lines to myself, that the two cited moral principles may provide a reason why the commands of God make actions right or wrong.

imposes no obligation. Nor does the command of an owner of vast estates not to use some of his unwanted corn to feed the starving. At least, most people would accept these moral judgements. Some might urge that if God is our creator, he is so much more truly the author of our being and the owner of the land than are human parents and property-owners that there are no limits to the obligations which would be produced by his commands.[21] But most would surely judge that even God could not remove my obligation to keep a solemn promise when the keeping of it would cause pain to no one, or my obligation not to torture the innocent. But if God has the properties which we have discussed so far and there is some action A which it would still be our duty not to do even if God commanded it; then, as we saw earlier, God would not command us to do A. For then commanding us to do A would be commanding us to do wrong. Since, it is plausible to suppose, to command to do wrong is morally wrong, God who necessarily wills the good would not incite to evil.

I have argued in the last few paragraphs for the truth of certain moral principles. It would follow from the truth of these principles that an omnipresent spirit, who is perfectly free, the creator of the universe, omnipotent, and omniscient, would have a right to command men to do many things, though perhaps not quite everything. It would also follow that in so far as he did not have the right to command, it would be for logical reasons that he did not have this right (because it is an analytic truth that certain actions are right or wrong, whatever any person may command). It would also follow that, being omniscient and perfectly free, he would not command that which he had no right to command.

It is possible that one might wish to describe this situation in terms rather different from those which I have used, and to confine the word 'obligation' to describe an act which, once he has been commanded to do it, it would be wrong for an agent not to do (and similarly to confine talk of acts which one 'ought' to do or are one's 'duty' to do to acts made wrong not to do by a command). Then one could say that although many acts are wrong, even though there is no obligation not to do

[21] As William of Ockham seems to have held. See F. C. Copleston, *A History of Philosophy*, vol. iii (London, 1953), pp. 104 f.

them, many other acts are made wrong, and so there is an obligation not to do them, because they are forbidden by God (i.e. God commands us not to do them). Scotus claimed[22] that although acts were often good or bad in themselves apart from considerations about God, God's commands made it obligatory to do them or obligatory not to do them. The same point is, involved in what Professor Anscombe claims in her article 'Modern Moral Philosophy'[23] when she claims that the concept of obligation only has a sense within a law concept of ethics, that is within a concept of ethics in which to be obliged is to be commanded. My argument suggests that commands sometimes make acts right or wrong and make acts which are right or wrong anyway right or wrong in a new respect. We could well reserve the word 'obligation' to refer to an act which it is wrong not to do, and which is made thus by a command. I have not myself used 'obligation' in this way, because I do not think that normally its use is restricted in this way. But there would be a point in so restricting its use in order to give a name to a certain kind of act which otherwise does not have one.

It follows from the arguments of this chapter that—given that there is an omnipresent spirit, perfectly free, creator of the universe, omnipotent, and omniscient—not merely is it coherent to suppose that he is perfectly good and the source of the obligatoriness of many duties, but that it would be incoherent to suppose anything else. An individual's being perfectly good and the source of the obligatoriness of many duties follows from his possession of the other properties just listed.

[22] See Copleston, *A History of Philosophy*, vol. ii (London, 1950), p. 547.
[23] *Philosophy*, 1958, **33**, 1–19.

12

Eternal and Immutable

THE argument of Part II so far has been that it is coherent to suppose that there exists now an omnipotent spirit, who is perfectly free, the creator of the universe, omnipotent, omniscient, perfectly good, and a source of moral obligation—so long as 'omnipotent' and 'omniscient' are understood in somewhat restricted senses. I shall consider in this chapter two further suppositions which the theist makes—that this being is an eternal being and is immutable.

Eternal

The property of being creator of the universe is different from the other properties which we have considered so far in the following respect. To say that there exists now a being with the other properties does not entail the existence of such a being at any other time. A being with all the other properties could come into existence yesterday and cease to exist today—though his ceasing to exist today could not have been something which was against his choice; otherwise he would not have been omnipotent before ceasing to exist. However, if a creator of the universe exists now, he must have existed at least as long as there have been other logically contingent existing things. For a creator of the universe is (see pp. 130f.) one who brings about or makes or permits other beings to bring about the existence of all logically contingent things which exist, i.e. have existed, exist, or will exist. On the assumption that an agent can only bring about effects subsequent to his action, he must have existed at least as long as created things.

However, traditionally theists believe not merely that this

spirit, God, exists now or has existed as long as created things, but that he is an eternal being. This seems to mean, firstly, that he has always existed—that there was no time at which he did not exist—and that he has always had the properties which we have been considering. Let us put this point by saying that they believe that he is backwardly eternal. The supposition that a spirit of the above kind is backwardly eternal seems to be a coherent one. If, as I have argued, it is coherent to suppose that such a spirit exists at the present time, then it would seem coherent to suppose that he exists at any other nameable time; and, if that is coherent, then surely it is coherent to suppose that there exists a being now such that however far back in time you count years you do not reach the beginning of its existence. The above spirit could surely be of that kind. Then he would be backwardly eternal. Various writers have suggested that endless life would be tedious, boring, and pointless. An omnipotent being could, however, if he so chose, ensure that his life was not tedious or boring. And given, as I have argued, that there are true moral judgements, there will often be a point in doing one thing rather than another.

The doctrine that God is eternal seems to involve, secondly, the doctrine that the above spirit will go on existing for ever, continuing for ever to possess the properties which I have discussed. I will put this point by saying that he is forwardly eternal. This too seems to be a coherent suggestion. We, perhaps, cease to exist at death. But we can surely conceive of a being now existent such that whatever future nameable time you choose, he has not by that time ceased to exist; and the spirit described above could be such a being. A being who is both backwardly and forwardly eternal we may term an eternal being.

The above seems the natural way of interpreting the doctrine that God is eternal, and it is, I have urged, a coherent one. However, there is in the Christian theistic tradition an alternative way of interpreting this doctrine, and I shall consider this alternative after considering the doctrine of God's immutability.

Immutable

Closely connected with the doctrine of God's eternity is the doctrine of his immutability. Theists traditionally claim that God is immutable, that he cannot change.

We can understand 'immutable' in a weaker or stronger way. In the weaker way to say of a person that he is immutable is simply to say that he cannot change in character. To say of a free and omniscient creator that he is immutable is simply to say that, while he continues to exist, necessarily he remans fixed in his character. We saw in Chapter 11 that of logical necessity a person who is perfectly free and omniscient will be perfectly good. Hence a person cannot change in character while he remains perfectly free and omniscient. According to traditional theism God is eternally perfectly free and omniscient, and so it follows that he will not change in character. Given the doctrine which I shall discuss later that God necessarily possesses such properties as freedom and omniscience, it will follow that he cannot change in character, and so is immutable in the weaker sense. God's immutability in this sense is of course something which theism has always wished to affirm.

Theists have, however, sometimes understood immutability in a much stronger sense. On this understanding to say that God is immutable is to say that he cannot change *at all*. The doctrine of divine immutability in this sense is often combined with the doctrine of divine timelessness. But for the moment I shall consider it independently of the latter doctrine. To investigate the coherence of the suggestion that a person with the properties so far delineated be immutable in this strong sense, we must begin by asking what it is to change.

There is a famous but clearly unsatisfactory criterion of change, which Professor Geach has called the Cambridge criterion.[1] According to this a thing x changes if some predicate 'φ' applies to it at one time, but not at another. Thus my tie has changed if it was clean yesterday, but is not clean today. But although everything which 'changes' in the ordinary sense does seem to 'change' by the Cambridge criterion, the converse is not true. Sometimes a predicate 'φ' applies to an object x at one time, but not at another without that thing having 'changed' in the ordinary sense of the word. Socrates may at one time be thought about by Smith and at a later time not be thought

[1] P. T. Geach, 'What Actually Exists', *Proceedings of the Aristotelian Society*, Suppl. Vol., 1968, **42**, 7–16. Reprinted in his *God and the Soul*, pp. 65–74; see pp. 71 f.

about by Smith, without Socrates having changed. Or John may be at one time taller than James and at another time John may not be taller than James—without John having changed at all. It may be simply the case that James has grown.

Real change must be distinguished from mere Cambridge change. An attempt to bring out the difference has been made by T. P. Smith.[2] He claims that the Cambridge criterion is perfectly satisfactory for non-relational predicates. A relational predicate is one which expresses a relation to some individual. Thus 'moves', 'talks', 'is green', 'is square' are non-relational predicates; whereas 'hits John', 'thinks of the man in the moon', 'opens the door', etc. are relational predicates. Where we have a relational predicate of the form ' . . . Ry' (viz. ' . . . has relation R to y'), all that follows from x being Ry at one time and not being Ry at another is that either x has changed or y has changed or both have changed—given that ' . . . Ry' is not a predicate of spatial relation, such as 'is to the left of Jones', in which case we cannot conclude even that. So, given that ' . . . Ry' is not a predicate of spatial relation, x has changed if x is Ry at one time and not at another, and if y has not changed between these times. (If y has changed, x may have changed also, or it may not.) Thus if James has not changed, and John is at one time shorter than James, and at another and later time not shorter than James, then John has changed by getting taller. But something does not change merely because it is now thought about, and then not thought about by John. The criterion can only be applied to yield results in the case of relational predicates if we already have some understanding of what it is for something to change (for one can only conclude that x has changed if one knows that y has not). Nor, if we know that y has changed can we conclude whether or not x has changed merely from knowing that x has a certain relation to y at one time but not at another. But the criterion does bring out to some limited extent what is involved in real as opposed to mere Cambridge change.

Now given this understanding of change, what is it to say that God does not change at all ? This would not rule out God at one time not being worshipped by Augustine, and at a later time being worshipped by Augustine. For in such a case,

[2] T. P. Smith, 'On the Applicability of a Criterion of Change', *Ratio*, 1973, **15**, 325–33.

intuitively, Augustine changes but God does not. It might seem that it rules out God acting—for acts take place at particular times; in acting God changes from not doing a certain action to doing that action. This difficulty could be avoided if one said that all that God brings about he has chosen 'from all eternity' to bring about. The effects (e.g. the fall of Jerusalem, the fall of Babylon) which God brings about occur at particular times (587 B.C. and 538 B.C. respectively). Yet God has always meant them to occur at those times—i.e. there was no time at which God did not intend Jerusalem to fall in 587 B.C. When 587 B.C. arrived there was no change in God—the arrival of the moment put into effect the intention which God always had. This view would need to be made more sophisticated to deal with the suggestion that God's bringing out one state of affairs, say A, rather than another, say B, was due to his reaction to the behaviour of men (e.g. men may have behaved badly and so God gave them drought instead of rain). The view in question would have to claim that in such circumstances 'from all eternity' God had intended that A-occur-if-men did so-and-so, and that B-occur-if-men did such-and-such.

If God had thus fixed his intentions 'from all eternity' he would be a very lifeless thing; not a person who reacts to men with sympathy or anger, pardon or chastening because he chooses to there and then. Yet, as we saw in Chapter 10, the God of the Old Testament, in which Judaism, Islam, and Christianity have their roots, is a God in continual interaction with men, moved by men as they speak to him, his action being often in no way decided in advance. We should note, further, that if God did not change at all, he would not think now of this, now of that. His thoughts would be one thought which lasted for ever.

It seems to me that although the God of the Old Testament is not pictured as such a being, nevertheless a perfectly free person might act in fact only on intentions which he had had from all eternity, and so in a strong sense never change. However, a perfectly free person could not be immutable in the strong sense, that is *unable* to change. For an agent is perfectly free at a certain time if his action results from his own choice at that time and if his choice is not itself brought about by anything else. Yet a person immutable in the strong sense would be unable to perform any action at a certain time other than what he had previously intended to do. His course of action being fixed by his past choices, he would not be perfectly free. Being perfectly free is incompatible with being immutable in the strong sense. We could attempt to save the coherence of the supposition that God is both perfectly free and immutable (in the strong sense) by pleading that words are being used analogically, but there seems no need whatever for this manoeuvre here, because there is no need whatever for the theist to say that God is immutable in the strong sense.

Why should many theists have wished to suppose that God is immutable in the strong sense? The belief that God is immutable in this sense does not seem to me to be much in evidence in Christian tradition until the third or fourth century A.D. It came, I suspect, from neo-Platonism. For a Platonist things which change are inferior to things which do not change. Aquinas, claiming that God is altogether unchangeable, gives as one of his reasons that 'anything in change acquires something through its change, attaining something not previously attained. Now God . . . embracing within himself the whole fullness of perfection of all existence cannot acquire anything.'[3] Being perfect already he can lack nothing. However, an obvious answer to this point is to suggest that the perfection of a perfect being might consist not in his being in a certain static condition, but in his being in a certain process of change. Only neo-Platonic dogma would lead us to suppose otherwise. That God is completely changeless would seem to be for the theist an unnecessary dogma. It is not, I have suggested, one implicit in the Old or New Testaments. Nor, I would think, is it one to which very many modern theists are committed, unless they have absorbed Thomism fairly thoroughly.

Timelessness

Armed with the results of the last few pages, I now return to consider an alternative interpretation of the doctrine that God is eternal, alternative to the simple interpretation that God's eternity consists in his always having existed and his going to exist for ever. This simple interpretation, I urged earlier, was a coherent one.

[3] *Summa Theologiae*, vol. ii, 1a.9.1.

The alternative interpretation of God's eternity is that to say that God is eternal is to say that he is timeless, that he exists outside the 'stream' of time. His actions are timeless, although they have their effects in time. His thoughts and reactions are timeless, although they may be thoughts about or reactions to things in time. His knowledge is timeless, although it includes knowledge of things in time. There is no temporal succession of states in God. Another way of putting these points is to say that God has his own time scale. There is only one instant of time on the scale; and everything which is ever true of God is true of him at that instant. In a sense, however, that instant of time lasts for ever. In this chapter I wish to consider whether it is a coherent claim that God is timeless and whether it is one which the theist needs to make.

Most of the great Christian theologians from Augustine to Aquinas taught that God is timeless. The best-known exposition of this doctrine occurs in the last section of the *Consolation of Philosophy* of the sixth-century Christian philosopher Boethius. Let us look at Boethius's exposition. God, Boethius says, is eternal, but not in the sense that he always has existed and always will exist. Plato and Aristotle thought that the world always had existed and always would exist. Christian revelation had shown that the world had a beginning and would have an end in time. But even if Plato and Aristotle had been right, that would not mean that the world was eternal in the sense in which God is eternal. 'Let us say that God is eternal, but that the world lasts for ever.' God, however, is eternal in being present at once to all times which from our view at any one time may be past or future. God is thus outside the stream of temporal becoming and passing away. Boethius's much-quoted definition of eternity is that it is 'the complete and perfect possession at once of an endless life'. 'For it is one thing to be carried through an endless life which Plato attributed to the world, another thing to embrace together the whole presence of an endless life, a thing which is the manifest property of the divine mind.'[4] The obvious analogy is to men travelling along a road; at each time they can see only the neighbourhood on the road where they are. But God is above the road and can see the whole road at once. Taking man's progress along the road as his progress through

---

[4] Boethius, *On the Consolation of Philosophy*, 5.6.

time, the analogy suggests that while man can enjoy only one time at once, God can enjoy all times at once. God is present to all times at once, just as he is present to all places at once. This doctrine of God's eternity provided Boethius with a neat solution of the problem of divine foreknowledge. Because all times are present to God, God can just as easily see our future acts as other men can see our present acts. But this does not affect their freedom. Just as the fact that we see a man acting now does not mean that he is not acting freely, so God's seeing a man acting in the future does not mean that the man will not act freely. For God does not ever see what are from our point of view future acts, *as* future. He always (on his time scale) sees them as present, and hence the difficulties discussed in Chapter 10 concerning God's present knowledge of our future free actions do not arise.

This doctrine of divine timelessness is very little in evidence before Augustine. The Old Testament certainly shows no sign of it. For Old Testament writers, as has been noted, God does now this, now that; now destroys Jerusalem, now lets the exiles return home. The same applies in general for the New Testament writers, although there are occasional sentences in the New Testament which could be interpreted in terms of this doctrine. Thus in the Revelation of St. John the Divine God is described more than once as 'Alpha and Omega, the beginning and the end' and also as he 'which was and is and is to come'. But it seems to be reading far too much into such phrases to interpret them as implying the doctrine of divine timelessness. Like the doctrine of his total immutability, the doctrine of God's timelessness seems to have entered Christian theology from neo-Platonism, and there from Augustine to Aquinas it reigned. Duns Scotus seems to have rejected it and so did William of Ockham. It seems to have returned to Catholic theology from the sixteenth century onwards, but to have had comparatively little influence in Protestant theology. Post-Hegelian Protestant theology explicitly rejects it. For Hegel the Absolute or God was essentially something in process and Tillich acknowledges his debt here to Hegel, by claiming that Hegel's 'idea of a dialectical movement within the Absolute is in agreement with the genuine meaning of eternity. Eternity is not timelessness'.

Tillich claims that God is not outside the temporal process, for, if he were, he would be lifeless. Only a God who acts and chooses and loves and forgives is the God whom we wish to worship, and the pursuit of these activities, since they involve change of state, means being in time. 'If we call God a living God, we affirm that he includes temporality and with this a relation to the modes of time.'[5] Exactly the same point is made by Barth,[6] though he argues not only from the general fact that God is a living God but also from the particular fact of the Incarnation. The Incarnation means, according to Barth, that God acts at a particular temporal moment. Only a temporal being can do this. 'Without God's complete temporality the content of the Christian message has no shape'.[7,8]

The reasons why theists would wish to adopt this doctrine are interior to theism. That is, it is felt by some theists to be better consonant with other things which they wish to say, to say that God is timeless than to say that he lives through time. However, it seems to me that the reasons which the scholastics had for putting forward the doctrine of timelessness were poor ones. A major consideration for them seems to have been that this doctrine would provide backing for and explanation of the doctrine of God's total immutability. For if God is timeless he is totally immutable—although it does not follow that if he is totally immutable he is timeless. Aquinas seems to have thought that the latter did follow: 'something lacking change and never varying its mode of existence will not display a before and after'.[9] God's eternity (in the sense of timelessness), he claimed, 'follows upon unchangeableness, and God alone . . . is alto-

---

[5] *Systematic Theology*, vol. i, p. 305.

[6] Also by O. Cullman in *Christ and Time* (London, 1951), Pt. I, Chs. 3 and 4. Cullman owes an obvious debt to Barth.

[7] K. Barth, *Church Dogmatics*, II (i) (Edinburgh, 1957), p. 620.

[8] For a fuller statement of the history of the doctrine in Christian theology, see Nelson Pike, *God and Timelessness* (London, 1970), esp. pp. 180–7, and the opening pages of an article of mine, 'The Timelessness of God', *Church Quarterly Review*, 1965, 323–37 and 472–86. The later philosophical part of this article now seems to me mistaken both in its argumentation and in its conclusion. It mistakenly assumed that the only proper kind of explanation was scientific explanation, and reached the conclusion, which I now regard as mistaken, that the timelessness of God was a doctrine needed by Christian theism. Pike's book, in contrast, is a very careful systematic treatment of this issue which reaches the opposite conclusion, which now seems to me the correct one.

[9] *Summa Theologiae*, vol. ii, Ia.10.1.

gether unchangeable'.[10] However, this seems mistaken. A totally immutable thing could just go on existing for ever without being timeless—especially if other things, such as the universe, changed, while the immutable thing continued changeless. The change of other things would measure the passage of time during which the immutable thing changed not. Still, the timelessness of God would explain God's total immutability, if he was totally immutable. But we have seen no reason why the theist should advocate God's total immutability.

A second reason why the scholastics adopted the doctrine of timelessness is, as we saw for Boethius, that it allowed them to maintain that God is omniscient in the very strong sense which was discussed in Chapter 10. God outside time can be said never not to know our free actions, even though they may sometimes be future from our point of view. Since they are never future for God, he sees them as present and this does not endanger their free character. In view of the general Christian tradition that God's omniscience includes knowledge of future free human actions, the doctrine of timelessness does seem to have the advantage of saving the former doctrine against obvious difficulties. I urged in Chapter 10, however, that the view that God's omniscience includes knowledge of future free human actions is easily detachable from the theistic tradition.

A further reason why a theist might want to adopt the doctrine, although, as far as I know, it was not one put forward by the scholastics is the following. A man, especially a modern man, might feel that a temporal being was as such less than perfect in that his mere existence in time would mean that he was as it were continually losing parts of his existence all the while. As today ends and tomorrow begins, the being has lost today—his existence today is dead and gone, for ever unrecallable:

> Time, you old gypsy man, will you not stay,
> Put up your caravan just for one day?

But *why* does the continual passage of time mean loss for those who live in it? Obvious answers are—that they get older and so weaker, that new experiences are not so exciting as old ones, and that they draw nearer to death, which, they fear, is the

[10] Ibid., Ia.10.3.

end. All of these are indeed proper reasons for regretting the passage of time; and if the passage of time had these consequences for God, he would indeed have cause for regret. But these are mere factual consequences of the passage of time for mortal finite man; an omnipotent being need not suffer them. But still, it might be felt, there are some consequences of life in time which even an omnipotent being would have to suffer. These are that the moment certain states, experiences, and actions are past, they are for ever unrepeatable. If he performed a certain A on one day, he could not perform exactly that action on another day—he could only perform one qualitatively similar. This is true of logical necessity. States, experiences, actions, etc. are individuated by the time of their occurrence. An 'action' is a numerically different individual 'action' from a similar action tomorrow, because of the criteria which we have for distinguishing one 'action' from another. But what real loss does this fact mean? If I can tomorrow have states and do actions qualitatively as similar as I like to those of today, why should the passage of time cause me regret? And anyway, even if this limitation is a logically necessary one for all beings in time it is one which a being who lives and acts, chooses and reacts in anything like a literal sense will—of logical necessity— have to endure. Such a being may still be as close as it is logically possible for a being to be to being perfect.

So much for the reasons why a theist might wish to claim that God is timeless. I have urged that they are not very good reasons. Further, the claim that God is timeless, as I have expounded it, seems to contain an inner incoherence and also to be incompatible with most things which theists ever wish to say about God.

The inner incoherence can be seen as follows. God's timelessness is said to consist in his existing at all moments of human time—simultaneously. Thus he is said to be simultaneously present at (and a witness of) what I did yesterday, what I am doing today, and what I will do tomorrow. But if t_1 is simultaneous with t_2 and t_2 with t_3, then t_1 is simultaneous with t_3. So if the instant at which God knows these things were simultaneous with both yesterday, today, and tomorrow, then these days would be simultaneous with each other. So yesterday would be the same day as today and as tomorrow—which is clearly nonsense. To avoid this awkward consequence we would have to understand 'simultaneously' in a somewhat special stretched sense. The 'simultaneity' holding between God's presence at my actions and those actions would have to differ from normal simultaneity.

The second difficulty is that so many other things which the theist wishes to say about God—that he brings about this or that, forgives, punishes, or warns—are things which are true of a man at this or that time or at all times. If we say that P brings about x, we can always sensibly ask *when* does he bring it about? If we say that P punishes Q, we can always sensibly ask *when* does he punish Q? If P really does 'bring about' or 'forgive' in anything like the normal senses of the words, there must be answers to these questions even if nobody knows what they are. Further, many of these things which the theist wishes to say about God seem to be things the doing of which at one time carries entailments of things being true at later or earlier times. If P at t brings about x, then necessarily x comes into existence (simultaneously with or) subsequently to P's action. If P at t forgives Q for having done x, then Q did x prior to t. If P at t warns Q not to do x, in such a way that Q has an opportunity to heed his warning, then there must be a time subsequent to t at which Q has this opportunity. And so on. So, superficially, the supposition that God could bring things about, forgive, punish, warn, etc. etc. without his doing these things at times before or after other times (often, times on the human scale of time) seems incoherent. Once again, the theist will need to say that God only 'brings about', 'forgives', etc. in senses very different from the normal, if the sentences in which God is said to do these things are to express coherent suppositions.

Generally, the theist's only hope for maintaining the inner coherence of his claim that God is timeless and its coherence with others of his claims would be to maintain that many words are being used in highly analogical senses. When he says that God is a 'person' or 'brings about' states of affairs, or 'knows' what happened yesterday 'at the same time as' he 'knows' what happens tomorrow and that he 'knows' all these things at and only 'at the same time as' they happen, the theist could claim that the words involved here are being used in highly stretched senses, so that there is no incoherence in what is being said and no incompatibility with other things which the theist wishes to say. When discussing the analogical use of words in Chapter 4, I warned that although a theist would be justified on occasion in using words in an analogical sense, nevertheless too many appeals to analogical senses of words would make sentences in which the words were used empty of content. In this case it seems to me that the theist has no need to make such an appeal. For as I have been urging, the theist has no need to incorporate the doctrine of the timelessness of God into his theism. He can easily do without it and all the difficulties which it brings,[11] and rely instead on the simple and easy coherent understanding of God's eternity which I delineated earlier.

The Personal Ground of Being

Apart from the property of necessity I have now considered all the main properties traditionally ascribed to God, properties which, in some sense which I shall be discussing shortly, are inalienable from him. Are there any logical relations between the predicates ascribing properties to God or are they just a string of predicates, such that it is coherent to suppose that there might be beings with different combinations of them? I argued in Chapter 11 that—of logical necessity—an omniscient and perfectly free person would be perfectly good, and that a perfectly good creator of the universe would be a source of moral obligation. So, if my arguments are correct, any being which had the other properties would—of logical necessity—be perfectly good and a source of moral obligation.

I wish now to argue for two further entailments between the properties discussed. The first is that any person who is omnipotent and omniscient will be of logical necessity an omnipresent spirit. A person who is omnipotent is able to bring about effects everywhere by basic actions. One who is omniscient at a certain time has justified true beliefs about all things which are going on anywhere at that time. Now if he depended

[11] The doctrine of the timelessness of God is connected in the Thomist system with various connected doctrines, expressed in Aristotelian terminology, that there is no potency in God, that God is pure act, and that God is one pure act. There seem to me similar reasons for adopting or rejecting these doctrines as for adopting or rejecting the doctrine of timelessness.

for his knowledge on the proper functioning of intermediaries such as eyes and ears, then if they were to behave in unusual ways, his beliefs would be false (as are ours when our eyes and ears malfunction). But if there were such intermediaries, as an omniscient being he would know if they were behaving unusually and so would correct his beliefs in the light of this knowledge. Malfunctioning of intermediaries could not lead an omniscient being astray. Hence an omniscient being does not depend for his knowledge on the correct functioning of intermediaries. Hence an omnipotent and omniscient person, in my senses of the terms, is of logical necessity an omnipresent spirit.

The other entailment for which I shall argue is that an eternally omnipotent person (who is also omniscient and perfectly free in our senses of these terms) is necessarily the creator of the universe. A person P who is omnipotent at a time t (in my sense [E]—see p. 160) is able to bring about the existence of any logically contingent state of affairs after t (the description of the occurrence of which does not entail that P did not bring it about at t), given that he does not believe that he has overriding reason for refraining from bringing it about. Now consider for any time t all the logically contingent things which exist at that time. At a time t' immediately precedent to t, an omnipotent being P would have had it in his power to bring about the non-existence of all those things—with the exception to which we will come shortly. In that case, if they exist, they only exist because he brought them about (or permitted them to exist) or made or permitted some other being to bring them about. For each time t there will be a precedent time t' of which this holds. Hence an eternally omnipotent being will at some time have brought about (or permitted to exist) or made or permitted other beings to bring about the existence of, all the things which exist.

The only kind of thing existent at t such that an omnipotent being P would not at t' have had the power to bring about its non-existence is anything such that P believes that he has overriding reason for refraining from bringing about its non-existence, viz. anything for which he believes that he has overriding reason for bringing about its existence. But then, although P's being omnipotent does not entail that he brings about the existence of such things, it follows from his being omnipotent, omniscient, and perfectly free that he will do so. For being omnipotent he will have the power to do so.[12] Being omniscient and perfectly free, he is perfectly good, and hence will bring about those things.

The complex argument of the last two paragraphs may be summarized as follows. If there is an omnipotent being, whatever exists at some time must have existed because he did not stop it existing. The only things which he could not stop from existing are any things which he has overriding reason to bring about. If he is also perfectly free and omniscient, of logical necessity he will bring those things about. I conclude that an eternally omnipotent person who is omniscient and perfectly free is of logical necessity the creator of the universe. Note that God being creator of the universe in my sense does not entail the existence of our universe or any other material universe— only that if any universe does exist God created it or permitted some other being to do so. Theists have always held that God did not have to create the universe.

So then I have claimed that a person who is eternally perfectly free, omnipotent, and omniscient will have the other divine properties which I have considered. He will be an omnipresent spirit, creator of the universe, perfectly good, and a source of moral obligation. I now define such a person as a personal ground of being.[13] The theist's claim is that there exists a personal ground of being. The arguments of Part II have been arguments designed to show that the concept of a personal ground of being is a coherent one. I claim that those arguments do show that.

Although the properties associated together in the property of being a personal ground of being do not, I think, entail each other in any further way, they do belong very naturally together. A person who brings about effects clearly does so in virtue of his powers or capacities. An omnipotent person is a person to whose powers there are no limits but those of logic. If all power is really to be in the hands of some agent, it is natural to suppose

[12] Unless the things are such as to entail that he does not bring them about. But a being can hardly have overriding reason for bringing about a state of affairs, the description of which entails that he does not bring it about; and an omniscient being will know this.

[13] The terminology is of course based on that of Tillich. See, e.g., his *Systematic Theology*, vol. i, Ch. 10.

that how that power is exercised lies also within his hands, and that involves him in being perfectly free. Now an omnipotent being must be able to acquire knowledge of anything, but he need not actually possess knowledge of everything. Yet he clearly has to possess some knowledge. He must, for example, surely know of the basic actions which he is performing, that he is performing them. I can only move my hand, or open my mouth, as basic actions, things which I do meaning to do them, if I know that I am doing them. Further, it would seem very odd to suppose that an omnipotent being might try to do something and yet fail to do it. Yet unless he knew all the truths of logic, this would be possible. For he might try to do something which was (unknown to him) logically impossible. If this is to be ruled out, any omnipotent being would need to know all the truths of logic. However, omnipotence does not seem to entail omniscience. An omnipotent being might well not know how many pennies I have in my pocket—so long as he could acquire that knowledge when he wanted to do anything about them. But given that he must have much knowledge, the most natural assumption about the knowledge of an omnipotent person is that there are no limits to it except those of logic, viz. that he is omniscient. If such a being came into existence at any time, there would clearly in a wide sense be limits to his power. Hence it seems natural to suppose that he is backwardly eternal. Forward eternity seems to fit not unnaturally with backward eternity.

There can only be one personal ground of being. This is because there cannot be causation in a circle. It is incoherent, philosophers generally agree, to suppose that A brings about the existence of B and that B in turn brings about the existence of A. Let us suppose A to be one personal ground of being and B to be another. Let us further suppose, as I shall argue below, that the existence of a personal ground of being is a logically contingent matter; that is, although it may be necessary in some sense, it is not logically necessary. Then A as creator of the universe will have brought about the existence of B, since B is a logically contingent thing apart from A. Conversely, B will have brought about the existence of A. But that is absurd. Therefore there can only be one personal ground of being. Henceforward instead of talking of 'a personal ground of being' we can talk of '*the* personal ground of being'. There can be at most one such.

'*God*' a proper name

In subsequent discussion it will be useful to have a name for the individual who is, on the theist's claim, the personal ground of being. Proper names are words such as 'Socrates', 'Aristotle', 'Disraeli', 'Stalin', 'Edward Heath', used to denote unique individuals. (In the cases cited the individuals are people, but they need not be. 'Red Rum' is the proper name of a horse, and 'Italy' of a country.) Proper names apply to individuals, so long as they remain the same individuals, however they may change in other ways. Proper names are contrasted with definite descriptions. A definite description is a phrase such as 'the Queen of England', 'the President of France', 'the world chess champion'. Like proper names, definite descriptions pick out unique individuals. But a definite description applies to a certain individual only while he has the characteristics set out in the description. These are characteristics which he may lose while continuing to be the same individual. Some writers tend to treat the word 'God' as a definite description shorthand for 'the one and only one perfectly free omnipresent spirit, who is the creator of the universe, omnipotent, omniscient, perfectly good, and a source of moral obligation', or something similar. In that case 'God' would apply to an individual only as long as he retained the stated characteristics. However, I propose henceforward[14] to use 'God' as the proper name of the individual, if there is one, who is the personal ground of being. I suspect that, in treating 'God' as a proper name, I am conforming to majority use.[15]

[14] It has been necessary to use the word 'God' earlier in this book, before it was convenient to introduce the distinction between proper names and definite descriptions. In general, however, throughout the book I have used 'God' only as a proper name, but one or two earlier statements will need to be read slightly differently in order to conform to this precise usage. Thus when on p. 4 I talk of there being 'different definitions of "God" ', this should be understood as claiming that there are different definitions, that is different descriptions, by which an individual who is then given the name 'God' is supposedly picked out.

[15] But not, however, to the use of Aquinas. He treats 'God' as a description roughly equivalent to 'a simple, perfectly good creator'. This is an indefinite description, in the sense that its applicability to a certain individual does not

The status and function of proper names has been the subject of a considerable amount of recent philosophical controversy, in which it would be better to avoid getting too deeply involved. However, I had better discuss briefly the question of what conditions have to be satisfied, where 'A' is a proper name. for 'A exists' or 'A existed' to be true or false. There are two plausible current theories on this issue—one is the descriptive theory, the other the causal theory of proper names.[16] I will present each in the most plausible version known to me.

Consider a proposition such as 'Moses existed' (more naturally perhaps expressed as 'Moses really existed' or 'There really was a man Moses'). The descriptive theory of proper names says that 'Moses existed' is true if and only if many of a set of descriptions currently believed to apply to Moses in fact apply to one individual. Thus we may pick out Moses by the identifying descriptions believed to apply to him—'Israelite who was brought up in Pharaoh's court', 'man who led the Israelites out of Egypt', 'man who led the Israelites through the wilderness', 'man who wrote (or whose teaching led to the writing of) the first five books of the Bible', etc. etc. If many of these descriptions are all true of a single individual, then that individual is Moses and 'Moses existed' is true. If there is no individual to whom many of these descriptions all apply, then there is no individual picked out by the name 'Moses' and 'Moses existed' will be false. In expounding the descriptive theory I have left many aspects of it vague—who has to believe that these descriptions apply? How many constitutes 'many' of the descriptions?—a majority? Or are one or two descriptions of especial importance so that satisfaction of them alone would be enough for the existence claim to be satisfied? What are we to say if more than one individual satisfies the des-

---

immediately entail that he is the only individual to whom it applies (in English indefinite descriptions are indicated by the occurrence of 'a' instead of 'the' in front of the description). Aquinas needs to produce an argument to show that there is only one God—this he does in *Summa Theologiae*, I.11.3; it does not follow immediately from the definition.

[16] For the descriptive theory see, e.g., J. R. Searle, 'Proper Names', *Mind*, 1958, 67, 166–73. For the source of the causal theory see Saul A. Kripke, 'Naming and Necessity' in D. Davidson and G. Harman (eds.), *Semantics of Natural Language* (Dordrecht, Holland, 1972). For elaboration of the latter and discussion of both, see the symposium by Gareth Evans and J. E. J. Altham, 'The Causal Theory of Names', *Proceedings of the Aristotelian Society*, Suppl. Vol., 1973, 47, 197–225.

criptions? I have merely given a skeleton of the theory. As I am expounding it, the theory does not claim that a word such as 'Moses' *means* 'whatever individual uniquely satisfies many of the following descriptions' followed by a number of descriptions *a*, *b*, *c*, *d*. For if that was what was meant, one could not coherently speculate about what would have happened if Moses had been killed at birth, as one clearly can, saying, for example, 'If Moses had been killed at birth, the Israelites would never have left Egypt'. For the supposition that a man had been killed at birth would involve, in most cases, the supposition that the descriptions believed to apply to him in fact did not. Hence the supposition that Moses had been killed at birth would involve a supposition that an individual both satisfied and did not satisfy *a*, *b*, *c*, and *d*. Rather, what the theory claims is that a word such as 'Moses' denotes whatever individual *in fact* satisfies a number of descriptions. Having thus identified the individual, we can then coherently conceive a situation when that individual did not satisfy those descriptions.

The alternative theory to the descriptive theory is the causal theory of proper names. According to this theory, for 'Moses existed' to be true there must have been an individual called to his face by some name 'M' and people who called him this. They then talked to others about 'M' and others understood by 'M' whoever the former referred to by 'M'; and the others talked to yet others about 'M' and the yet others understood by 'M' whoever their informants understood by 'M'. In the course of time 'M' may become, through mishearing or bad transliteration, some other word. Then for 'Moses existed' to be true there must be a continuous causal chain of the kind outlined between the naming of an individual to his face as 'M' and our talk of 'Moses'. If there is, then 'Moses existed' is true; otherwise it is false.

There is no need to discuss in general terms which of these theories is true. I suspect that for some 'A' one theory may give a correct account of the truth conditions of statements of the form 'A exists', and that for other 'A' the other theory may give a correct account of statesments of the form 'A exists'. It seems, however, fairly clear that for the admittedly special case 'God exists'—given that 'God' is a proper name—the descriptive theory gives a satisfactory account. The history of the word 'God' down the ages is quite irrelevant. Men could have put forward in our time the theory that there is an omnipresent, etc. spirit, suggested 'God' as the name of the postulated spirit, and then discussed whether God exists. Their question would be the same question as our question whether God exists. In fact, as the descriptive theory claims, we pick out 'God' by a set of identifying descriptions of the kind which I have been considering in this book—'omnipotent', 'omniscient', 'person', etc. 'God exists' is true if and only if there is an individual who satisfies many of these descriptions. 'Many' is somewhat vague. But clearly if there is one and only one individual who satisfies almost all of them, 'God exists' is true; if there is no individual who satisfies more than one or two of them then 'God exists' is false. If there is an individual who satisfies quite a few of the descriptions, but either no individual or more than one individual who satisfies almost all of them, then 'God exists' is a border-line candidate for being true; it would be as true to say that it is true as to say that it is false.

Having thus analysed the meaning of the proposition ordinarily expressed by 'God exists' (on the supposition that 'God' is a proper name), I propose to use 'God' somewhat more narrowly in future, as the name not of whatever being satisfies most of such descriptions as have been considered in his book, but as the name of whatever individual satisfies the description 'the personal ground of being'. If there is such an individual, then 'God exists' is true; if there is no such individual, then 'God exists' is false. I am thus sharpening up the use of the word 'God', a sharpening needed for my exposition.

PART III

A NECESSARY GOD

13

Kinds of Necessity

THE argument of Part II has been that it is coherent to suppose
that there exists eternally an omnipresent spirit, perfectly free,
the creator of the universe, omnipotent, omniscient, perfectly
good, and a source of moral obligation—so long as 'omnipotent'
and 'omniscient' are understood in somewhat restricted senses.
Such a being I have called a personal ground of being, and I
have argued that there can only be one such being. I am
treating 'God' as the name of the personal ground of being, if
there is such a being. My argument has in no way relied on
supposing that words are used in analogical senses. I have
supposed that the words used above to denote the properties
of the being in question are used in perfectly ordinary senses
or are defined by words which are so used. If the claim of
theism is simply that there exists a personal ground of being then,
I believe, I have proved this claim to be coherent. However, my
proof may not be accepted by all reasonable men for the reasons
given in Chapter 3; they may not find my detailed spelling-out
of the circumstances in which it holds coherent, and they may
not find my claims about what entails what cogent. The only
way to convince such opponents would be by yet more detailed
argument, and the size of this book precludes that. Nevertheless,
I hope that I may have convinced many reasonable men.

However, most theists, and certainly most theologians, have
put forward two further claims which they have made central
to their theism, and to prove these claims coherent or incoherent
will prove far more difficult. The first such claim is that God
does not just happen to exist. It is not a matter of fortunate
accident that there exists God; he exists necessarily. The other
is that God is necessarily the kind of being which he is; God
does not just happen to have the properties which he does. It is

not by chance that he is omnipotent or omniscient. Being omnipotent or omniscient is part of God's nature. There are, as we shall see in Chapter 14, different ways of understanding God's nature. But we shall generally understand it as being a personal ground of being. The theist's claim is then that God is necessarily a personal ground of being. So the theist makes two claims about God's necessity. But what does it mean to say that the things stated are necessarily so? This chapter is devoted entirely to analysing six different kinds of necessity, to setting out six different criteria for a proposition being necessary. With the tools forged in this chapter we can go on in Chapter 14 to investigate on which if any criteria of necessity the theist can coherently make the claims which he wishes to make about God's necessity. Finally, in Chapter 15 I come to the question of which if any of the combinations of properties which I have been discussing an individual would have to have in order to be worthy of worship. The property of being worthy of worship, being a moral property, must be a supervenient property; that is, an individual will possess it in virtue of possessing some natural properties. I shall consider the question of whether the God of traditional theism which I have been describing so far is, if he exists, worthy of worship; whether a being with fewer or other properties than I have been considering would be worthy of worship; or whether only a being with slightly different properties would be worthy of worship.

So in this chapter I come to discuss kinds of necessity. Many writers of earlier decades in the English philosophical tradition have assumed that the only kind of necessity is logical necessity. There is not the slightest reason for supposing that this is so. In ordinary conversation we talk quite naturally and correctly of various things being necessary which are in no way logically necessary. We may naturally and truly say 'In order to get from London to Paris in less than four hours it is necessary to go by air' or 'to obtain social security benefits it is necessary to fill in a form'. Yet neither of the things referred to in these propositions is logically necessary. However, it is not clear that the necessities claimed in these propositions are necessities of a kind of much interest to philosophers. Nevertheless, there are many propositions and states of affairs which philosophers at various times have called 'necessary', when in so doing they

seem to have been using 'necessary' in a not unnatural way but
in a way in which 'necessary' is not the same as the 'logically
necessary'. What is necessary is what must be, what has to be,
what cannot but be. Because the philosophers have wanted to
say that the things of which they talked must be, had to be,
could not but be, they naturally said that they were 'necessary',
but they did not intend to claim that they were logically
necessary.

If a state of affairs is necessary, then the proposition which
states that that state of affairs holds will be necessary; and
conversely, if a proposition is necessary, then the state of affairs
which it states to be the case is necessary. Necessity *de re* entails
necessity *de dicto*, and conversely. So we can in effect analyse
kinds of necessity possessed by states of affairs or propositions
by analysing only the kinds of necessity possessed by propositions. This I shall do. I shall distinguish six different kinds
of necessity, six different criteria on which a proposition is
necessary.

I shall illustrate the different criteria of necessity with examples of propositions which, someone might reasonably claim,
are necessary on each. It will in general be more important for
me to illustrate with moderately plausible examples the
different criteria of necessity, especially the criterion which I
shall call criterion [B], rather than to prove that the examples
are indeed examples of propositions necessary under a specified
criterion of necessity. I shall, however, attempt a proof for
some examples. The immediate relevance of the examples to
the main theme of this book is unlikely to be apparent until
the next chapter.

My first criterion of necessity is simply the criterion of logical
necessity: [A] A proposition is necessary if and only if it is
analytic.

A considerable part of Chapter 2 was devoted to analysis
of the concept of the analytic or logically necessary. I gave there
three equivalent analyses of the analytic. One of them was that
a statement is analytic if and only if it is coherent and its negation is incoherent. Since on my definition a proposition is a
coherent statement, we can say that a proposition is analytic
if and only if its negation is incoherent.

My second criterion of necessity picks out a kind of necessity which seems to be the kind of necessity which a number of philosophers have written about in the last two or three years when they have written about propositions which are not analytic being necessary. This is:

[B] A proposition is necessary if and only if it is incoherent to suppose that the individuals in fact picked out by the referring expressions in the sentence which expresses it do not have the properties and/or relations claimed by the proposition.

I understand by a referring expression a proper name, or a definite description which picks out the individual or individuals which the proposition is 'about'. Now in either case, whether the referring expression is a proper name or a definite description, the proposition will presuppose rather than state the existence of the individuals referred to. Propositions are often 'about' individuals, attributing to them properties or relations. 'The President will be away next week' is about the President, and 'his boss is very irritable' is about the boss. It is of course sometimes unclear which constituents of sentences pick out the individuals which they are about. Is 'among those who called last week was the representative from the trade union' about the representative or is it about those who called last week? Sometimes only the context can reveal (by showing what is the subject of conversation) and sometimes not even the context can reveal. But the undoubted fact that it is sometimes not clear which, if any, expressions are referring expressions does not call into question the equally undoubted fact that it is often clear enough which expressions are referring expressions.

As an example of a proposition necessary on criterion [B] but not on criterion [A] we may take:

(1) The number which is the number of the planets is greater than 6.

The negation of (1) is the statement that states that the number which is the number of the planets is not greater than 6. This seems to be a coherent statement given the understanding of coherence outlined earlier. Yet the referring expression 'the number which is the number of the planets' in fact picks out the number 9 and it is not coherent to suppose that 9 is no greater than 6. So (1), though not analytic, seems necessary on criterion [B]. The converse situation is illustrated by:

(2) The author of Hamlet wrote Hamlet.

The negation of (2) is the statement which states that the author of Hamlet did not write Hamlet and that is incoherent. On the other hand, it is clearly coherent to suppose that the person in fact picked out by 'the author of Hamlet', i.e. Shakespeare, in fact did not write Hamlet. Although it is necessary that whoever wrote Hamlet wrote Hamlet, it is by no means necessary that the man who actually did should have done so. So (2), although analytic, is not necessary on criterion [B]. It is easy to construct other examples of the same pattern as (2). Although 'the Prime Minister is Prime Minister' cannot but be true, the Prime Minister might never have become Prime Minister—he might have become a professional musician instead. Like necessity of type [A], necessity of type [B] arises because there are limits to what can be coherently thought. If a referring expression is to pick out an individual, there have to be criteria which distinguish that individual from others. Hence it will not be coherent to suppose that individual not satisfying those criteria. It is from that incoherence that type [B] necessity arises.

The difference between [A] and [B] turns crucially on what constitutes the negation of a proposition in which a referring expression occurs. The cases which I have considered so far are all ones in which the referring expression is a definite description—e.g. 'the author of Hamlet'. As the above examples illustrate, I understand by the negation of a proposition in which a definite description serves as a referring description, the proposition which says that for *whomsoever* that definite description picks out things are not as the original proposition said. Thus the negation of 'the φ is ψ' says that it is not the case that whoever is uniquely φ is ψ. We could have understood by the negation of such a proposition the proposition which says that for the individual to whom the definite description in fact applies things are not as the original proposition said. But in that case there would be no difference with respect to such propositions between criterion [A] and criterion [B]. Those propositions which satisfied the one would satisfy the other, and conversely. Yet is it clearly useful to distinguish the two kinds of necessity, and that involves understanding negation in the way specified. A similar point applies with respect to propositions in which the referring expression is a proper name. I analysed briefly in the last chapter criteria in virtue of which a proper name applies to an individual. I understand by the negation of a proposition in which a proper name serves as a referring expression the proposition which says that for *whomsoever* the criteria for the application of that proper name pick out, things are not as the original proposition said. There are other ways in which the negation of such a proposition as '*a* is φ' (e.g. 'Socrates is snub-nosed') could be understood. But this way is parallel to the similar way of understanding the negation of propositions in which reference is made by means of a definite description, and it does enable useful distinctions to be made between two different criteria of necessity. Subsequent examples will show what this difference amounts to in the case of propositions in which reference is made by means of proper names.

It is Kripke[1] as much as anyone[2] who in the last year or two has drawn our attention to the complexity of examples such as (1) and (2)—although his concern has been somewhat more with the possibility of propositions being necessary without being *a priori* (and conversely), than with the possibility of propositions being necessary without being analytic (and conversely). But Kripke does not in his discussion provide precise definitions of the terms involved—'necessary', 'analytic', and '*a priori*'.[3] I have attempted to provide a criterion of necessity—criterion [B]—which will, I suggest, classify as necessary many of those propositions which Kripke wishes to call necessary. Apart from (1) above, (3), (4), and (5) below are examples of propositions of different kinds which, Kripke suggests, we might wish to classify as necessary.

(3) Nixon is a human being.[4]

(4) The table in front of Kripke was not from the very beginning of its existence made of ice.[5]

(5) Tully is Cicero.[6]

---

[1] See his 'Identity and Necessity' in M. K. Munitz (ed.) *Identity and Individuation* (New York, 1971); and 'Naming and Necessity' in D. Davidson and G. Harman (eds.), *Semantics of Natural Language*.

[2] See also A. Plantinga, *The Nature of Necessity* (Oxford, 1974), for work along similar lines. In citing propositions similar to (3), (4), and (5) below Plantinga writes that he is concerned with necessity 'in a broadly logical sense', but he does not amplify this remark.

[3] See the discussion on 260–4 of 'Naming and Necessity'.

[4] 'Naming and Necessity', 268 f.

[5] 'Identity and Necessity', 152.   [6] Ibid., 156 f.

On the assumption that (3), (4), and (5) are true, Kripke
suggests that perhaps they are necessary. (3) is necessary,
Kripke suggests, because nothing would be Nixon unless that
thing were a human being. Nixon only exists as long as he is a
human being. (4) is necessary because a table would not be
that table if it had been made from ice. (5) is necessary because
'Tully' and 'Cicero' in fact pick out the same person and that
person must be identical with himself.

If we adopt criterion [B] of necessity, it seems highly plausible
to suppose that at any rate (4) and (5) are necessary propositions. (5) is necessary because it is not coherent to suppose that
the individual in fact picked out by both 'Cicero' and 'Tully'
is not self-identical. Note by contrast that none of these propositions is analytic on my definition of 'analytic' nor would they
generally be so regarded. (5) is not analytic because it is coherent to suppose that the various criteria for picking out the
individual to whom 'Tully' refers and the various criteria for
picking out the individual to whom 'Cicero' refers might pick
out different individuals. In fact they pick out the same individual, and because it is not coherent to suppose that that
individual be not self-identical (5) is necessary on criterion [B].

The necessity of (4) is worth discussing a little more fully.
It seems to derive from continuity of matter being necessary
for the sameness of an (inanimate) material object. If my car
disappeared from Keele and a car of very similar appearance
turned up in London, the latter could only be my car if it was
made of the same matter as the former, or if the former had
turned into the latter by gradual replacement of matter. It is
this that seems to be behind the principle suggested by Kripke
that 'if a material object has its origin from a certain hunk of
matter, it could not have had its origin in any other matter'.[7]
Kripke supposes that the wooden table in front of him was
originally made of wood, and asks:

Could *this table* have been made from . . . water cleverly hardened
into ice-water taken from the Thames river? We could conceivably
discover that, contrary to what we now think, this table is indeed
made of ice from the river. But let us suppose that it is not. Then,
though we can imagine making a table. . . from ice, identical in

[7] 'Naming and Necessity', 350, n. 56.

appearance with this one, and though we could have put it in this *very* position in the room, it seems to me that this is *not* to imagine *this* table as made of . . . ice, but rather it is to imagine another table, *resembling* this one in all external details, made . . . of ice.[8]

This seems to be because for a table to be the same table as this table it must have matter continuous with that of this table. Clearly we can in general suppose that things develop in ways other than the ways in which they actually develop—this table might have been cut up for firewood last week. And among the suppositions which we can make are that their matter gradually changes—the bits of wood of this table might gradually have been replaced by bits of ice while the table remains this table. These suppositions about things happening to this table are suppositions about things happening to the table which was in fact materially continuous with this table. We trace back the table to some earlier stage of its history and suppose it to develop in a way different from the way in which it actually developed. Yet if we suppose the table to have been made originally of ice, we are not doing this, because in that case there is no earlier stage of the table in fact continuous with this table at which we are supposing that being made of ice became true of it. I conclude that on criterion [B], (4) is a necessary proposition.

(3), as Kripke realizes, is a more dubious case. Could not Nixon turn into an alligator and yet remain Nixon? However, if we do regard (3) as necessary, it will surely be because we do not find it coherent to suppose that the individual in fact picked out by 'Nixon' be anything other than a human being.

If it was a necessary truth on criterion [B], (3) would be an example of a class of propositions necessary on criterion [B]— those which state an essential kind to which an individual belongs. It will be important for us to investigate this class of propositions in a little detail. A proposition states an essential kind to which an individual belongs if the proposition states what sort of a thing the individual is (e.g. 'is a person', 'is a car', 'is a number') and if it is not coherent to suppose that that individual no longer be that sort of thing yet continue to exist by being something else instead. Thus (6) and (given that it is

[8] Ibid., 314.

uttered in appropriate circumstances) (7) below state an essential kind to which an individual belongs.

(6) $\sqrt{2}$ is a number

and

(7) What Smith was talking about is a number

both come out as necessary, if Smith was talking about $\sqrt{2}$. For $\sqrt{2}$ could not cease to be a number; nothing would count as $\sqrt{2}$ unless it were a number. Yet (7), unlike (6), is not analytic.

In thinking of something a as a continuing individual, and perhaps giving it a name, we have certain criteria which have to be satisfied for a future individual b to be the same individual as a. Among those criteria is the criterion of sameness of form— for b to be the same individual as a they must, for some φ, both be φ. For example, if a is a number, b must be too; if a is a concept, b must be too; if a is an equation, b must be too. (This notion of sameness of form will need tightening up later.) If a certain individual (e.g. $\sqrt{2}$) is a number, it cannot cease to be a number while continuing to exist as something else. The concept of being British could not cease to be a concept and become something else instead. But such things are of course things which exist of logical necessity. What of logically contingent things? What of tables and chairs and cars and houses and people? If something is a table can it cease to be a table and become something else instead? Suppose that 'Amanda' is the name of my car. What then is the status of

(8) Amanda is a car?

Does it state an essential kind to which Amanda belongs or could Amanda cease to be a car and become a ship or a bed instead? Of course the matter out of which Amanda was made could be made into the matter of a ship or a bed, but would that thing be Amanda or not? In our normal way of thinking, *I think*, if something ceases to be a car, it ceases to be. And thus (8) turns out to be necessary on criterion (8). It contrasts with such propositions as

(9) Amanda is green
(10) Amanda is driven by petrol.

which are not necessary on criterion [B]. Amanda could be

repainted, or have her method of propulsion changed, while remaining Amanda.

What goes for cars *seems* to go for tables and chairs, houses and trees. These are essential kinds in that if an individual belongs to one of these kinds, it could not cease to do so, while continuing to exist. Buckingham Palace could not cease to be a house and become a road; although the matter of which it is made could come to be the matter out of which a road is made. Yet it must be admitted that in all such cases there is a considerable border-region, where it seems equally legitimate to affirm and to deny that the same thing continues to exist. Suppose Amanda is made into a lorry? Has Amanda ceased to exist and its matter been made into the matter of a new individual? Or is it rather that Amanda is now a lorry? There is no obvious right answer. But if the metal of Amanda is melted down to make a gate, then clearly Amanda is no more. Again, if my favourite chair has its back taken off and is used as a table, does it exist any more or not? Neither answer seems *obviously* right. Yet if the chair is chopped up and the bits used to make a rabbit hutch, it is no more. We must conclude that although necessarily in thinking of something as a continuing individual we have criteria for a future individual being the same individual, they are ones fuzzy at the edge.

For inanimate material objects, these criteria are the twin criteria of continuity of matter and sameness of form. We may analyse sameness of form as belonging to the same minimal essential kind. If 'a is φ' states an essential kind to which a belongs, then so does any other proposition of the form 'a is ψ' which is entailed by 'a is φ'. If 'a is a castle' states an essential kind to which a belongs, then so does 'a is a building'. Among essential kinds, we can distinguish minimum essential kinds. 'a is φ' states a minimum essential kind to which a belongs if there is no proposition 'a is ψ' which states an essential kind to which a belongs and which entails 'a is φ' but is not entailed by 'a is φ'. If 'a is φ' states the minimum essential kind to which a belongs, we may say that it states the miniessential kind to which a belongs or that a is miniessentially φ. Now for material objects a and b at different times to be the same object there has to be continuity of matter between them, and for some φ they have to be both miniessentially φ. For suppose a, Amanda, which is a car, to be made into a lorry *b* instead. Continuity of matter is preserved. But is sameness of form? Sameness of form cannot consist in their both belonging to some common essential kind—for clearly they both belong to the essential kind of motor vehicle, and yet that does not settle the issue whether they are the same individual. What is at issue is whether being a motor vehicle is the narrowest essential kind to which both have to belong—in which case they are the same individual—or whether one or other has to belong to a narrower essential kind, e.g. the kind of car, in which case they are not the same individual.[9]

An (inanimate) material object *a* is the same individual as *b* if and only if it has continuity of matter and has the same form, i.e. belongs to the same minimum essential kind. I have now in effect discussed both these criteria. Both criteria are fuzzy at the edges in that there are border-line cases where they do not provide definite answers about whether objects are or are not the same. Thus for continuity of matter between *a* and *b*, the matter of *b* has to be the same matter as that of *a* or to result from the matter of *a* by gradual replacement of the latter—but how gradual is gradual? If almost all the matter of a car is replaced at once we have a different car; if just a bit of the matter is replaced we have the same car—but it is unclear what to say if just the chassis and the bodywork, but no other parts, are replaced at one time (as I brought out earlier in Chapter 7). The same applies to the criterion of sameness of form. It is not always perfectly clear to which minimum essential kind an individual belongs—e.g. whether Amanda has 'car' as its minimum essential kind or not—although for any particular individual the unclarity concerns only the question of to which of a small range of essential kinds that individual belongs. Thus it is clear enough that Amanda does not have 'green thing' as a minimum essential kind.

In describing the world, we pick out, and often have names

[9] My concept of a minimum essential kind is very close to Wiggins's concept of a substance sortal. Wiggins distinguishes 'substance-sortals' as concepts which apply to 'an individual x at every moment throughout x's existence, e.g. human being' from 'phrase-sortals, e.g. boy or cabinet-minister' which 'do not'. Presumably Wiggins means not 'do not', but 'need not'—for a human being can remain a boy for all his existence, as he may die at the age of 13. See David Wiggins, *Identity and Spatio-Temporal Continuity* (Oxford, 1967).

for, individuals of certain miniessential kinds, and describe the
history of the world by describing what happens to them. Our
scheme of names is in no way an unavoidable one. There are
many other schemes which will convey the same information.
Thus, I have argued, we pick out and name individuals belonging to the miniessential kinds of cars and boats, but not to a
miniessential kind of motor vehicles. 'Amanda' names an
individual, my car, which is miniessentially a car. So if my car
is dismantled and made into a boat, the right way to describe
this is:

(11) Amanda ceased to exist, and the bits of Amanda were
      made into a boat.

But we could have picked out and named individuals belonging
to the miniessential kind of motor vehicle. 'Amanda' could,
as before, have named an individual which was in fact my car,
but one which was miniessentially a motor vehicle, and so not
essentially a car. Then if my car had been dismantled and made
into a boat, the right way to describe this would have been, not
as before, but:

(12) Amanda was a car, but has now become a boat'.

yet given the two different meanings of 'Amanda', (11) and (12)
seem to be logically equivalent propositions. We do not lose
or gain any ability to convey information by choosing a different
scheme of miniessential kinds in terms of which to pick out
individuals and describe their fate. Which scheme of essential
kinds a culture uses will depend in part on what kinds of
continuity are of importance for it and in part on what kinds of
continuity are frequent and noticeable.

Yet although we could use alternative schemes of essential
kinds without losing any ability to convey information about
the world, we cannot describe a world of material objects unless
we have and apply the concept of two objects being made of
roughly the same matter. For, whatever scheme of essential
kinds is used, two material objects a and b are only the same if
they consist of the same matter or if the matter of b is obtained
from that of a by gradual replacement. For to give information
about a world of material objects[10] we have to trace the history

[10] I do not discuss whether the public world could without loss of information

of such objects, and we can only do that if we can make a judgement about when two material objects at different times are the same.

However, if the argument of Chapter 7 is correct there are in the world kinds of logically contingent things for the continuation of which continuity of matter is not essential. For a person P_2 to be the same person as a person P_1 he does not have to have continuity of matter with (and so the same body as) P_1. P_2's being the same person as P_1 is, we found, something ultimate, not analysable in terms of such publicly observable features as continuity of matter or similarity of memory claims.

Let us introduce the term 'continuity of experience' to denote the peculiar relation which holds between persons at different times. More formally, I define it as follows. An individual a at t_1 and an individual b at t_2 are related by the relation of continuity of experience if and only if a is an animate being, b is an animate being, and the animate being which a is has the same experiences and does the same actions as the animate being which b is. By an animate being I mean a being which has experiences and does actions. The relation of continuity of experience can hold between animate beings at certain times when those animate beings are not actually having experiences or doing actions at those times. In saying that the relation does hold between such dormant beings, one is saying that if they were conscious and so having experiences and doing actions, then the experiences and actions of the one would be the experiences and actions of the other. Then, clearly, if a and b are both persons they will be the same person if and only if they are related by the relation of continuity of experience. So the argument of Chapter 7 can be regarded as showing that this relation is one indefinable in terms of publicly observable features. However, as I have defined 'continuity of experience', this relation could hold

---

be described in other ways than as a world of material objects. Phenomenalists have thought that the world could be described instead in terms of actual or possible sense-data. Other philosophers have thought that the world could be described in terms of the qualities which characterize points of space. Both groups of philosophers have to cope with the difficulty that it is very difficult to identify their entities ('sense-data', 'points of space') without reference to material objects—e.g. to identify a point of space you have to specify its distance and direction from some material object.

between chimpanzees, between frogs, between snails, indeed between animate beings of any one kind.

The question arises whether the relation can hold between animate beings of different kinds. One is certainly inclined to suppose that it can hold between a caterpillar *a* and a butterfly *b*. The animate being which *a* is can have the experiences had by and do the actions done by the animate being which the butterfly *b* is. But one may say that really *a* and *b* are animate beings of the same kind; and the question of whether two animate beings are of the same kind is one which we had best avoid. However, without prejudging that question, we can ask between beings how different from each other can the relation hold? For example, can it hold between a person John and an alligator *b*? Can the animate being which John is come subsequently to have the experiences and do the actions of an alligator? Now no doubt John's body could grow scales, his arms could grow short, he could lose his voice, etc. so that there existed an individual with an alligator-body. But if the sort of things the resulting individual thought and the sort of actions which the resulting individual did were those of a person, then he would be a person, although unfortunately cursed with an alligator-body. I am not asking whether the animate being which John is could subsequently have the experiences of and do the actions of such an individual. It seems fairly clear that he could. What I am asking is whether that being could have the experiences and do the actions of an individual who really was an alligator—had alligator-like feelings about things and did actions typical of alligators.[11] I am inclined (just) to think that this is a coherent supposition. Religions which postulate re-incarnation, as well as Western fairy-tales, tell us of animate beings who are persons subsequently doing the actions and having the experiences of frogs, alligators, chimpanzees, etc. Those beings fear being in such a situation, and they are thought of as having reason to do so. The detailed stories seem to me (just) coherent fillings-out of such suppositions, although I admit to some hesitation about the matter. However, I will leave unresolved this issue whether the kind of experiences and

---

[11] There is fortunately no need for me to consider the question whether having a body is a necessary condition for having alligator thoughts and feelings, i.e. whether there can be disembodied alligators.

actions which alligators do could come to be fitted on to an animate being who is a person. In due course this discussion of it will serve to illustrate a similar issue of crucial relevance to the main theme of this book.

So we have individuals of a certain kind, persons, for the identity of which over time a different criterion must be satisfied from those which apply to inanimate material objects. The same would *seem* to apply to animals too (although, once again, I do not press the point). What makes two chimpanzees the same is not, it would seem, continuity of their bodies, but something different which is not entailed by bodily continuity, that the animate beings which those chimpanzees are have the same experiences and do the same actions. In saying this, I am not denying the obvious point that bodily continuity is over-whelming evidence that two chimpanzees are related by the relation of continuity of experience, evidence which in the case of animals (as opposed to persons) one cannot conceive of being outweighed by evidence of memory and character (because there is so little of this in the case of animals). Generally then, however, for animate beings, the relation of continuity of experience replaces the relation of continuity of matter. For animate beings, I suggest, two individuals are the same individual if and only if they are related by the relation of continuity of experience and belong to the same minimum essential kind. We can see this from examples. Let 'John' and 'James' both be names of an individual who is miniessentially a person. Then John and James are the same individual if and only if the animate beings which they are have the same experiences. By contrast let 'Cyril' be the name of an individual who is miniessentiallly a caterpillar and 'Sam' be the name of an individual who is miniessentially a butterfly. Let them be related by the relation of continuity of experience—the animate being which Cyril is will have the experiences and do the actions which Sam does. But they are still not the same individual, for Cyril ceases to be when the caterpillar which Cyril is ceases to be.

We saw earlier that there are different possible schemes of essential kinds in terms of which we can describe the world of inanimate material objects, and the same applies to the world of animate beings. What schemes are possible depends on which individuals can be related by the relation of continuity of experience. But suppose that an animate being which is a being of one kind (e.g. a person) can have the experiences and do the actions of a being of any other kind (e.g. an alligator), then we *need* only pick out and name individuals who are miniessentially animate beings. We need only names such as 'John' for individuals who could pass from being persons to being alligators or snails, in order to describe the world of animate beings. However, we can still pick out and name also individuals such as Cyril and Sam above, individuals who belong to narrower essential kinds than the essential kind of animate being. If, on the other hand, animate beings of certain kinds cannot have the experiences and do the actions of animate beings of some other kinds—e.g. animate beings who are persons can only have the experiences and do the actions of persons—then there cannot be individuals who are miniessentially animate beings, but only individuals who belong to some narrower minimum essential kind—e.g. individuals who are miniessentially persons. However, we can still name and pick out as well individuals who belong to yet narrower minimum essential kinds. Even if an animate being who is a person can do the actions and have the experiences of a subsequent person, however different in character from him, we may still wish to pick out and name individuals which belong to a minimum essential kind of persons-of-such-and-such-character-appear-ance-or-physiology. Thus suppose a person to change sex—one might give a name to that person while a male, and a different name to that person while a female, and so pick out two individuals, one of whom ceases to be and the other of whom comes to be when the change of sex occurs. Again, 'Dr. Jekyll' may name an individual who exists only during a certain phase of the existence of the person which Dr. Jekyll is;[12] when that person behaves in a Hyde-like manner, we may say that Dr. Jekyll has ceased to exist. But if 'Dr. Jekyll' is the name of an individual who is miniessentially a person, then we would have to describe the change differently as 'Dr. Jekyll now behaves in a Hyde-like way'.

[12] Some philosophers have called such individuals 'selves'. The point that we sometimes use names to denote selves is well made in Brian Smart, 'Persons and Selves', *Philosophical Studies*, 1974, **26**, 331–6.

This concludes my lengthy discussion of criterion [B] of necessity. In the process I have discussed the limits to what can happen to individuals of various kinds, and developed a number of technical terms for discussing such issues. I have suggested one or two results—e.g. that the animate beings which persons are can become alligators or chimpanzees—but nothing in the main argument of this book depends on such results. The point of the discussion was to describe and illustrate various kinds of necessity which might exist, in order to have available technical vocabulary to apply in the next chapter to the main points at issue.

I pass to my next criterion of necessity—criterion [C]. A number of ancient and medieval philosophers have spoken of propositions about the past and present being necessary, in virtue of the fact that no action of ours can now affect their truth value (and the sort of 'can' involved here seems to be a logical 'can'—they were talking about what we call logical possibility). In contrast, propositions about the future have been said to be contingent because we can do something now to make them true or false. More precisely, this suggests the following criterion for being a necessary proposition according to which a proposition is necessary at this or that time, for example:

[C] A proposition p is necessary at a time t if and only if p is true and it is not coherent to suppose that any agent by his action at or subsequent to t can make p false.

If it is coherent to suppose that an agent by his action at a time t can bring about any state at a time earlier than t, the description of which is coherent, the only propositions which are necessary on criterion [C] would be those which are necessary on criterion [A], and conversely, viz. those, the negations of which are incoherent. However, as we saw in Chapter 8, the view of most philosophers is that it is not coherent to suppose that agents can ever by their actions at t bring about a state of affairs prior to t. In that case all true propositions about events at some time become necessary on criterion [C] when that time is past. For example, 'the Second World War ended in 1945' became necessary in 1945 and remained necessary thereafter, although it was not necessary before 1945. Then criterion [C] picks out at any time a class of necessary propositions larger than that picked out by criterion [A]. Criterion [C] differs from criteria [A] and [B] and also from subsequent criteria which I shall consider in picking out propositions which are necessary at a time as opposed to eternally.

Another kind of necessity is suggested by the writings of some recent writers on the philosophy of religion.[13] Their discussion of God's necessity suggests the following criterion of a necessary proposition:

[D] A proposition p is necessary if and only if it is true, but the truth of what it states is not (was not, or will not be) dependent on anything, the description of which is not entailed by p.

A state of affairs S_1 is dependent on another state S_2, if the existence of S_2 makes a difference to whether or not S_1 exists. This will be so if S_2 brings about S_1 (S_1 would not have existed but for S_2) *or* S_2 makes it more probable that S_1 will exist[14] (makes the world more conducive to the existence of S_1). By [D] of course all analytic propositions such as 'all bachelors are unmarried' come out again as necessary. They do not depend for their truth on anything the description of which is not entailed by them. 'All bachelors are unmarried' does not depend for its truth on the genetic characteristics or social habits of bachelors. You may want to say that it depends for its truth on all unmarried men being unmarried. But then the description of that fact, the proposition 'all unmarried men are unmarried', is entailed by 'all bachelors are unmarried'. But analytic propositions are not the only propositions which come out as necessary on criterion [D]. If there is no God or any

---

[13] See, e.g., John H. Hick ('Necessary Being', *Scotish Journal of Theology*, 1961, **14**, 353–69), and R. L. Franklin ('Some Sorts of Necessity', *Sophia*, 1964, **3**, 15–24), who have written along similar lines. Both of these authors find God's necessity in his ultimacy, his independence of other things, which is where criterion [D] finds necessity, as well as in various other characteristics, which I have included within my concept of the personal ground of being in the last chapter. However, Hick seems to equate God's independence with 'aseity'. He writes that 'The core of the notion of aseity is independent being. That God exists *a se* means that he is not dependent on anything for his existence.' If this is what 'aseity' is to mean, then it means necessity on criterion [D] and is, I argue, a coherent concept. However, as I point out in Chapter 14, etymology naturally suggests a different meaning for 'aseity'.

[14] i.e. makes it physically more probable that S_1 will occur, *not* makes the evidence favour the claim that S_1 has occurred. For 'physical probability' and how it differs from probability of other kinds see my *An Introduction to Confirmation Theory* (London, 1973), Ch. 2.

similar being,' 'the universe exists' would be a necessary proposition. For in that case the universe would not depend for its existence on anything else. The existence of the universe would be an ultimate brute fact. Also, if there were no God or similar being and atoms were indestructible and there were exactly ten billion billion of them, then 'there are ten billion billion atoms' would be a necessary proposition on criterion [D]. The kind of necessity picked out by criterion [D] we may call ontological necessity.

Another way in which 'necessary' has been used in the past—although it may seem to us an unnatural one—is this. A being is said to be a necessary being if he is by nature eternal and imperishable. The scholastics called the angels and stars necessary beings for this reason. A being is 'by nature' eternal and imperishable if it will continue to exist for ever, and never decay—but for divine action. For the scholastics God differed from other necessary beings in being an 'unconditioned' necessary being —i.e. unlike them, he did not owe his necessary existence to anything else. The necessity of a proposition is then a matter of the eternal truth of what it states. We can capture this kind of necessity more precisely by the following criterion:

[E] A proposition is necessary if and only if it is a true proposition which states how things are at some time and if things always will be and always have been as it states that they are at that time.[15],[16]

Most true propositions which state how things are at some specific time describe things which will cease to be the case or were once not the case. Thus 'there is now a Labour Government' describes a state of affairs which once did not hold. Likewise 'it is now spring' or 'John is ill' describe states of affairs which have come to be and will pass away. But if the universe has always existed and will always exist (whether or not God keeps it in existence), then 'the universe exists' is a necessary proposition on criterion [E] (and so too is 'the universe exists eternally'). So too is 'there are atoms' if there are atoms,

---

[15] If we wish to provide an account as close as possible to the scholastic one, we could add 'since the first moment at which they were as described', and also 'but for the supernatural account of God', but I ignore these complications.

[16] In his 'God and Necessity' (in B. Williams and A. Montefiore (eds.), *British Analytical Philosophy*, London, 1966) Anthony Kenny gives a version of this definition on 148 et seq.

there always have been atoms, and there always will be atoms hereafter. Any analytic proposition comes out as necessary by criterion [E]. But on both criteria [D] and [E] of 'necessary' not all necessary propositions are analytic. I shall not subsequently be concerned with necessity of kind [E], but I thought that in view of its history in discussions of the philosophy of religion I ought to describe it in order to distinguish it from the other kinds of necessity with which I am concerned.

One further kind of necessity remains to be distinguished by a criterion [F]. I shall call this physical necessity:

[F] A proposition *p* is necessary if and only if it is true and there exists a full explanation of what it states to be the case. The concept of a full explanation was introduced in Chapter 8. If there is a full explanation of some state of affairs then that state could not but occur. In that sense, it occurs necessarily. The explanatory factors, causes, and reasons (whether those cited in scientific explanation or those cited in personal explanation) made that state occur. A proposition is necessary on criterion [D] if there is no explanation at all for the occurrence of what it states to be the case—a proposition is necessary on criterion [F] if there is a full explanation of what it states to be the case. A proposition is necessary on neither criterion either if it is false or if there exists only a partial explanation of what it states.

In the theist's view 'there is a universe' is physically necessary, because there is a full explanation of the existence of the Universe in terms of the action of God who brought it about. Again, if physical states produce their effects entirely predictably in accord with natural laws, then an event, such as today's motion of the earth about its axis was physically necessary because there is a full explanation of its occurrence in terms of natural laws and such initial conditions as the earth having the velocity and mass it did at the beginning of yesterday, the planets and other heavenly bodies being as they were at that time. If a state of affairs is physically necessary then its cause physically necessitates that state (see p. 134).

Propositions necessary on criteria [A] or [B] are not necessary on criterion [F], for there is no scientific or personal explanation of why they hold. Such explanations exist only for logically contingent matters. It will be seen that some propositions which are necessary on criterion [F] are necessary on criterion [C] or on criterion [E] and some are not.

I have now distinguished six alternative criteria for a proposition being a necessary proposition. In the next chapter I shall consider whether it is on any of these criteria of necessity that the theists wish to claim that 'God exists' is a necessary proposition, i.e. that God is a necessary being, and whether this claim is a coherent one. I shall go on to consider on which criterion of necessity the theist wishes to claim that 'God is a personal ground of being' is a necessary proposition, and whether this claim is coherent.

'Necessary' propositions are contrasted with 'contingent' ones. A natural definition of a contingent proposition is that a contingent proposition is any proposition which is not necessary and is not the negation of a necessary proposition. Each way of understanding 'necessary' then has a different way of understanding 'contingent' contrasted with it. Necessary propositions of these various kinds are to be distinguished from *a priori* propositions. As mentioned in Chapter 2, an *a priori* proposition is—very roughly—one which is true and can be known to be true merely by considering what it says, without 'looking at the world' to see if it is true. No doubt some analytic propositions are *a priori*. I can know that all bachelors are unmarried without doing a social survey on the habits of bachelors. But it is open to argument whether all analytic propositions are *a priori*;[17] and there is no reason to suppose that propositions which are necessary only on other criteria of necessity are *a priori*.

[17] I discuss this matter in my 'Analyticity, Necessity, and A Priority', *Mind*, 1975, **84**, 225–43.

14

A Necessary Being

I STATED at the end of Chapter 12 that we have to investigate two further claims of theism—that God exists necessarily and that God is necessarily the kind of being which he is. Chapter 13 was devoted to analysing six different kinds of necessity, to setting out six different criteria for a proposition being necessary. Armed with these tools we can now in this chapter come to investigate on which, if any, criteria of necessity the theist can coherently make the claims which he wishes to make about God's necessity.

That God is in some sense a necessary being is not often stated in creeds; but it has been recognized by many philosophers that something of this sort must be true if the God whose existence is affirmed in creeds is to be worthy of worship. The requirement that God be a necessary being and be necessarily the kind of being which he is was stated by Findlay in a well-known article[1] as follows:

We can't help feeling that the worthy object of our worship can never be a thing that merely *happens* to exist, nor one on which all other objects merely *happen* to depend. The true object of religious reverence must not be one to which, merely, no *actual* independent realities stand opposed: it must be one to which such opposition is totally *inconceivable*. . . . Not only must the existence of other things be unthinkable without him, but his own non-existence must be wholly unthinkable in any circumstances.

This kind of point was well recognized by Aquinas. He expressed the claim that God is a necessary being by saying that in

[1] J. N. Findlay, 'Can God's Existence be disproved?', *Mind*, 1948, **57**, 176–83.

God there is no distinction between nature and existence. He is using here Aristotelian terminology, which needs some explanation. In the case of a material object such as a chair, one can distinguish the nature (or form) of the chair, and the matter, the wood, out of which it is made. The coming into existence of the chair consists in the 'union' of the form of a chair with certain matter. It is not necessary that such unions take place; chairs may, but need not, come to exist. There are, however, Aquinas taught, also immaterial beings, such as angels. Like material objects, they may exist, but do not have to exist. However, their coming into existence cannot consist in a union of matter and form, for they have no matter. They are pure form. Their coming into existence consists in existence being joined to their form (or nature). God, however, is different. Like the angels, he is pure form, and so 'God is to be identified with his own essence or nature'.[2] But, unlike that of the angels, the nature of God must exist. That nature, alone of natures, could not not exist. So 'it is God's very nature to exist'. 'God is not only his own essence, but also his own existence'.[3] God's nature, according to Aquinas, includes some such properties as his omnipotence, omniscience, and perfect goodness. Hence, according to Aquinas, God is necessarily a being of roughly the kind which I have discussed so far.

Why have theists wished to make these claims? Basically because they have seen that God cannot be the cause of his own existence or of his being the kind of being which he is. Since no other agent can be the cause of these things, it follows if it is not to be a matter of chance that God happens to exist and be the kind of being which he is, then it must be somehow in the nature of things, unavoidable. For a being whose existence and nature was a chance matter would hardly deserve worship. We see this motivation in the quotation from Findlay. In order to see clearly what kind of necessity is here involved, it is worth while pausing a moment to see why it is that God cannot be the cause of his own existence or of his being the kind of being which he is. Men have occasionally claimed that God is the cause of his own existence or of his being the kind of being which he is, although this is not a claim normally made by traditional theologians.

[2] Aquinas, *Summa Theologiae*, vol. ii, Ia.3.3.
[3] Op. cit., Ia.3.4.

Etymology would suggest that this is what is meant when God is said to have 'aseity'[4] (his existence deriving from himself, *a se*).

Aseity

Our account of this matter will depend crucially on what kind of being we suppose God to be; or, rather, put in the technical terminology of the last chapter, to which minimum essential kind we suppose God to belong. The traditional view, as stated for example by Aquinas,[5] is roughly, we have seen, to put the matter in my terminology, that he belongs to the minimum essential kind of personal ground of being or to some narrower kind which entails his being essentially a personal ground of being. (I shall, however, largely ignore this latter possibility until my concluding pages, as the problems of coherence are similar to those which arise with the supposition that God is miniessentially a personal ground of being.) I shall return shortly to the issue of whether this is a coherent supposition, but let us suppose for the moment that it is. In that case, God is necessarily (on criterion [B]) an eternal being; necessarily if he exists at one time, he exists at all times. Hence if any agent does bring about God's existence, he need only bring about that existence at one moment of time. For once God exists at a moment of time, he exists at all moments of time. On the other hand, no moment of time would be early enough for an agent to bring about God's existence. For any moment *t*, if the agent brought about God's existence at *t*, this could not ensure God's existence at any earlier time—given, as I earlier assumed (p. 150), that a cause cannot bring about a state of affairs earlier in time. So any moment of time at which an agent brought about God's existence would be too late to ensure his eternal existence. I conclude that it is not logically possible that any agent could bring about God's existence if God is necessarily an eternal being. What holds generally holds in particular when the agent is supposed to be God himself. If God is miniessentially a personal ground of being God could not bring about his own existence. Clearly, too, God could not bring it about that he is a personal ground of being. If he is

---

[4] Theologians have, however, often understood this term in quite different senses.
[5] If God's eternity is understood in my way and not his.

miniessentially a personal ground of being, it will be incoherent to suppose that he could fail to be such a being. An agent can only bring about what would have been otherwise but for his agency. But whatever God did he could not fail to be a personal ground of being, if this is what he miniessentially is.

However, one could have different views of God's nature. While holding that God is in fact a personal ground of being the theist could hold that this is not what he miniessentially is. One alternative which a theist might hold is that God is miniessentially what I shall call simply a divine being. I define a divine being as a backwardly eternal being who is perfectly free, omnipotent, and omniscient. Given that a divine being exists, nothing brought him into being, for he has always existed. Further, how things are in future depends on his choice. However, his existence at a given time would not appear to entail his future existence. Whether he existed in future would be up to him, and he could, if he so chose, commit suicide. However, if in fact he is forwardly eternal, that is as a result of his continual choice. If he goes on existing for ever, he would be a personal ground of being, but not miniessentially so. One who is miniessentially a personal ground of being does not, however, have the power to commit suicide, for he is the kind of being which, once he exists, it is not coherent to suppose that he cease to exist; and so, even though omnipotent, he does not have the power to bring about his non-existence. When discussing the properties of a being who is miniessentially divine, I wrote just now that 'his existence at given time would not appear to entail his future existence'. However, there is one reason why it might. An individual who is perfectly free and omniscient cannot, as we have seen, do what is morally wrong. If committing suicide would be morally wrong for such a being (and if it were so, it would, by the arguments of Chapter 11, be a logical truth that it was so), then his existence at a given time would entail his existence at all future times—for he alone, as omnipotent, could deprive himself of existence. In that case the concepts of an individual who is miniessentially divine and of an individual who is miniessentially a personal ground of being would coincide. In order to continue to investigate the properties of a being who is miniessentially divine but not miniessentially a personal ground of being, I shall assume that it would not always be morally wrong for a backwardly eternal being who is omnipotent, omniscient, and perfectly free to commit suicide.

There are yet other views which a theist might hold about God's nature, about what God miniessentially is. He might hold that God is miniessentially simply a person. That he is eternal, omnipotent, omniscient, and perfectly free would then be accidental properties of God; he would still be the individual he is if he were to lose his omniscience or his omnipotence by his own choice. But on this view (if we assume that there are no moral obstacles—viz. that it would not be morally wrong for him so to do), God could deprive himself of his omnipotence or his perfect freedom or his omniscience. One thing which it would then be possible for God to do is to bring about the existence of things long before they come into existence—e.g. by his action in 1900 make it the case that there would be an earthquake in 1975. He could have made the world and programmed into it its future development, in such a way that even he could not ever interfere with it. We may call such an act an act of binding the future. Binding the future is one way of making oneself no longer omnipotent. One who holds that God is miniessentially a personal ground of being or miniessentially divine must hold that he does not have the power to do such things. For on both of these views God could not cease to be omnipotent while continuing to exist. An individual who is miniessentially divine cannot deprive himself of his omnipotence, omniscience, and perfect freedom while continuing to exist. An individual who is miniessentially a personal ground of being cannot cease to exist.

If God is miniessentially something less than a personal ground of being, then God's failure ever to deprive himself of his properties or to commit suicide would be simply a matter of his free choice at each moment of endless time. He always chooses to continue in existence with all his powers intact. If that were so, it would follow from the results of Chapter 10 that neither any human being nor God himself could know that God would go on existing for ever or retain his powers. For I showed there that no person, not even God himself, can know which future free actions God will do, and that means, which free actions from among those which are logically possible. So if God is in fact a personal ground of being (viz. a person eternally omnipotent, omniscient, and perfectly free), but not miniessentially so,[6] neither he nor anyone else could know that he was a personal ground of being.

Traditional orthodoxy has supposed that God does not have the power to commit suicide or to deprive himself of any of such properties as I have considered. Aquinas lists suicide among the things of which the omnipotent God is incapable.[7] He also holds that God cannot deprive himself of such properties as omnipotence.[8] As I have said, the traditional view is that God is miniessentially something like a personal ground of being, and I shall after the next few pages concentrate on the coherence of claims about God's necessity on this supposition. This is partly simply because it is the traditional view, and it is the coherence of traditional theism which I am examining in this book, and partly because, as I shall urge in the next chapter, God is more obviously worthy of worship on the traditional view. Before doing so, I will, however, make the point that even if the theist does hold a different view of God's nature, of what God miniessentially is, he still cannot say that God is the cause of his own existence or of his being the kind of being which he is.

It might be supposed that if God is miniessentially a divine being, he could indeed be regarded as the cause of his own existence. For his existence at each moment could be explained by his action of bringing it about at each earlier moment. Certainly in that case God would be the cause of his own existence at any named moment of time. But, I shall claim, it does not follow from this that he is the cause of his eternal existence, his existence throughout endless time. I shall claim that given that there is a time at which he exists, God's action explains his subsequent existence, but that what God's action cannot explain is the fact of his existence at all.

Before making this claim, it will be necessary for me to make more clear than I have done so far in this book the sense in which I am using the expression '*the* cause'. In saying that some person or state of affairs is *the* cause of some effect, I meant only

---

[6] Or mini-essentially a being of a narrower kind than a personal ground of being and so essentially a personal ground of being.

[7] *Summa contra Gentiles*, 2.25.21.

[8] 'God cannot make a thing to be preserved in being without himself', ibid., 2.25.10 (Bk. II trans. James F. Anderson under the title *On the Truth of the Catholic Faith*, Bk. II, New York, 1956).

that (given the reason, viz. the law or intention—see p. 134) the former physically necessitated the latter. In speaking of '*the* cause' I meant only to distinguish the object or state of affairs in question from the effect, or the reason for the efficacy of the effect, or from any component states which might make up the total causal state, and so are parts of the cause. It would, however, have been more precise—although unnecessary at the earlier state of discussion—to talk not of '*the* cause' but of 'a full cause'. For clearly, given a certain set of reasons (e.g. scientific laws), an effect may have in the above sense many causes. For if, given a natural law L, S_1 brings about S_2 and S_2 brings about S_3, S_1 also brings about S_3, and so S_3 has as causes both S_1 and S_2 (although S_1 is a more remote cause than S_2). Likewise a cause C_1 may bring it about that a certain reason operates, so as to make another cause C_2 bring about E; and so C_1 will also be a cause of E. An effect may have many full causes, and it can therefore be misleading to talk of any one of them as *the* cause. A state or event can have many full causes, so long as all but one are remote causes, in the sense that each brings out the existence or efficacy of some other cause.

With this clarification, let us investigate the argument that if God is the cause of his existence at each moment of time, then he is the cause of his existence at all moments of time, *viz*. his eternal existence; understanding by 'the cause' 'a full cause' in the sense above defined. The argument depends for its soundness on the principle that S is the cause of the occurrence of a collection of states if and only if it is a collection of the causes of each.[9]

---

[9] This claim is made by Hume (though without his allowing for the fact that an effect may have more than one full cause): 'In . . . a chain . . . or succession of objects, each part is caused by that part which preceded it, and causes that which succeeded it. Where then is the difficulty? But the *whole* you say, wants a cause. I answer that the uniting of these parts into a whole, like the uniting of several distinct countries into a kingdom, or several distinct members into one body, is performed merely by an arbitrary act of the mind, and has no influence on the nature of things. Did I show you the particular causes of each individual in a collection of twenty particles of matter, I should think it very unreasonable, should you afterwards ask me what was the cause of the whole twenty. This is sufficiently explained in explaining the cause of the parts.' (*Dialogues concerning Natural Religion*, ed. H. D. Aiken, New York, 1948, pp. 59 f.) The same argument is put forward, among modern writers, by Paul Edwards. He writes that 'if we have explained the individual members' of a series 'there is nothing additional left to be explained' ('The Cosmological Argument' in *Rationalist Annual*, 1959, pp. 63–77; see p. 71).

This principle clearly holds for any finite set of effects, where none of the causes of any members of the collection of effects is itself a member of the collection of effects. If the cause of a is a', b is b', of c is c', of d is d',—a, b, c, d, a', b', c', and d' being distinct states—then the cause of $a+b+c+d$ is $a'+b'+c'+d'$. If the cause of one lamp lighting up is its being connected to a battery, and the cause of a second lamp lighting up is its being connected to a different battery, then the cause of the two lamps lighting up is the two being connected to batteries. This principle seems also to hold where the collection of effects is infinite, and none of the causes of any member of the collection of effects is itself a member of the collection of effects. If the cause of the existence of every double-star system in the Universe is the breaking up of a single star, then the cause of the existence of the double-star systems is still the breaking-up of single stars, even if the number of double-star systems is infinite.

However, this principle must be modified if it is to take account of cases where the cause or part of the cause of some member of a collection of effects is itself a member of that set. For when b is the cause of a, and c is the cause of b, we say that the cause of $a+b$ is c, not $b+c$. If c is the lighting of a fuse, b is an explosion caused by c, and a an explosion caused by b, then the cause of $a+b$ is just c. Again, if b and c are conjointly the cause of a, d is the cause of b, and e is the cause of d, then the cause of $a+b+d$ is not $b+c+d+e$, but merely $c+e$. To take account of this point, the previous principle must be expressed more generally as follows: S is the cause of the occurrence of a collection of states if and only if it is a collection of the causes of each, which are not members of the former collection. Hence if the universe has existed for only a finite time, and if the cause of a state of the universe at any moment is its state at any preceding moment (and it has no causes other than such states), and if the earliest state of the universe has no cause, then the whole series has no cause. The same conclusion follows if we suppose that the universe is eternal, and that the cause of a state of the universe at any moment of time is its state at any preceding

---

Both of these writers use the argument in an attempt to show that if the existence of the universe at each moment of time has a cause (viz. its existence at prior moment), then its existence at all moments of time has a cause. My argument in the text shows that the argument does not show this.

moment (and it has no cause other than such states). The whole series has no cause, for there are no causes which lie outside the series. This conclusion does not follow, however, if we suppose, as the theist does, that for each state of the universe there is a cause outside the series, viz. God who makes a previous state produce it. The theist supposes this in supposing God to bring about the operation of laws of nature. In that case, since each state of the universe has a cause outside the series—God who brings about each state by making another state bring it about —the cause of the whole infinite series is God acting at an infinite series of moments of time. It follows from all this that if God's existence at each moment of time is brought about by God acting at a prior moment of time (and God's existence has no other cause than his actions), that the whole series of God's states at each moment of infinite time, that is God's eternal existence, has no cause. For nothing from outside the series is in any way responsible for the existence of the members of the series. Certainly given that at some time God is, his subsequent existence will indeed be due to his actions. But what has no cause, and so is inexplicable, is the non-existence of a time before which God was not.

A similar point can be made if we suppose God to have the power to deprive himself of some of the properties which I have been discussing. Although we could then say that God was the cause of his possessing those properties at any given moment of time, because (in virtue of his possessing those properties) he brought it about at the prior moment that he possess these properties at the succeeding moment; what we could not say is that he is the cause of his eternal possession of all those properties. For it is only in virtue of his possessing certain of those properties at a given moment that he has the power to bring about his subsequent possession of the properties. What is inexplicable is the non-existence of a time before which God lacked those properties.

So, generally, even if we suppose that God is miniessentially something less than a personal ground of being, he still could not be the cause of his own eternal existence and of his being eternally the kind of being which he is. That is also the case, we have seen, on the more traditional view, with which we shall continue normally to operate, that God is miniessentially a personal ground of being. So if he cannot say that God is not the cause of his own existence, the theist wishes to say that he exists necessarily and not by accident, and that he is necessarily the kind of being which he is. On which criteria of necessity can the theist say that? I assume henceforward, unless stated otherwise, that God is miniessentially a personal ground of being (or miniessentially something which entails his being a personal ground of being—but for simplicity of exposition I largely ignore that possibility).

God's Necessary Existence

On what criterion of necessity can the theist coherently claim that 'God exists' is a necessary proposition? Given that God is miniessentially a personal ground of being, the claim that 'God exists' is necessary is the claim that God's eternal existence is necessary. On what criterion can the theist claim that?

To say that 'God exists' is logically necessary, necessary on criterion [A], is to say that it is not coherent to suppose there is no being picked out by the description 'the personal ground of being', i.e. that 'there does not exist a personal ground of being' is an incoherent statement.

There have been some very sophisticated discussions of the suggestion that 'God exists' is a logically necessary proposition, in connection with the traditional ontological argument which in effect makes this claim.[10] It does this because it purports to prove the existence of God to be a deductive consequence of logically necessary premises; and whatever follows from logically necessary premises is itself logically necessary. There have been some very thorough discussions of the traditional ontological argument, and variants thereof, over the past twenty years; and although almost all philosophers argue that it is not a good argument, it has proved very difficult indeed to show exactly where it goes wrong.[11]

However, there is one traditional criticism of the ontological

[10] The ontological argument is a famous argument for the existence of God put forward by Descartes and (probably also) by St. Anselm. The traditional version runs roughly as follows: 'God is by definition a most perfect being. A being which exists is more perfect than one which does not. Therefore God, being most perfect, exists'. For ancient and modern versions of the argument and criticisms of it, see, e.g., the collection edited by A. Plantinga, *The Ontological Argument* (London 1968). For a new version see A. Plantinga, *The Nature of Necessity*, Ch. 10.

[11] For a very careful analysis of where the traditional argument does go wrong see Jonathan Barnes, *The Ontological Argument* (London, 1972).

argument which is of special relevance to our concerns. This is the criticism that nothing can exist of logical necessity, from which it follows of course that its conclusion 'God exists' cannot be logically necessary. The claim is that the only propositions which can be logically necessary are those which say in effect that *if* so-and-so is the case, then such-and-such is the case— e.g. 'red things are coloured', which says in effect that 'if anything is red, then it is coloured'. Logical necessity is only a matter of relations between concepts (e.g. the concepts of being red and coloured)—it cannot be a matter of logical necessity that a concept is instantiated (e.g. that there exists something which is red). Hence it would not be coherent to suppose that there be a logically necessary being.

This criticism, however, clearly will not do. For, as we saw in Chapter 8, some things do exist of logical necessity. There exists a prime number between 9 and 13—and it is a logically necessary matter that there does. There exists a number greater than one million—and it is a logically necessary truth that there does. There exist concepts which include other concepts (e.g. the concept of a bachelor which includes the concept of being married). And so on. Certain numbers and concepts and similar things (such as logical truths) have logically necessary existence. But of course the slogan 'nothing exists of logical necessity' was not really intended to rule out the logically necessary existence of numbers and concepts. It was intended to rule out the logically necessary existence of men and tables, wars and vegetables, cabbages and kings. But it is not easy to formulate the slogan more carefully so that it rules out all that it ought to rule out and allows all that it ought to allow. It will not do just to say 'No material object exists of logical necessity', for, although this slogan is no doubt true, it does not rule out the logically necessary existence of fields of force or ghosts—which presumably it ought to. And even if the slogan were reformulated in a careful way so as to rule out the necessary existence of fields of force and ghosts but not of numbers and concepts, it is not now completely obvious whether or not it ought to be formulated so as to rule out the logically necessary existence of God. The original slogan was simple enough to look right intuitively —but once we have to produce a more complex slogan, it becomes less obvious that the slogan is true.[12]

So I do not think that there is any quick proof of a general slogan of the above type which would rule out the logically necessary existence of God. Nevertheless, it is, I think, easy enough to show fairly conclusively that 'God exists' is not logically necessary, necessary on criterion [A]. For to say this is, as we saw, to say that (s) 'there exists a personal ground of being' is logically necessary. But if this were so, any statement entailed by (s) would also be logically necessary. (s) entails such statements as the following: 'it is not the case that the only persons are embodied persons', 'it is not the case that no one knows everything about the past', 'it is not the case that no one can make a weight of more than ten million pounds rise into the air'. Hence if (s) is logically necessary the negations of these later statements will be incoherent. But fairly obviously they are not. Fairly obviously 'the only persons are embodied persons', 'nobody knows everything about the past', and 'no one can make a weight of more than ten million pounds rise into the air' are coherent claims, whether false or true. Hence (s) is not logically necessary. Of course there just might be contradictions buried in the statements which we have been considering, but in the absence of argument to the contrary we ought to assume what clearly appears to be the case that there are no such buried contradictions, and so that (s) is not logically necessary. Atheism is a coherent supposition. 'God exists' is not necessary on criterion [A]. I do not think that the vast majority of theists who have wished to claim that God's existence is necessary have really wished to claim that it is logically necessary. For the theist the existence of God is a tremendous thing, the most fundamental truth about the universe. It seems to trivialize it to say that it holds for the same reason as does the truth that all bachelors are unmarried.

What of criterion [B]? To say that 'God exists' is necessary on criterion [B] is to say that the description 'the personal ground of being' in fact picks out an individual, God, such that it would be incoherent to suppose him not to exist—not that it would be incoherent to suppose any personal ground of being not to exist, but that it would be incoherent to suppose the

---

[12] For more detailed argument along these lines, see R. M. Adams, 'Has it been proved that all real existence is contingent?' *American Philosophical Quarterly*, 1971, **8**, 284–91.

individual God, who is in fact the personal ground of being, not to exist. Despite the difference, however, exactly the same points apply. For, given that God is miniessentially a personal ground of being, it is incoherent to suppose that God exists without there existing a personal ground of being. If it is also incoherent to suppose God not to exist, then it is incoherent to suppose there not to exist a personal ground of being. So anyone who claims that 'God exists' is necessary on criterion [B] is committed to the claim that 'God exists' is necessary on criterion [A] and we have seen that the latter is not a plausible claim.

Necessity on criterion [C] is relative to time.' God exists' is necessary at time t on this criterion if it is true and it is not coherent to suppose that any agent by his action subsequent to t could make it false. Now given that no agent can bring about a past state of affairs, it is not coherent to suppose that any agent could by his action at any time make 'God exists' false. For any time at which the agent acted, if there was God before then, it would not be coherent to suppose that there could fail to be God thereafter (given that God is miniessentially a personal ground of being). So any time at which any agent acted would be too late to bring about the non-existence of God. Hence if 'God exists' is true, it is necessary on criterion [C] at all moments of time. The theist may certainly coherently make this claim.

'God exists' is necessary on criterion [D] if and only if it is true and it does not depend for its truth on anything which is not entailed by it. The theist must claim that 'God exists' is necessary in this way. For we have seen that God as creator brings about (or permits the existence of or makes or permits some other agent to bring about) the existence of all logically contingent states of affairs, apart from his own existence and anything entailed thereby. There cannot be, as we saw earlier, causation in a circle. Since all logically contingent things depend on God for their existence, he cannot depend on them. All logically necessary propositions are entailed by every proposition; and so even if one wants to say that 'God exists' depends for its truth on the truth of some logically necessary propositions, since all such are entailed by 'God exists', this dependence does not affect God's necessary existence on criterion [D] of necessity. So 'God exists' is, if it is true, necessary on criterion [D], for it does not depend for its truth on anything which is not entailed by it. Its necessity follows from its truth. The theist must also claim that 'God exists' is necessary on criterion [E]. For to say this is just to say that God always has existed and always will exist. The theist must, however, deny that 'God exists' is necessary on criterion [F], for he denies that God's existence is necessitated by anything else.

I conclude that, on the supposition that God is miniessentially a personal ground of being, the theist is committed to 'God exists' being necessary on criteria [D] and [E] and (at all times) on criterion [C]. He is committed to 'God exists' not being necessary on criterion [F], and he cannot coherently claim that it is necessary on criteria [A] or [B]. However, in claiming that God's existence is necessary, he clearly wants more than necessity on criterion [E]. He is claiming more than that God exists eternally. For he may well hold that 'the universe exists' is also necessary on criterion [E], but he will certainly deny that the universe has the kind of necessity which God has.

Necessity on criterion [D] seems to me to be the kind of necessity which the theist wishes to attribute to God's existence. To say that 'God exists' is necessary on this criterion is to say that God does not depend for his existence on himself or on anything else. No other agent or natural law or principle of necessity is responsible for the existence of God. His existence is an ultimate brute fact. Yet being the sort of being which he essentially is, everything else in the universe depends on him, and must do so—for he is by his nature the ultimate source of things. Hence his existence is not merely *an* ultimate brute fact, but *the* ultimate brute fact.'[13] All other logically contingent facts depend on this one. There is no chance here, because the nature of things is that what is and what is not depends on the will of God, and that can only be if he exists. But then is it not fortunate chance that that is the nature of things? Fortunate, maybe. But not chance, because that is how the world works. True, it is logically contingent that that is how the world works. But it is the ultimate principle of its operation.

---

[13] When it is stated that [God] is a necessary being, this means that he is a being without a cause, and that he is the cause of other then himself'—Avicenna, in his *al-Risālat al-'Arshīya*, a passage trans. by A. J. Arberry in *Avicenna on Theology*, (London, 1951), p. 32.

If we suppose that God is miniessentially divine rather than miniessentially a personal ground of being, we reach similar conclusions. In this case, as we have seen, God's continued existence, given that he once exists, would be due to his own choice. What would not be due to his own choice would be the non-existence of a moment before which God was not. The necessary proposition, the theist must then claim, is not 'God exists' but rather 'there does not exist a moment before which God was not'. This latter proposition would not be necessary on criteria [A], [B], or [F]. If it is true, it would be necessary on criterion [D], and again its necessity on this criterion follows from its truth. For it belongs to the nature of God, given that he is miniessentially a divine being, that he is backwardly eternal. The proposition would also be necessary at all moments of time on criterion [C]. Given that God is in fact, although not essentially, a personal ground of being, the proposition in question would also be necessary on criterion [E]. Once again, however, it seems that necessity on criterion [D] is the necessity which matters for the theist when he claims that God is a necessary being. (The same conclusion holds if we suppose that God belongs miniessentially to some narrower kind which entails his being a personal ground of being.)

God's Being Necessarily a Personal Ground of Being

Given that God is miniessentially a personal ground of being, on what criterion of necessity can the theist coherently claim that 'God is a personal ground of being' (i.e. 'If God exists, he is a personal ground of being') is a necessary proposition?

Clearly this proposition is necessary on criterion [B]. For to say this is just to say that it is incoherent to suppose that God be anything else than a personal ground of being; and that follows directly from his being miniessentially a personal ground of being. It is also necessary on criterion [A]. For the criteria for applying the name 'God' to an individual are that he be the personal ground of being. It is not coherent to suppose of any individual picked out by that description that he be not a personal ground of being. Hence 'God exists' is necessary on criterion [A]. Like all propositions necessary on criterion [A], it will be also necessary on criteria [C], [D], and [E], but not necessary on criterion [F].

If we suppose that God is miniessentially divine, God's necessarily being the kind of being which he is will be a matter of the necessity of 'God is divine'. This is naturally interpreted as 'whenever God exists, he is divine'. It then comes out as necessary on criteria [A], [B], [C] (for all moments of time), [D], and [E], but not on criterion [F].

Let us now continue with our main supposition that God is miniessentially a personal ground of being. On that supposition 'God is a personal ground of being' is necessary on criterion [B] and that surely gives the theist all he could possibly want in the way of necessity. For it links to God the properties which I have been discussing in this book by a very strong bond indeed; by the bond of the incoherence of supposing that God could lack them. In this case, God is certainly not a being 'on which all other objects just *happen* to depend' (to use Findlay's words quoted earlier).

So I conclude that, given that God is miniessentially a personal ground of being, the theist can coherently claim that God is a necessary being on criterion [D] and that he is necessarily the kind of being which he is (a personal ground of being) on criterion [B]. Indeed both these claims follow deductively, on the given assumption, from 'there exists a personal ground of being'. These claims seem to be what the theist is getting at when he claims that God is a necessary being and that God is necessarily the kind of being which he is. (I shall, however, return in the final chapter to this matter of whether these claims are what the theist is really getting at.)

However, we need now to look more carefully at the assumption made so far and ask if it is a coherent one. The assumption is that God is miniessentially a personal ground of being. The assumption is the claim that the individual who is the personal ground of being is essentially this—he would not be that individual unless he were the personal ground of being—but that he does not need to belong to any narrower kind in order to be that individual (e.g. he does not need to have created the sun and the moon in order to be the individual which he is; they might never have existed and God still be God). On this assumption the name 'God' applies to an individual such that to be that individual an object would have to be a personal ground of being. Now there seems nothing incoherent in this suggestion, as it stands. There are as we saw in the last chapter different possible schemes of essential kinds in terms of which to describe the world of animate beings. We certainly could treat being a personal ground of being as an essential kind, and only suppose an individual of this kind to exist at some time, given that always a certain animate being had been divine (in the sense defined on p. 257) and would always continue to be. If any animate being who had always been divine at some time ceased to be divine, then there would never have been an individual of the kind of personal ground of being. Words purporting to refer to such individuals would not in fact do so. This would be like supposing there to be laws of nature (i.e. laws which govern the behaviour of objects at all points of time and space) and then coming to have good reason to believe that no laws operate beyond the solar system or the present temporal era. We should then have to retract our claim that laws ever existed. Yet in claiming that God is essentially a personal ground of being, the theist wishes to claim more than that always a certain animate being has been divine and will continue to be so, and that that animate being is, as long as he is divine, the individual God (i.e. that the name 'God' applies to an animate being who is always divine in virtue of his being always divine). Most theists, such as Aquinas, who put forward the traditional view that God is essentially what I have called a personal ground of being, do not merely wish to claim this. Their claim is, rather, that the animate being which God is could not be anything else than always divine, is necessarily always divine. The necessity (on criterion [B]) is not merely the necessity that unless a certain animate being were always divine, he would not be the individual God; but rather the necessity that a certain animate being is of a certain kind, such that if any animate being is of that kind he could not be other than eternally divine, i.e. a personal ground of being. The animate being who is God, the theist claims, could not ever have been anything else. In effect the theist understands his claim that God is miniessentially a personal ground of being as having built into it a further assumption that necessarily (on criterion [B]) any individual who is related to God by the relation of continuity of experience is identical with God.

To take an analogy. Suppose that the name 'Dr. Jekyll' picks

out a man who always behaves in a Jekyll-like way; it is only
applicable to a man if he so behaves. Dr. Jekyll would not
exist unless there were a being who always behaved in a Jekyll-
like way. But even if in fact Dr. Jekyll exists, it will still be
coherent to suppose that the animate being which Dr. Jekyll
in fact is might behave in a Jekyll-like way up to a certain time
and not thereafter. Whether Dr. Jekyll exists would not be
known until the end of the life of the man who behaved in a
Jekyll-like way. For were that man at some time to cease to
behave in a Jekyll-like way and to behave in some other way
instead, Dr. Jekyll would never have existed. Hence even if in
fact Dr. Jekyll exists we can still make sense of the supposition
that the animate being who is in fact Dr. Jekyll might cease to
behave in a Jekyll-like way and so never have been Dr. Jekyll.
In the case of God, a theist such as Aquinas rules out anything
analogous to this possibility.

So the theist wishes to claim both that God is miniessentially
a personal ground of being and also that he is necessarily
identical with any individual who is related to him by the
relation of continuity of experience. Superficially these claims
seem to be inconsistent. Consider the person P who is, on the
theistic hypothesis, in fact eternally divine and so the personal
ground of being. Superficially it is coherent to suppose of any
particular person either that he is omnipotent or omniscient
eternally, or that he is omnipotent or omniscient only up to a
certain time and not thereafter. Superficially it is coherent to
suppose of any person who is in fact eternally divine and so a
personal ground of being, that he might not ever have been
divine, or might have been divine only for a certain time. Now
since at any time t_1 P is in fact the personal ground of being,
God at any time t_2 is related to him by the relation of continuity
of experience. Hence, the theist claims, P is necessarily identical
with God. But God, being miniessentially a personal ground of
being, could not cease to be divine; whereas P, it would appear,
could cease to be divine. So God cannot be necessarily identical
with P. Hence the contradiction—the contradiction between a
proposition expressed by the sentence 'God is miniessentially
a personal ground of being' and a proposition expressed by the
sentence 'God is necessarily [on criterion [B]] identical with
any individual who is related to him by the relation of con-

tinuity of experience' arises because the semantic and syntactic rules for 'person' limit the kind of 'persons' which there could be. For it seems that, given those rules, the only 'persons' which it is coherent to suppose that there could be are ones which could have or lack omnipotence, omniscience, or perfect freedom, while remaining the same persons.

The only way in which the theist can maintain the compatibility of propositions expressed by the quoted sentences is by playing, at long last, the analogical card. This card is, as we saw in Chapter 4, a perfectly proper card to play but it must not be played too often. It is a joker which it would be self-defeating to play more than two or three times in a game. The theist must say that in saying that God is both miniessentially 'a personal ground of being' and also necessarily identical with 'any animate being with whom he is related by the relation of continuity of experience', he is using the expressions, or, rather, the words by which these technical terms were introduced, analogically. I defined (p. 224) a 'personal ground of being' as a 'person' who is 'eternally perfectly free, omnipotent, and omniscient'. The three latter terms were also given fairly technical definitions, but the definitions ultimately relied on various ordinary words in common use such as 'is able', 'brings about', 'knows', etc. I defined the relation of continuity of experience (p. 245) as holding between individuals a at t_1 and b at t_2 if and only if 'a is an animate being, b is an animate being, and the animate being which a is has the same experiences and does the same actions as the animate being which b is', an animate being being 'a being which has experiences and does actions'. Now we could suppose any of these terms to be being used analogically and thereby begin to reconcile the superficially incompatible claims in the way outlined in Chapter 4. The historical tradition, including that part of it described in Chapter 5, is that no one word is given special analogical treatment. It seems more natural, as well as fairer to the historical tradition, to suppose that a number of connected words have their meanings given somewhat of an analogical extension. The most central term seems to me to be 'person'. If we suppose that this word preserves many of its syntactic links with other terms, then a loosening-up of its meaning will clearly go with a loosening-up of the meanings of many of the other words involved in giving meaning to the claims discussed in this paragraph. This process will clearly make it easier for the theist to make the two apparently incompatible claims which we saw that he wishes to make.

The concept of 'person' is, as we saw in Chapter 7, introduced into language partly by examples. We ourselves, our brothers and sisters, etc. are said to be 'persons'. The concept of 'person' is also made more rigorous by the introduction of syntactic rules linking it to such other words as 'thought' and 'action'. A 'person' is (analytically) an animate being who has 'thoughts' and does 'actions' of a certain complexity—which can be illustrated by examples. The examples will be examples of human thoughts and human actions. To be a thought of the requisite complexity a thought has to resemble standard examples of thoughts which we humans have in the respect in which they resemble each other and to the degree to which they resemble each other. To be an action of the requisite complexity an action has to resemble standard examples of actions which we humans do in the respect in which and to the degree to which they resemble each other. For 'thought' and for 'action' there are syntactic rules which link them to other words, e.g. if someone performs an 'action', then he 'brings about' an effect; if someone 'knows' that so-and-so, then he 'thinks' that so-and-so, etc. Such connections with neighbouring terms mean that there is a close connection between the concept of 'person' and other concepts involved in the definition of 'a personal ground of being'.

Now suppose that for 'person' and all of these closely related terms we modify the semantic rules in the way described in Chapter 4. That is, we retain the same standard examples of 'persons', 'thoughts', 'actions', etc. but insist that in order to be a 'person' or 'thought' or 'action' something only needs to resemble the standard examples more than it resembles things which are clear cases of 'non-persons', 'non-thoughts', etc., but does not need to resemble the standard examples as much as they resemble each other. The standard examples of 'non-persons' are those ordinary things which we unhesitatingly and naturally say are not persons, e.g. houses or trees or tables. Suppose further that (with a certain exception) we retain all the syntactic rules linking these terms with each other and with other terms; as before, a 'person' is (of logical necessity) an animate being who has 'thoughts' and performs 'actions' of a certain complexity. A 'person' who 'knows' p, 'believes' p. And so on. The exception is as follows. We abandon any syntactic rules which by themselves (without help from semantic rules) allow us to deduce from 'God is miniessentially a personal ground of being' that 'God is not necessarily [on criterion [B]] identical with any animate being with whom he is related by the relation of continuity of experience'. In this way we prize the network of interrelated terms—'person', 'animate being', 'thinks', 'actions', 'brings about' further away from the standard examples of their application, and slightly break up the logical relations between them. Thereby we give all of these words somewhat analogical senses.

All of this allows us to suppose that there can be kinds of 'persons' very different from those with which we are familiar, much more different than our present rules for the use of 'person' would allow us to suppose. We saw in Chapter 7 how we can indeed coherently suppose that there are 'persons' different from the kinds of 'persons' with which we are familiar— given our present rules for the use of the word. We are here supposing a further extension of use, allowing us coherently to suppose the existence of 'persons' *very* different from those with which we are familiar. The issue now, with the analogical use of the word, is whether there can be a kind of 'person' such that an individual who is a person of that kind is a personal ground of being and could not coherently be supposed to be anything else. The earlier contradiction arose from the fact that any persons of which we could coherently conceive would have to be not too dissimilar from persons with which we are familiar; and those are such that we can imagine them gaining or losing power or knowledge. Once we loosen up the meanings of words can we allow as coherent the supposition that there is a person of the kind just described? We have abandoned any syntactic rules which by themselves have the consequence that 'God is miniessentially a personal ground of being' entails 'God is not necessarily identical with any animate being with whom he is related by the relation of continuity of experience'. If the first entails the second, this can now only be in part in virtue of the semantic rules. The issue is whether it is coherent to suppose that a being resemble ordinary persons more than houses, trees, desks, etc. and yet have power, knowledge, etc. undetachable from him, and be such that it is not coherent to suppose that he exist at all unless you suppose that he exist eternally. The issue is whether the new semantic rules (together with the remaining syntactic rules) allow us to make the inference in question, or whether they allow as coherent the first proposition being true while the second one is false.

The theist in postulating that God, being necessarily eternally omnipotent, omniscient, and perfectly free, is in effect postulating, to speak metaphorically, that God is power and knowledge. This point is made by Aquinas when he states that 'power wisdom, and the like which are accidental to other things, belong to [God] by nature'.[14] For how this can be Aquinas appeals to his doctrine of analogy: 'Power and wisdom are not ascribed to God and to us in the same sense . . . For this reason it does not follow that, because they are accidental in us they will be accidental in God also.'[15] I have argued that Aquinas's doctrine of analogy is unsatisfactory and that we need a different understanding of this notion. Yet Aquinas's intuition that we attribute 'power', 'wisdom', etc. to God in such a way that they are not detachable is one which the theist needs and one of which he can begin to make sense on a different doctrine of analogy.

While to make this supposition is, as we have seen, to use words analogically, it is not to make a kind of supposition which is altogether remote from mundane thinking. We considered in the last chapter the suggestion that a person might become an alligator. Let us consider the suggestion that he might become a worm. This looks less likely to be coherent. Suppose that we were tempted to regard it as an incoherent supposition. Why would we do this? We would say that worms have such lowly thoughts that they are not the kind of thoughts which it makes sense to suppose being had by somebody who was in fact capable of (e.g.) arguing about morals or doing philosophy. Different kinds of animate being have different kinds of thought. Likewise they perform actions of different kinds. I do not myself find such argument entirely plausible

[14] *Summa Theologiae*, vol. ii, Ia.6.3.
[15] Op. cit., Ia.3.6. ad 1.

even for the case of persons and worms, but I can see its force. It provides an example of a supposition similar to that which the theist must make about God. For the theist is also claiming that God is an animate being of a certain kind which can only have thoughts of certain kinds and perform actions of certain kinds. He could not have thoughts other than true thoughts or perform actions other than ones which effect their desired result.

Again, in claiming that God is necessarily the kind of person which he is, the theist claims that God is a necessarily eternal being. Being what he is, he cannot cease to be. Clearly, only with a stretched sense of 'person' can the theist coherently make that claim. But to make this claim is also to make a kind of claim which is not altogether remote from mundane thinking. On a common understanding of 'law of nature', as we saw earlier, if something is now a law of nature, it governs the behaviour of objects at all times and places. If something is at any time a law of nature, it is always a law of nature. A supreme principle of physical necessity could not cease to operate. The failure of a principle to continue to operate would only prove that it had never been a supreme principle. Likewise the failure of a being to be any longer omnipotent would only show that he had never been a personal ground of being.

Many empiricist philosophers have held that no statement about how things are at a certain time entails any statement about how things are at any other time. Certainly to say that something is now blue does not entail that it will be blue tomorrow or was blue yesterday. But this principle does not seem to hold generally. There are many statements which are indeed really about how things are at a certain time, but which do carry entailments about how things are at some other time—in the terminology of Chapter 10, they are not totally about the former time but have a covert reference to some other time. 'P is now 10 years old' entails 'P was born ten years ago' and also 'P cannot be born at any future time, at any rate unless he dies first between now and then'. If P is innocent of the murder last year of Q, with which crime is he now charged, then P did not murder Q last year. If P blows up the Houses of Parliament at t, then the Houses of Parliament do not exist at a time immediately after t. If a person is older than most other people in the town, it follows that there was an earlier time at which he was alive and most other people in the town were not. If a person is now unbeatable at chess, it follows that he will not lose a game within the next two minutes. So there is no reason in principle why a claim to the effect that there exists now a person of a certain kind should not carry entailments about past and future. But a person of the kind with which we are concerned would have to be a person of a very different kind from ordinary persons.

It follows, incidentally, from God being necessarily (on criterion [B]) a personal ground of being that God could not have been a mere man instead of being the personal ground of being, and could not cease to be the personal ground of being, and become a man instead.[16] It follows too that necessarily (on criterion [B]) neither you nor I nor any existing individual apart from God, if he exists, could have been the kind of being which God is, if he exists. For God is necessarily the personal ground of being. What a thing is not, it cannot be necessarily. Hence neither you or I could have been necessarily the personal ground of being; and if we were to wish that in this way we had God's nature, we would be wishing an incoherent wish.

In giving words analogical meanings in the ways outlined, although I have loosened up the meanings of those words, I have not emptied them of meaning. There are still statable and precise rules for their use. For that reason information is still conveyed by the use of the words although not as much as would have been conveyed if the words had been used in the normal senses. Many words which the theist uses, he may claim, are used in perfectly ordinary senses—all conjunctions such as 'if' and 'then', and topic-neutral words such as 'necessarily' and 'state of affairs', and also 'good'. For the application of these words there are the same syntactic rules and the same standard examples. The other words which I have been discussing

---

[16] It should be noted that this does *not* rule out the possibility of an incarnation of the kind in which traditionally orthodox Christians believe. What it rules out is God becoming man and being the personal ground of being no longer. What it does not rule out is God becoming man while remaining the personal ground of being as well. Traditionally orthodox Christians believe that God did the latter in becoming Christ. This belief may or may not be incoherent but whether that is so is not something affected by the argument of *this* chapter.

have had their meanings loosened, but the loosening-up is not too great, since most of the syntactic rules remain.

However, can we now prove the coherence of 'God is miniessentially a personal ground of being, and also necessarily identical with any individual with whom he has continuity of experience' (given the new analogical senses of the words by which the expressions just used are defined)? I cannot now myself prove either that the quoted statement is coherent or that it is incoherent. The stretch of meaning of the words involved has left me without arguments of the normal kind for or against coherence. An argument for coherence would consist in spelling out one way in which the quoted statement could hold, describing a possible word in which it is true. To some extent I have been doing that for the last few paragraphs, and it will, I suspect, become clear to many readers that a lot more such 'spelling-out' is not going to help too much. There will still be a big question mark in the minds of most readers as to whether my 'spelling-out' is itself coherent. There is no better prospect for the success of a proof of incoherence. Such a proof would involve showing that the quoted statement contains a self-contradiction. Now we dropped any syntactic rules which by themselves allow us to deduce from 'God is miniessentially a personal ground of being' that 'God is not necessarily identical with any individual with whom he has continuity of experience'. So one could only prove an incoherence by relying on semantic rules; that is by showing it incoherent to suppose that there is a being who resembles ordinary persons more than he resembles houses, trees, etc. and yet is an individual of a kind who could not cease to be or lose his omnipotence, omniscience, etc. But it would be very hard to show that. For who knows what kinds of beings there can be wildly dissimilar from those known to us? There is not the slightest reason to suppose that humans can list the kinds of being which it is logically possible that there be. There may be kinds of being of which most of us have never thought, and none of us could form more than the vaguest idea. Some such beings may well be more like persons than like trees or houses or tables and yet have the disputed property as well.

None of this shows that the supposition in question is such that the concepts of coherence or incoherence do not apply to it.

It is a meaningful claim for it is made by an indicative sentence using meaningful words (since the words of the sentence have clear semantic and syntactic rules for their use), which (for the reasons given in Chapter 6) makes a statement. All that I am suggesting is that it is beyond the powers of humans directly to prove the coherence or incoherence of the suggestion. My inability to produce such a proof may of course be merely a result of my philosophical incompetence, but for the reasons given above and also because of the similarity of the situation to the two cases of analogical predication discussed in Chapter 4, I do not think so. In those two cases also we could not see any straightforward proofs of coherence or incoherence. We saw there that the only hope of making progress would be to produce indirect argument for coherence. An indirect argument for the coherence of a statement is provided by evidence, on normal inductive criteria, of its truth. So here, if we had normal inductive evidence in favour of the existence of a being of the above kind that evidence would point to the coherence of our supposition. Whether there is evidence in favour of the existence of a being who is the personal ground of being, understood in the way spelled out in the last few pages, is an issue which lies outside the scope of this book. All that I claim to have shown is that theists often make (in their own words) a claim such as that expounded above, that if this claim is to be coherent they must be using words in analogical senses, and that the only hope of evidence of the coherence (or incoherence) of the claim seems to be from any evidence there might be of its truth.

I have reached the conclusions of the last paragraph by making (p. 272) certain assumptions about which words were given an analogical sense and just how this was done. Clearly one could make slightly different assumptions—e.g. that the semantic rules for the use of 'person' remain as at present, while the syntactic rules for 'person' (especially for 'is the same person as') change radically; and similarly for 'knows', 'brings about', etc. So long as the right syntactic rules were dropped, similar conclusions to those of the last paragraph would probably follow. However, the account which I have given seems to me to fit best with the historical tradition, e.g. with the kind of remarks which I quoted from Aquinas on page 275 and which other theologians have echoed. My main point, however, is that there is at least one way, and probably many others, in which the theist, by claiming that words are being used in analogical senses, can say both 'God is miniessentially a personal ground of being' and 'God is necessarily identical with any individual with whom he has continuity of experience', making thereby claims not too dissimilar from those which would be made if words had their normal senses, without there being any evident proof of coherence or of incoherence. I do not see any way in which this could be done so that there is an evident proof of coherence, in view of the evident stretch of meanings which would be necessarily involved.

If the theist wishes to maintain that God is miniessentially something more than a personal ground of being, that is that he has essential properties additional to those which I have described, the same conclusions follow. Words would need to be stretched in a similar way, perhaps further, for this to be a coherent claim.

If the theist wishes to maintain, not that God is miniessentially a personal ground of being, but that God is miniessentially divine, as I suggested (p. 257) that he might wish to do, similar considerations apply. Superficially, 'God is necessarily divine' is incompatible with 'God is necessarily identical with any animate being with whom he is related by the relation of continuity of experience'. For if the latter is true, could not God gain or lose powers while remaining the person which he is? But if he is necessarily divine, he cannot do this. So a similar appeal must be made to analogical senses of words if the theist's claims are to be coherent. The theist's claims in this case are, however, less far removed than are the earlier claims from claims which we can understand and formulate. It is easier to make sense of the notion of a being who, while he exists, is necessarily divine, but who can deprive himself of existence; than it is to make sense of the notion of a being who, if he exists, is necessarily the sort of being that he is for evermore and cannot deprive himself of existence. However, as we have seen, this latter supposition is not without similarities in non-theological schemes of thought.

15

Holy and Worthy of Worship

In Part II and the other chapters of Part III I have discussed the coherence of various claims which theists make. In Part II I argued that it is coherent to suppose that there exists eternally an omnipresent spirit who is perfectly free, creator of the Universe, omnipotent, omniscient, perfectly good, and a source of moral obligation—that is a personal ground of being. In Part III we have seen how the theist normally wishes to make one further crucial claim—that God is miniessentially a personal ground of being (as well as being necessarily identical with any individual with whom he has continuity of experience). From this there follows the theist's doctrine that God exists necessarily (on criterion [D] of necessity) and that he is necessarily (on criterion [B]) the kind of being which he is, viz. a personal ground of being. If this claim of Part III is to be a coherent claim, the words in which it is expressed have to be taken in an analogical sense. Given that the words are so taken, I was unable to prove in any direct way either that this claim was coherent or that it was incoherent. However, I pointed that there could be an indirect proof of coherence in so far as there was inductive evidence for the truth of what was claimed.

Various thinkers who would still rightly be called 'theists' have, however, held slightly different views about God's nature from the one with which I have been mainly concerned. Some for example, have held different views from the ones which I expounded on what the omnipotence or omniscience or eternity of God amounts to. I have urged that these thinkers have only held these views because of beliefs that God would not be worthy of worship if he was 'omnipotent' or 'omniscient' or 'eternal' only in the senses which I found coherent and not in the senses in which they wished to make their claim. Other thinkers who would also rightly be called 'theists' have held different views about God's necessity from the view which I developed. Some have held a view which I held to be incoherent—that 'God exists' is logically necessary. I suggested briefly in the last chapter that the theist does not need to hold this view if he is to claim that his God is worthy of worship, and I shall develop that point further in this chapter. Other theists perhaps hold a view that God is miniessentially rather less than a personal ground of being. I shall argue in this chapter that God would be more obviously worthy of worship if he is miniessentially a personal ground of being than if he is miniessentially divine.

Worthy of Worship

Theism, as well as making the claims which I have so far discussed, does make this further claim—that God is worthy of worship by men. The theist normally claims that God is worthy of worship both in virtue of his having such essential properties as I have discussed and also in virtue of his having done of his own free will various actions (e.g. rescued the Jews from Egypt and brought them to the Promised Land). In claiming that God is worthy of worship by men, the theist may be making the stronger claim that men ought morally to worship God, or the weaker claim that it would not be morally wrong if they did worship God. Most theists would wish to make the stronger claim, and for that reason I shall examine it, and I shall understand the claim that God is worthy of worship in this sense; the stronger claim does of course entail the weaker claim. Moral claims, as we saw in Chapter 11, are supervenient. They hold or fail to hold, that is, in virtue of natural facts. I shall investigate briefly in this chapter whether a God who is miniessentially a personal ground of being would, if he exists, be worthy of worship by men. In the process I shall consider the general question of what properties a being needs in order to be worthy of worship. The answers will support earlier claims which I made about which beings would be worthy of worship, and allow us to see whether a being who was miniessentially less than a personal ground of being would be worthy of worship. In order to do this I shall need to argue for the truth of certain moral principles. As in Chapter 11, where I needed to argue for certain moral principles, my arguments will inevitably seem rather brief. Adequate argument in favour of such moral principles could only be given in the context of a book about morality. As I urged in Chapter 11, moral argument consists of such processes as drawing-out at length the consequences of moral principles and, if possible, confronting opponents with real-life situations. However, although my arguments will be more brief than some opponents will require, I hope that they will be sufficient to convince many, and that even those who are unconvinced will feel the force of the arguments. Once again, I plead as my excuse for the brevity of my arguments considerations as to what is a desirable length for this book.

What is it then to worship a being? The concept of worship is a very vague one.[1] Many different acts constitute worship according to their context—taking-off shoes, singing, dancing, saying certain things, etc. 'Worship' is paid to beings about whom worshippers have very different kinds of beliefs; and it is not clear which uses of 'worship' are metaphorical and which are literal. Christians, Jews, and Muslims certainly worship God; but the ancient Greeks and Romans and primitive tribes today are said to 'worship' many gods of very limited powers, and humans are often said to 'worship' men or women or ideals or organizations. Which of these uses are metaphorical is unclear. However, I am concerned only with the kind of worship which theists offer to their God. To offer to a being worship of this kind is surely to show explicit respect towards a being acknowledged as the *de facto* and *de iure* lord of all things. Which public behaviour will constitute such worship will depend on the conventions in the society for showing respect. One way of showing such respect is explicit confession in words of the being's status and of man's nothingness with respect to him. Another way is bowing or genuflecting before some representation or believed manifestation of his presence.

When ought a man to offer such worship?[2] The theist argues that the duty to worship is a consequence of certain moral

---

[1] For some of its nuances see Ninian Smart, *The Concept of Worship* (London, 1972).

[2] The account which I give of the duty to worship is very similar to that given by Aquinas in his account of the duty of what he calls 'religion' in *Summa Theologiae*,

principles. The main one is that one ought to show explicit respect to those persons with whom one has to do, having regard to the qualities and status which they possess. The meaning of this principle should come out in the examples by which I illustrate it. The principle seems to me correct and I shall seek to defend it.

Let us bring out the different facets of this principle. First, one ought to show to all persons with whom one has to do a certain explicit respect just because they are persons. This respect is their due because they have feelings and moral awareness, because they make a difference to the world; and such respect is, I suggest, more their due if (as many of us believe) they have free will in the sense which I delineated in Chapter 8—that is, if to some extent what they do depends ultimately on them and not completely on their genes, upbringing, and environment. No one better expressed the obligation to treat other persons with respect that did Kant. A rational being must regard himself, Kant claims, as a member of a 'kingdom of ends', the 'ends' being the other rational beings who are 'ends in themselves'. He claims that 'rational beings all stand under the law that each of them should treat himself and all others, never merely as a means, but always at the same time as an end in himself'.[3] Treating other persons as ends in themselves of course involves many things. It involves not killing them without just cause, or stealing from them property or spouses. It also involves, I suggest, showing them explicit respect when we have to do with them. We show explicit respect to persons in many ways. We shake hands with those we meet, or smile at them, or say friendly words to them. Thereby we accept them as persons and acknowledge openly our recognition of their presence, their status as persons, and their needs. We do this too in various other ways. We open doors for people which they could have opened for themselves, listen to what they have to say when we are not immediately interested in their conversation, reply to

---

2a.2ae.80 and 81. He quotes with approval Cicero's definition of 'religion' as 'offering service and ceremonial rites to a superior nature that men call divine' and claims that 'religion is a virtue because it pays the debt of honour to God'. (See *Summa Theologiae*, vol. xxxix, London, 1964 (trans. Kevin D. O'Rourke), 2a.2ae.81. 1 and 2.)

[3] I. Kant, *Groundwork of the Metaphysic of Morals*, trans. H. J. Paton under the title *The Moral Law* (2nd edn., London, 1953), p. 101.

their letters when we have nothing interesting to say to them. In sum, we treat them with courtesy. But do we have a moral obligation to do so? A man might admit that he may have moral obligations of cruder kinds to his fellows, such as paying his debts to them or not injuring them, but deny that he has any obligation to pay them explicit respect. I myself think that there is such an obligation, and I suggest that a man will see this if he reflects on the differences between a society without such courtesy and a society with it. (Of course the forms of courtesy will vary with the conventions of society—e.g. whether one recognizes another person by shaking hands or bowing or smiling.)

However, there is clearly an even stronger case for a duty to pay explicit respect to benefactors. It goes with the duty of doing what pleases the benefactor which I discussed in Chapter 11. If a man has done much for us, he is entitled to our explicit respect. By virtue of their status benefactors are entitled to a special degree of respect. We show this by our mode of address, by giving them places of honour, perhaps by the occasional present. Sometimes to show him respect is the only return one can make to a benefactor for what he has done. Now of course some men may think that there is no obligation on the recipient of benefit to show respect to the benefactor. They should, however, reflect on that fact that all societies from Tsarist Russia to Communist China, from primitive tribes to capitalist U.S.A., have shown such respect and thought it right to do so. They have shown such respect often when the benefactors were in no position to confer further benefit. They give to benefactors medals, or titles, or dinners, or 'benefit matches' when they retire and are too old to confer further benefit—which shows that there is not too obvious a crude selfish motive for the conferring of such respect. A society which did not recognize its benefactors would surely morally be a significantly worse society than one which did. The greater the benefit which we receive, and the more costly it was for the benefactor to give it, the greater the respect which he deserves. By contrast, in so far as there is a selfish motive for the benefactor's behaviour (e.g. in so far as he acts simply in order to gain our explicit respect or to gain a reward from some other person), the less he deserves our respect. From the general duty of respect to benefactors there follow particular and strong duties of respect to those on whom we depend much for our existence, growing, and flourishing.

There are clearly special duties of respect which we have to those who have particular intimate relationships with ourselves, and this means two classes of people—those who have given to us what they could not give to others, some specially intimate personal aspect of themselves; and those who are what they are largely because of how we have made them. For the first reason there is a special duty of respect owed to parents, and to wife or husband. One who failed to show explicit respect to his spouse who had given so much uniquely to him would indeed deserve condemnation. For the second reason, I suggest, there is a special duty of respect (though one perhaps less often recognized) to all those who are what they are because of the way in which we have made them, in particular to children who have been formed by us humans, ignorant of what their true well-being consists in, and unsatisfactory promoters of even our limited vision of what that well-being consists in.

But further, there seem to be special duties of respect to persons who are not closely connected with ourselves, but who are greatly worth-while people or who have done very worthwhile things. The wise, the good, and the brave deserve recognition by us even though they have not especially benefited ourselves. Again societies which have failed to acknowledge, to show recognition of, great achievement (except when it is immediately beneficial to that society) are societies of which we think the worse. He who saves the life of another, educates the young well, finds out the secrets of the Universe or of men's past, who runs fast or flies high, sings, paints, or writes well, deserves to be acknowledged for these things by his neighbours—even though they have not benefited in any direct way by these activities. A society which recognizes only direct benefit to itself is obviously morally poorer than one which recognizes greatness and great achievement of all kinds. A society which does the latter does not merely recognize its members as persons but recognizes them for the persons which they are, and values them for that too.[4] It is for reasons such as these that the old are deserving of special respect. They have done much and

---

[4] This paragraph should *not* be read as a plea for a 'birthday honours list'. It is

suffered much, learnt much and handed on their knowledge. Persons deserve respect peculiar to their status and achievements. To pay the same kind of respect and the same amount of respect to all would not be to show recognition of the features in respect of which each person deserves respect.[5] To treat children with the same kind of respect as parents would not be to recognize the features for which they deserve respect. And *if* there were a significant difference between men and women in the features for which they deserve respect, a society ought to have different ways of paying that respect. Similarly, to pay the same respect to him who has achieved a moderate amount as to him who has achieved very much is to fail to acknowledge the features of each in virtue of which each deserves respect.

It should be added that a duty to respect any person for his beneficence to us or for his greatness or other features would of course be lessened in so far as that person was morally bad, and in particular if he was exercising his beneficence or greatness in ways in which he had no right to exercise them. A person who gave us what he had stolen from someone else, or exercised a sovereignty which he had achieved by murdering the rightful claimant to that sovereignty would deserve little, if any, respect.

It follows from these considerations about the duty of respect that a person who had most of the properties which I have been discussing would deserve to be shown considerable respect. If he is our creator, he is a person with whom we have to do; and since we depend on him for our being, he is indeed our benefactor. If he is omnipotent, omniscient, or perfectly free, and so perfectly good, he deserves respect for his unequalled greatness and goodness. But to worship, as we have seen, is more than just to show respect. It is to show respect towards a person

---

another matter which I do not discuss in detail as to what it is the right way to honour greatness. The paying of respect ought not to be too automatic, too formal, or too lacking in the personal touch or in genuine sacrifice. The only point which I am making is that respect is due; I do not say how it should be paid.

[5] 'Honour is due on account of excellence. Since God infinitely surpasses and completely transcends all other things his excellence is unparalleled. Therefore he should receive a special kind of honour; as in human affairs we give different kinds of honour for different types of excellence, one for a parent, for example, another for a king and so on'—Aquinas, *Summa Theologiae*, vol. 39, 2a.2ae.81.4.

acknowledged as *de facto* and *de iure* lord of all. Such a person deserves a peculiar kind of respect for two reasons. Firstly, whatever our dependence on other beings, they depend on him. He is our ultimate benefactor, and has the right to be such. Secondly, he has incomparable greatness; if greatness deserves respect, he deserves a peculiar respect.

Which properties would a being need to have in order to have lordship of this kind? First, in order to be supremely great and the ultimate source of our well-being, he must be perfectly free, for if he is in any way pushed into exercising his powers sovereignty is not fully his. But given this, there must be no limits to his power other than those of logic; otherwise his lordship would not be supreme. That means that he must be omnipotent in my sense [E]. But what of the limits of logic? Ought not a being who was truly lord of all things have the power to overcome those limits—to change the past, to make a man both to be and not to be at the same time, to be able to do what he believes to be morally wicked while remaining perfectly free? But in asking that God should be able to make something both to be and not to be at the same time, one is clearly asking for something the description of which makes no sense. It looks as if one is asking for God to be able to do something, but in an important sense there is no something for which one is asking. The words in which we attempt to describe the something cancel each other out, fail to be coherent. The same applies in the end to things which are less obviously incoherent, such as changing the past. A being who is perfectly free and omnipotent in my sense [E] has as much control over things as it is logically possible that a being could have. I have urged above that such control deserves respect, because the being who has it is our benefactor and great. Such a being deserves it more than any other being could.

As I urged on page 128 it would not detract from his greatness if God were able to give to other beings the power to create; nor would it detract from our dependence on him, so long as the other beings only exercised their creating power when he permitted them so to do—which would be so, if he is a personal ground of being. Nor, as I urged on page 161 does it detract from his dignity if he cannot act in ways which he judges to be irrational. For all that this means is that his choice is unin-

fluenced by causal factors beyond his control; he acts in the light
of his own unbiased judgements about how things are. That
makes him more in control of things than he would otherwise be.

What of omniscience? Does a person need this in order to
deserve worship? As we saw in Chapter 12 (p. 225) he would
need quite a lot of knowledge in order to be omnipotent. But
to be omnipotent an individual need not know all things; he
need only to be able to acquire knowledge of anything he chose.
Likewise an individual who is omnipotent and perfectly free
would be no less our benefactor and no less great for lacking
knowledge of some small item, so long as he could acquire such
knowledge at will. He would be no less worthy of worship if
through his own choice he preferred not to know how many
pennies I have in my pocket. His greatness derives not from
what he does know but from what he can come to know, just
like that, if he so chooses. That being so, an omnipotent and
perfectly free person would seem to be no less worthy of
worship if in order to secure his own future freedom and that
of humans he limits his knowledge of future free actions, in the
way suggested in Chapter 9.

Does an individual need to be eternal in order to have the
lordship which deserves worship? It seems to me that he will
be less in control of things, and hence less great if he is not backwardly eternal. Fully to deserve worship, he must always have
existed; he cannot have come into existence at some moment
of past time. For if he came into existence at some moment of
past time, his lordship over things would be limited. How
things were before that moment would not have depended on
him. Does he need to be forwardly eternal, to continue to exist
for ever?

It seems to me for a reason which I shall give shortly that a
being who is miniessentially a personal ground of being would
deserve worship more than a being who is miniessentially
divine. A personal ground of being is, as such, forwardly as well
as backwardly eternal. One who is miniessentially a personal
ground of being is therefore necessarily forwardly eternal. Now a
being K who was miniessentially divine could, if he so chose,
commit suicide. If he did, then there could come into existence,
either uncaused or because K had brought it about, an individual L who was necessarily (on criterion [B]) omnipotent,

omniscient, and perfectly free. L would be a divine being in all respects except that he was not backwardly eternal. In all other respects L would be like K. L could move the stars as well as K could. Although L could not have come into existence without K's consent, K would not be all that special; the lordship over all things would not be so tied to K as to be inalienable. By contrast, if there is a being G who is miniessentially a personal ground of being, no other being could exercise complete control of the Universe. G would have a logical uniqueness of a kind not possessed by K. The nature of things would be that how things are can be determined ultimately by G and by no one else. There could not be any other being who finally determined how things are. That would be the nature of the world. By similar argument G as miniessentially a personal ground of being would be more evidently a unique lord of all than some being H who could deprive himself of his omnipotence while continuing to exist. For if H did deprive himself of omnipotence, some other being J might come into existence exercising omnipotence. It would not then be the nature of things that power was tied uniquely to H, as it would be to G. I conclude that one who is miniessentially a personal ground of being would be especially deserving of worship, for if he rules the Universe and is our benefactor and is supremely great no other being could have had this status. The lordship over all things is peculiarly his. For it would not be coherent to suppose that anyone else could have been lord. The deepest synthetic truth would be that lordship is *his*—deepest, because all others depend upon it.

God, as miniessentially a personal ground of being, would not of course exist of logical necessity. However, the theist surely does not require that the object of his worship be a logically necessary being.[6] For if the existence of God is the tremendous exciting thing which theists believe it to be it is not to be expected that anything can show why God exists. Yet why something exists of logical necessity can be shown in terms of the incoherence of supposing that it does not exist; men can be

---

[6] That God would need to exist of logical necessity in order to be worthy of worship was a claim made by Findlay in the article cited on p. 254. Findlay assumed that the only kind of necessity was logical necessity and hence argued that there could not be a being worthy of worship. Peter C. Appleby argues against Findlay's claim in 'On Religious Attitudes', *Religious Studies*, 1970, **6**, 359–68.

brought to see why it exists, how it could not but exist. But then a being which exists of logical necessity does not seem to be truly ultimate, itself without explanation of any kind, that which explains all other things. All other things which exist of logical necessity, such as numbers, concepts, and logical truths are pale lifeless things which cannot exercise causal influence. God would seem greater and so more worthy of worship, not less, if the necessity of his existence is not of kind [A].

So a personal ground of being would be supremely our benefactor and supremely great and good and so deserving of the peculiar respect which men give in worship—at least so long as he had a right to exercise the lordship which he does. Such a person will, however, indeed be not merely *de facto* but *de iure* lord of all. I suggested in Chapter 11 that God's creating the inanimate universe *e nihilo* and keeping it in existence makes him *de iure* its owner and so its ruler. I argued further that his creating men and keeping them in being gave him certain rights over them, but I suggested that these rights were limited rights. Since moral truths are a species of logical truths, as I argued in Chapter 11, God's rights being limited would arise from his creating animate beings, and especially from his creating animate beings with free will. A person's *de iure* lordship would evidently be diminished or would cease if he exercised that lordship in morally repugnant ways. But clearly, a personal ground of being, being perfectly good, will not do that. So a person who is uniquely creator and sustainer of the Universe and also perfectly good would be its *de iure* lord—except in so far as his creating animate beings of limited free will means that he has in part abrogated the lordship. Has he done this to such an extent that he no longer deserves worship? Would he deserve worship more, the fewer free beings he creates? This seem implausible. He has as much *de iure* lordship as he logically can in a universe in which there are other free beings. That there are such limits to his lordship arises from his own choice. It is a good thing that he create such beings. Their obligations to worship surely cannot be less in so far as in making them he hands over to them some small part of his *de iure* lordship. If God were less than miniessentially a personal ground of being, he would still have considerable *de iure* lordship. In so far as he creates and sustains the world, it is to a considerable extent his to do with as he wishes. But if he is miniessentially a personal ground of being, the world depends for its existence uniquely and supremely on him, as we have seen, and so his *de iure* lordship is at its logically possible maximum.

I conclude that if God, a miniessentially personal ground of being, exists, he is in virtue of his nature supremely worthy of worship—more than any other being could be in virtue of his nature. (The same point holds if God has essential properties additional to those of one who is miniessentially a personal ground of being.) I made earlier the point that persons deserve respect both for what they are and for what they have done. It follows that a person who, by his nature, deserved men's worship, would deserve it more if he had done certain things for them, in particular he would deserve it if he had done for men any of the things which the great theistic religions claim that he has done —e.g. if in some sense he came to earth and redeemed men from sin, as Christianity claims.

The duty to worship, as I have expounded it so far, arises from a general duty to pay respect to persons of various kinds. It may plausibly be urged that there is another and a very different reason for worship. For worship of God is public acknowledgement of his existence and rightful sovereignty. It might be urged, although I do not press this, that there is a duty on a'l men to acknowledge at any rate to themselves, perhaps overtly (i.e. by a public act even if in a private place), perhaps even publicly, their most fundamental beliefs. A man owes it to himself and to his fellows to confess his deepest convictions. If that is so, then the believer in God has a duty to acknowledge this belief. An obvious way of doing this and showing the seriousness of such acknowledgement is by the public expression of that belief in worship.

Holiness

One who was miniessentially a personal ground of being (or something which entails this), would not merely be worthy of men's worship; he would have most, and probably all, of the properties which make up holiness, classically described by Rudolph Otto in his *The Idea of the Holy*.[7] Holiness, according

[7] Trans. J. W. Harvey (2nd edn., London, 1950).

to Otto, evokes the religious attitude in him who recognizes its presence. A holy being is a perfectly good being who is also something else, which Otto calls "numinous",[8] and the main purpose of Otto's work is to describe this other element in holiness. A numinous being is one on whom we depend,[9] something fearful,[10] overpowering,[10] vital,[10] wholly other,[11] and attractively fascinating.[12] A personal ground of being is our creator, and so we depend on him completely. Since our destiny is in his hands, he is indeed to be feared. His over-poweringness is a matter of his might or power; and a personal ground of being, being omnipotent, has all that a being could have of that. A personal ground of being, as I have analysed this concept, is a being who acts in time and can respond to the human condition with anger and mercy; he would therefore have the kind of vitality or energy which Otto describes and sees as an essential feature of the 'living' God of the Bible. A personal ground of being is certainly 'wholly other'. He is a person of a kind very different from ourselves— necessarily (on criterion [B] eternal, omnipotent, omniscient, and perfectly free. He is a necessary being (on criterion [D]), the ultimate source of how things are. Kant has described well the enormity of what the theist is claiming when he attributes such necessary existence to God:

Unconditioned necessity, which we so indispensably require as the last bearer of all things, is for human reason the veritable abyss. Eternity itself, in all its terrible sublimity, as depicted by a Haller, is far from making the same overwhelming impression on the mind; for it only *measures* the duration of things, it does not *support* them.[13]

The final element of the numinous which Otto picks out is the element of fascination. The holy is something, union with which will give man his fullest happiness, complete satisfaction, perfect bliss. Whether a personal ground of being will in this way satisfy man's deepest longings obviously depends on man's nature, and without a full analysis of this (which would take a book to itself) I hesitate to pronounce any definite conclusion about the matter. However, it would not be surprising if man's deepest longings were satisfied by union with a personal ground

---

[8] Ibid., Ch. 2.   [9] Ibid., Ch. 3.   [10] Ibid., Ch. 4.
[11] Ibid., Ch. 5.   [12] Ibid., Ch. 6.   [13] *Critique of Pure Reason*, B641.

of being. For man is not a solitary animal; he seeks to share his life with others. He values the company of other persons for their goodness, their interestingness, and their spontaneity. Yet often he finds those other persons profoundly unsatisfying, simply because they do not have enough of those characteristics for which he values them. They are in part mean and selfish, dull and of limited understanding, predictable and never do much. It would not therefore be surprising if man's ultimate satisfaction was to be found in union with a person who, being perfectly good, did not spoil his companionship by being mean or selfish; who, being omniscient, would ever have interesting things to tell us which he could see in virtue of his deep understanding of how things are; and who, being perfectly free and omnipotent, would be unpredictable, ever a source of novelty, and the ultimate source of all things.

I conclude that an individual who is miniessentially a personal ground of being (or something more) certainly has most, and probably all, the marks of holiness. Such an individual, if he exists, would be truly holy and worthy of worship.

Conclusion

As we have seen, various thinkers who would rightly be called 'theists' have held slightly different doctrines of God. In this book I have analysed these different doctrines. We have seen the different things which can be meant when a man claims that there is a God. Some of these doctrines I have shown to be incoherent, and others to be coherent. I have also developed a doctrine very close to the central tradition of theistic thought—that there is a God who is miniessentially a personal ground of being, or something which entails this. This doctrine I have been unable either to prove coherent or to prove incoherent by normal direct means. This is because the words in which the doctrine is expounded are words used in analogical senses, and when a claim is expounded in such words it is very difficult to prove by normal direct means its coherence or incoherence. However, I also showed that if we had good inductive evidence for the truth of this central doctrine of theism, we would thereby have indirect evidence of its coherence. Only by such a route is there a hope of showing coherence.

How ought theist and atheist to regard this conclusion? The atheist, I think, ought to regard it as a demonstration that traditional theism is a more subtle doctrine than many atheists have supposed; one which cannot be defeated by *a priori* arguments of the kind considered in this book. The best hope for the atheist is to show that the evidence of experience does not make it probable that there is a God; indeed, perhaps, even to show that some such evidence as the existence of evil in the world makes it wellnigh certain that there is not a God. The atheist's best hope for defeating theism lies not in attempting to prove it incoherent, but in attempting to show it false on the evidence of experience.

The theist, however, ought not to regard the conclusion of this book as in any way a setback for his claims. It is, on the contrary, just what long traditions of theological thought would lead him to expect. Clearly, he must believe that his claims are coherent and so cannot be proved incoherent. But if there were a straightforward proof of their coherence, this would mean, as we saw in Part I, that the claims of theism could be spelled out at greater length in sentences, the meaning of which men could grasp fully and understand completely. They would understand theism, and so accept that it was coherent through hearing sentences which they fully comprehended describing circumstances in which theism is true. Yet theologians of all theistic traditions have long emphasized the inability of man in any way fully or adequately to understand what is being said when it is claimed that there is a God. From St. Paul's 'we see through a glass darkly'[14] this has been a constant theme of the Christian theology of God. (Indeed for many hundreds of years Christian theology was dominated by *via negativa*, which, as we saw in Chapter 5, claimed that the only thing which you could say about God was what he was not.) If a direct proof could be given of the coherence of theism, the theist could hardly say this sort of thing, for it would be clear enough what was being said by one who claims that there is a God. But even if a direct proof of the coherence of some statement cannot be given, that does not mean that a man may not reasonably believe it to be coherent. For, as we have seen, clearly he may if he has good inductive grounds for believing it to be true. Whether the theist

[14] I Cor. 13: 12.

has such grounds is beyond the scope of this book. However, a long tradition of Christian thought has maintained that there are such grounds. Those in this tradition maintain that there are reasonable grounds for believing a claim which they far from fully understand, the claim that there is a God. Those in this tradition may also claim that these grounds are their grounds for believing that this claim is coherent; that the lack of direct proof of coherence does not mean that they do not reasonably believe the claim to be coherent. By contrast, those theists who claim to believe that there is a God 'by faith', in a sense of the latter expression which entails that they do not have good inductive grounds for this belief, will, if I am right, have to face the consequence that they do not have good grounds either for believing that the claim which they make is a coherent or logically possible one.

An account of the nature of God such as I have given is an account close to the central tradition of theism on the nature of God. Many theists hold that there are other essential properties of God, additional to those which I have described, some of which may be knowable by man (e.g. that he is 'three persons in one substance), and some of which may not be known to man at all. If any additional properties are entailed by the property of being a personal ground of being, then God is miniessentially a personal ground of being. If there are additional properties not so entailed, then God is merely essentially a personal ground of being, but miniessentially something more. I have not commented much on this latter possibility during the past forty pages, except to emphasize that similar results hold to those which hold if God is miniessentially a personal ground of being. The need for the stretch of meanings of words, and the consequent difficulty of proving incoherence or proving coherence by direct proof, remains. Most theists are very far from claiming that they know all there is to know about God's nature, although they do normally, as we have seen, claim that being a personal ground of being (in an analogical sense) is essential to God's nature. What other essential properties God has, man with his present language, knowledge, and capacities may be entirely unable to describe, especially in view of the unclarity in man's mind even about what it is to be a personal ground of being.

The account which I have given of God would, if it were not

merely coherent but true, vindicate Aquinas's claim that 'no created intellect can see God's essence', that is can come to know what God is like, 'by its own natural powers'.[15] Man does not have the concepts in terms of which to think about God adequately. He must stretch words in order to talk about God and does not fully understand what is being said when the words are stretched. However, that is not to say that he might not grow in experience and understanding so as subsequently to 'see God's essence', that is to come to know what God is like. Traditionally, many theists have believed that some creatures do one day come to this 'vision'. They have, however, also wanted to say that even if creatures do come to know what God is like, that knowledge would remain in an important respect limited. Aquinas claims that although a created mind could one day come to 'see' God's essence, it could not ever 'comprehend' it, that is understand perfectly what it is like to be God. And that too would not be surprising if there were a lot more to God than could be described, even analogically, by words which men can understand. Maybe some truths about God are ones which involve concepts which only a personal ground of being can grasp.

[15] *Summa Theologiae*, Ia.12.4.

Index